China's Foreign Relations in the 1980s

Published in cooperation with
The Asia Society, New York

China's Foreign Relations in the 1980s

EDITED BY
HARRY HARDING

YALE UNIVERSITY PRESS
NEW HAVEN AND LONDON

Published with assistance from the foundation
established in memory of Philip Hamilton McMillan
of the Class of 1894, Yale College.

Designed by Sally Harris
and set in Times Roman type by
Brevis Press, Bethany, Connecticut.
Printed in the United States of America.

Library of Congress Cataloging in Publication Data

Main entry under title:
China's foreign relations in the 1980s.
    Includes index.
    1. China—Foreign relations—1976–   —Addresses,
essays, lectures. I. Harding, Harry, 1946–
DS779.27.C5   1984   327.51   84-3677
ISBN 0-300-03207-2

The paper in this book meets the guidelines
for permanence and durability of the Committee
on Production Guidelines for Book Longevity
of the Council on Library Resources.

10 9 8 7 6 5 4 3 2 1

Contents

Foreword / vii

1 MICHAEL H. HUNT — Chinese Foreign Relations in Historical Perspective / 1

2 KENNETH LIEBERTHAL — Domestic Politics and Foreign Policy / 43

3 BRUCE REYNOLDS — China in the International Economy / 71

4 STEVEN I. LEVINE — China in Asia: The PRC as a Regional Power / 107

5 JONATHAN D. POLLACK — China and the Global Strategic Balance / 146

6 HARRY HARDING — China's Changing Roles in the Contemporary World / 177

Contributors / 225

Index / 229

Foreword

Ever since its establishment in 1975, the China Council of the Asia Society has undertaken an ambitious program of public education aimed at promoting greater awareness and understanding of China across the United States. As part of that program, the China Council has commissioned a series of books and monographs on major themes in China's domestic and foreign affairs. Previous volumes in the series have included *Dragon and Eagle,* a study of Sino-U.S. relations on the eve of normalization edited by Michel Oksenberg and Robert Oxnam, and *The China Difference,* a collection of essays edited by Ross Terrill on Chinese culture and values and their transformation by the Chinese Revolution.* Both books were intended to make the insights of American China specialists accessible to members of the public professionally involved in international affairs, informed readers with a general interest in China, and students at major colleges and universities.

This book represents a further effort in the China Council's ongoing education program. It reflects the Council's conviction that the foreign relations of the People's Republic of China deserve closer attention and better understanding in the United States. Over the last

---

* Michel Oksenberg and Robert B. Oxnam, eds., *Dragon and Eagle: United States-China Relations, Past and Future* (New York: Basic Books, 1978); and Ross Terrill, ed., *The China Difference* (New York: Harper and Row, 1979). Other publications in the series include Richard C. Bush, ed., *China Briefing, 1982* (Boulder, CO: Westview Press, 1983); Richard C. Bush and James R. Townsend, comps., *The People's Republic of China: A Basic Handbook,* third edition (New York: Council on International and Public Affairs, 1982); and Harry Harding, *China and the U.S.: Normalization and Beyond* (New York: Foreign Policy Association and the China Council of the Asia Society, 1979).

forty years, China has evolved from a semi-colony to a candidate superpower whose voice is now heard on a wide range of global and regional issues, whose military and economic resources have grown substantially, and whose involvement in the international system has increased dramatically. What is more, China has abandoned the essentially hostile relationship with the West that it adopted in the 1950s and 1960s and has developed extensive economic, cultural, educational, scientific, and diplomatic ties with the United States, Europe, and Japan. As a result, China has become more closely involved with, and is arguably more important to, the United States than at any time since World War II.

The book is also designed to encourage Americans to take a broader and more balanced view of China. In the more than a decade since President Nixon's historic journey to China in 1972, we have often been obsessed with the immediate bilateral aspects of Sino-U.S. relations. To counterbalance this tendency, those of us involved in planning this book concluded that Americans should develop a new appreciation of the wider contexts that shape Chinese foreign policy and U.S.-China relations. Six themes, we believed, were particularly important:

- As one of the world's oldest and most creative civilizations, China's foreign relations today are strongly influenced by the traditional patterns of its interactions with foreign cultures. The Chinese historical experience encompasses a wide range of traditions, from the cosmopolitanism of the Han and Tang dynasties, to the smug self-satisfaction of the mid-Qing, to the revolutionary anti-imperialism of the twentieth century, all of which have left their imprint on the present.

- In China, as in other countries in the contemporary world, foreign policy is profoundly shaped by domestic political considerations, as well as by developments in the international arena. In the case of Peking, foreign policy is influenced by a long-standing controversy over the desirability of transforming China through extensive contact with foreign societies. While some Chinese leaders have been willing to promote the all-round modernization of their country through the import of foreign institutions and technology, others have sought to preserve what they regard as the purity of Chinese cultural values by restricting China's links abroad.

• A commitment to modernization has led China's post-Mao leadership to increase the level of foreign trade, welcome foreign loans and investment, and undertake a wide range of new international economic relationships. But these new foreign economic policies are closely linked to a set of sweeping domestic economic reforms that still face serious political opposition and technical obstacles. If the reforms fail or are repealed, China's involvement in the international economy may fall short of present expectations.

• Since the late 1960s, China has been an important factor in the global strategic balance, with a significant influence upon the competition between the Soviet Union and the United States. Although objectively weaker than either the Soviet Union or the United States, China is powerful enough to have a "swing value" in the global balance, and Peking's alignment in the East-West competition has been of intense concern to both Moscow and Washington.

• Notwithstanding its growing importance in the global strategic balance and the world economy, China remains essentially a regional Asian power, seeking to advance its regional security and economic interests. Despite recent improvements, differences of both interest and outlook between China and its Asian neighbors, coupled with the prospect that China's economic and military power will increase substantially over the next few decades, continue to complicate Peking's relations with the rest of the region.

• China's foreign policy since 1949 has embodied a complex mixture of change and continuity. Its alignments, resources, degree of involvement in world affairs, and satisfaction with the international system have all changed, sometimes dramatically, over the last thirty-five years. But there remain notable continuities in China's view of the world. Peking has consistently been concerned with maintaining its security and sovereignty against threats from abroad, mistrustful of stronger allies, and deeply ambivalent about turning abroad for economic assistance, advanced technology, or modern institutions. These continuities are likely to persist well into the post-Mao era.

The authors assembled to address these themes constitute an interdisciplinary group of younger specialists on Chinese foreign affairs. Each was asked to prepare, for a wide readership, a balanced and thoughtful briefing on one of these major elements of China's foreign relations. While each chapter deals with developments before the death of Mao Zedong in 1976, the book's emphasis is on China's international relations in the post-Mao era, with some projections of the future of Chinese foreign policy for the rest of this century.

In addition to promoting wider public understanding of Chinese foreign relations, this project also sought to address a further problem. Many Americans tend, understandably enough, to see China through American eyes. When they look at China, their images are strongly influenced by American preconceptions. stereotypes, and clichés, many of which have endured since Americans first encountered China at the end of the eighteenth century. United States China specialists have sought to overcome this difficulty by dedicating long years to learning the Chinese language and by immersing themselves in the study of Chinese history, culture, and society. But this laudable effort carries with it another danger: the danger of seeing China too much in terms of Chinese assumptions and viewpoints. American biases, in other words, can readily give way to Sinocentrism.

But China can usefully be examined through perspectives other than the American or the Chinese. In Europe and Asia, there are large numbers of talented China specialists who are actively engaged in their own research on Chinese affairs. There is also a substantial corps of businessmen, diplomats, and journalists who have rich experience in dealing with China—often much more extensive than that enjoyed by their American counterparts. A second purpose of this project, therefore, was to encourage a group of younger American scholars to learn more about these non-American and non-Chinese perspectives on China.

When the project was initially being designed in the spring of 1980, the original plan was to hold a week-long international conference at which draft chapters could receive comment and criticism from a selected group of American, European, and Asian scholars. But another idea, which seemed rather visionary at first, actually proved to be both more effective and more economical. That was to send the authors, together with a rapporteur, on a journey around the world to discuss their papers with colleagues at research institutions and public affairs centers abroad.

Thus, no fewer than five conferences were ultimately held in Europe and Asia during August 1981. In Tokyo, Peking, and New Delhi, the authors met with scholars, officials, and journalists from Japan, China, and India. In Singapore and Bellagio, Italy, they had the opportunity to exchange views with representatives from the ASEAN countries, Australia, and Western Europe. In each place, the Americans participated in a two- or three-day conference in which they presented draft chapters of the book for local comment. Formal discussion of the ideas in the book was supplemented by informal meetings and smaller, one-on-one sessions.

Despite the rigors of the journey, the plan proved successful in several ways. The American participants met with a much larger number of specialists—more than ninety in all—than could feasibly have been assembled in the United States and, equally important, had the opportunity to meet them on their home soil. The chapters in this volume were heavily revised on the basis of the comments and criticism received abroad. In addition, the group obtained a better understanding of the range of views about China that are held in Europe and Asia.* And finally, each participant's scholarly interests and research agenda may have been altered in ways that are not yet fully apparent. At a minimum, each made personal contacts and friendships that can be developed in the years ahead. At a maximum, some of the group may find their interest in China evolving into a broader concern with Asia as a whole.

---

* The formal report of the trip has been published separately: see Jonathan Kaufman and Harry Harding, "China and the World/The World and China" (New York: The China Council of the Asia Society, September 1983). See also Harry Harding, "Viewpoints of America's Friends and Allies," in U. Alexis Johnson and George R. Packard, eds., *China Policy for the Next Decade* (Cambridge: Oelgeschlager, Gunn and Hain, forthcoming).

The authors of this volume did not attempt to reach any consensus about the present dimensions of Chinese foreign policy or the likely prospects for the future. Nonetheless, some common projections about the future course of China's international relations do run through the book.

First, although most of the authors anticipate that economic and cultural relations between China and the West will continue to grow over the rest of the century, they also warn that these ties may encounter some opposition and resistance. Both Michael Hunt and Kenneth Lieberthal stress the long-standing controversy between cosmopolitan and populist approaches to China's development—a debate over the desirability of importing foreign techniques, institutions, and values as a means of increasing China's wealth and power. To be sure, China's current leaders seem committed to a strategy of modernization that is more cosmopolitan than at any time since 1949. But neither Hunt nor Lieberthal believes that the dispute over modernization strategy has been decisively resolved in favor of this new approach. Although a return to the extreme nativism of the Maoist period is unlikely, China may well witness a reversal of present policies in the direction of greater restrictions on China's contacts with the West.

Similarly, Bruce Reynolds suggests that China's new involvement in the international economy is closely related to a series of controversial domestic economic reforms that have been undertaken since the death of Mao Zedong. If these reforms succeed, then China will play an even greater role in the international economy in the decades ahead, and may become integrated into what he describes as an "emerging East Asian system of production." But the obstacles to the reforms, both technical and political, are formidable. If they succeed in blunting the reform effort, Reynolds predicts that China's trade will grow more slowly, and the forms of China's international economic undertakings will diversify much less rapidly, than might otherwise be expected.

Second, the authors also predict that China will increase its level of involvement in Asia, as modernization places more military and economic resources at Peking's disposal. Some of the authors, particularly Michael Hunt and Steven Levine, raise the possibility that China will become more nationalistic, assertive, and self-confident in its relations with its Asian neighbors. Moreover, as Levine points out, there remain substantial problems that divide China and its Asian neighbors, including long-standing territorial disputes, the presence of large numbers of overseas Chinese throughout Asia, China's past commitment to revolution, the existence of non-Chinese ethnic groups, such as the Uighurs and the Mongols, that straddle China's frontiers, and the possibility that a rapidly modernizing China may become a tough economic competitor for other developing Asian nations. All these factors complicate Peking's relations with the rest of the region.

But none of the contributors to the volume presents any apocalyptic visions of the future. They expect that domestic economic constraints, and a complex balance of power in Asia, will prevent China from pursuing what Liddell Hart has called the "acquisitive approach" to foreign policy, let alone achieving any form of hegemony over the region. In short, China will probably play a more active role in the economic and political affairs of Asia, but it will do so as one power among many and not as the dominant force in the region. And if Peking continues to act, in Levine's words, as a "responsible member of the international system promoting stability and order," then its new initiatives are likely to be welcomed by its Asian neighbors.

Finally, the authors anticipate that China will pursue its own independent way in foreign policy. According to Steven Levine, while objectively an Asian power, China will eschew any interest in pan-Asian ideologies, will forgo any further formal alliances with other countries in the region, and will look beyond Asia to seek an active role in global, and not merely regional, affairs. At the same time, Harry Harding expects that, although Peking will probably continue to portray itself as a Third World country and support the principle of international reform, China will avoid any extensive involvement in the politics of the nonaligned movement. While part of both Asia and the developing world, in other words, China will stay somewhat aloof from both.

Above all, the authors predict that China will avoid an alliance, or even a close alignment, with either superpower for other than brief periods of time. In so doing, it will persist in what Jonathan Pollack identifies as one of the guiding principles of Maoist foreign policy:

While attempting to avoid international isolation, China should never become too dependent on any foreign protector or benefactor. Instead, China will try to preserve its international independence and initiative to the greatest degree possible. Pollack also raises the possibility that the demands of domestic modernization will lead China to try to disengage itself from the global competition between the United States and the Soviet Union.

If these projections are correct, the implications for Americans are clear. China will, over the rest of the century, be neither a close friend nor a bitter foe of the United States. In many areas, the parallel interests of China and the United States will continue to bring the two countries together. In particular, Peking and Washington can be expected to maintain a common desire for peace and stability in Asia, for containment of Soviet expansion in the region, and for mutually beneficial economic, scientific, and cultural relationships. But the relationship between the two nations will be complicated if China continues to fear the contaminating influence of contact with the West, if Peking's concern with sovereignty leads it to assign high priority to an early resolution of the Taiwan issue, or if China adopts a more aggressive posture in Asia. Even under the best of circumstances, it is difficult to imagine a proudly independent China forming a close strategic alignment, for more than fleeting moments, with the United States.

Americans must therefore accept a complex relationship with China that contains elements of both tension and cooperation. We must learn how to live with a large measure of ambiguity in the relationship, manage the differences between the two countries, and build constructively on the similarities. Such a relationship will require a more sophisticated diplomatic strategy, and a more adequate public understanding of China, than we have enjoyed in the past. This book represents one attempt to contribute to the latter objective.

This project was made possible by the support and cooperation of a number of individuals and organizations both in the United States and abroad. It is a pleasure to acknowledge and to express our deep appreciation for their contributions.

Assistance in organizing the five international conferences was provided by the Japan Center for International Exchange, the Chinese People's Association for Friendship with Foreign Countries, the Institute of Southeast Asian Studies in Singapore, the India International Centre, and the Rockefeller Foundation conference site at Bellagio. The group was also hosted by the Ministry of Foreign Affairs and the National Institute for Research Advancement in Tokyo; and by the Institute of Modern History of the Chinese Academy of Social Sciences, the Foreign Trade Research Institute of the Ministry of Foreign Trade, and the Institute of International Studies in Peking. Special thanks are due Tadashi Yamamoto in Tokyo, Pu Shan, Zhang Xueling, and Zi Zhongyun in Peking, Kerniel Sandhu in Singapore, U. S. Bajpai in New Delhi, and Susan Garfield at Bellagio for their help in arranging the five conferences.

Financial support for the project was provided by the Rockefeller Foundation. Administrative assistance and no small number of substantive ideas were offered by Marshall Bouton, Richard Bush, Datus Smith, and Susan O'Sullivan of the Asia Society. Invaluable editorial advice was given by Marian Neal Ash and Charlotte Dihoff of Yale University Press and Sally Serafim.

Finally, special gratitude is owed the families of the six authors, who endured not only their absence during their trip abroad, but also their reminiscences once they returned home; and to Jonathan Kaufman, then of Harvard University and now with the *Boston Globe*, who served as an admirable rapporteur, administrator, troubleshooter, and traveling companion all along the route.

Without the advice and assistance of all these people and institutions, and the comments and suggestions of all those who participated so actively in the five conferences overseas, this volume would not have been possible. We owe a great debt to all of them, but none should be considered responsible for any of the remaining shortcomings of the book.

> Robert B. Oxnam
> *President, The Asia Society*
>
> Harry Harding
> *Senior Fellow, The Brookings Institution*

1 Chinese Foreign Relations in Historical Perspective   MICHAEL H. HUNT

In foreign relations, as in domestic affairs, the past wields its power over the present. China is no exception to this grand proposition; indeed, it is perhaps one of the most impressive instances of it. Even a casual visitor to the People's Republic of China (PRC) will see on every hand evidence for the importance of the past as a point of personal reference and public concern.

The influence of the past is visible at once in the enormous effort the state itself places on the promotion of history broadly understood. It of course assiduously nurtures the memory of the recent, politically relevant past in which the masses struggled against the twin oppressions of feudalism and imperialism. It supports a bureaucracy to keep the story straight, and it builds memorials to the martyrs and leaders of the revolution. But the state has also restored an impressive number of monuments and palaces, and it has carried out an ambitious program of archeological work to keep alive the rich legacy of earlier and supposedly disreputable slave and feudal societies.

If one looks further, beyond the ambit of the state, one is struck by a remarkable popular fixation and familiarity with the past in all its forms. It is evident in the appeal of the storytellers who still make their rounds, in the dynastic histories and tales of heroes and villains sold in bookstores and peddled on street corners, in the ability of highly literate Chinese (a larger proportion of the population today than ever before) to grasp the historical allusions that abound in classical painting and literature, and even in the dogged persistence of free-wheeling academic historians who in propitious times can air their unorthodox views.

In China, then, we have a society that retains a high degree of historical consciousness, which its political leaders must take into account. Those leaders seem to share the popular view of their nation's past, but they could neither control nor expunge it even if they wanted to. History will surely remain important to public life. Political controversy will continue to elicit historical allegories, while historical discussion will still command attention for its political implications. For us to discount in the years ahead the importance of the past in Chinese thinking on their foreign policy, as on domestic matters, will be to set ourselves outside the framework of discussion in China and deaden our sensitivities to the significance of what is being said.

However, simply asserting a broad relationship between past and present will not carry us far. We need to carry the argument a step further and consider the various ways historical influence may be relevant to the present. If we look at the foreign relations of the United States—a subject more familiar to most readers of this essay—we can perhaps identify the chief guises the relevant past may take.

Like all political entities, the United States has placed the highest premium on securing its borders and adjacent territories against external threats. Out of this fundamental concern has evolved a set of commitments to areas judged essential to American security, beginning with a broad expanse of the North American continent and later extending to Central America and the Caribbean—with the former integrated into the American nation and the latter defined ever more emphatically as an American sphere of influence. In this way a chain of cumulative decisions made during the nineteenth and into the early twentieth centuries helped shape a security agenda that remains of prime importance to American leaders today.

At another level, Americans have often used the past to make sense of the present. This exercise may involve dipping into the grab bag of historical experience for events offering instructive parallels to present-day problems—evident in the recurrent references to Munich throughout the Cold War used to demonstrate the folly of democracies capitulating to totalitarian aggression. Or it may be embodied in a more complex and deeply rooted conception of our own national character and purpose—for example the myth of American exceptionalism, still widely accepted today with important consequences for our vision of our foreign relations.

Finally, we might see persistent patterns of American behavior in foreign relations as yet a third facet of the still relevant past. Take for example the recurrent antipathy toward genuine revolutions abroad displayed by a people schooled in a liberal political culture. This hostility became apparent as early as the 1790s with the reaction to the French Revolution, and it reappeared in our response to revolutions in Mexico and Russia early in this century and in Cuba and elsewhere in Latin America in recent decades. Persistent patterns such as this do not alone explain American behavior, even in the specific cases cited. But, considered in relation to inherited strategic commitments and distinctive historical vision, they provide a sense of the enduring pulse of American interaction with the world.

The categories identified above—each providing a different historical perspective—should help us make some sense of China's external relations. Like us, the Chinese have had their enduring strategic concerns, though their ability to secure their borders and culture against challenge has varied over the millennia. During the last two hundred years, while the United States was moving away from colonial dependency and strategic inferiority and toward international ascendancy, the Chinese were going in the opposite direction. Territorial bounds defined in the eighteenth century, at a time of strong dynastic power, became ever more difficult to sustain, and encroaching powers shattered claims to imperial preeminence. This badly battered security line and an awareness of the urgency and at the same time the difficulty of restoring it have been a major legacy of the past to the PRC.

Confronted by this crisis, the Chinese had to redefine their place in the world, drawing on their historical experience for guidance. One important product of that process has been the myth of China's humiliation at the hands of the West and Japan, a myth that gripped the imagination of three generations of Chinese and stung them into an ever more critical analysis of the international order and Chinese society. The result has been an obsession with expunging the residue of a feudal-imperialist past. Though somewhat attenuated, this commitment remains an important element in official doctrine in the PRC today.

Finally, the foreign relations of China, like that of the United States, can be made to yield its own persistent patterns, produced by the attempt to realize long-sanctioned strategic goals in a complex and sometimes threatening international environment. Perhaps the most striking of these patterns—and the pattern most worth developing—is the conflicting impulses toward autonomy and dependency that have governed China's external relations. Autonomy carried the risk of costly isolation—diplomatic, economic, and technological. On the other hand, dependency seemed to many modern Chinese too high and humiliating a price to pay for foreign assistance. Chinese leaders repeatedly have had to come back to the problem of striking a balance between these two dangerous extremes.

The elaboration of these themes in Chinese foreign relations—the commitment to an inherited definition of security, the evolution of an historically conditioned world view stressing China's humiliation by foreigners in the recent past, and the influence of a long-lived tension in dealing with the outside world—constitutes the burden of this essay.

China's Multiple Traditions

Before we proceed, however, we need to clear away some of the underbrush that might obscure our perspective on the origins of contemporary Chinese foreign relations. One hardy weed, sustained by the liberal outlook of Americans, flowered during the early Cold War from seeds sown in the 1920s. This interpretation, built almost exclusively around twentieth-century events, concentrates on the world view of Communist China's leaders. It reduces their view to a function of an imported Marxist-Leninist ideology. As youths these men and women had been captivated by the Bolshevik revolution; they had immersed themselves in leftist ideological currents in France and the Soviet Union; later, they were tutored by Soviet advisers in China. During their years in the political wilderness from the late 1920s to the mid-1940s when they were learning to make revolution, their contacts with the outside world were limited, with the result that their conception of international relations remained rigid and distorted. Once in power, this interpretation tells us, those leaders predictably followed their ideological predilections: They followed the lead of the USSR, lashed out at "American imperialism," and gave their backing to like-minded Asian revolutionary movements. Peking's apparent surrender to Moscow and its determined defiance of prevailing international practice made Chinese leaders seem—at least by liberal standards—inflexible and dangerous ideologues. Only over the last decade has that image been charmed away by the apparent moderation and reason of a China ready to set aside its quarrel with the United States the better to hold the Soviet Union at bay. The more modest and tenable conclusion now to draw about the role of Marxist-Leninist ideology is that it has been but one source for policy and that, as a source, it can sustain not one policy but a wide variety of policies.

A second hardy growth that has closed off our vista is also a species of ideological interpretation. It differs from the first by emphasizing the tyranny of an indigenous tradition. The Chinese elite had long nursed a conception of their land as a "middle kingdom," to which adjoining states owed tribute as political and cultural satellites. China thus laid claim to a position of dominance and centrality in the Asian state system. Arriving during the nineteenth century, Americans and other Western observers and officials were appalled by the seemingly unshakable adherence of the Qing dynasty (1644–1911) to this anomalous hierarchical conception of interstate relations, and they seized on the apparent influence of the middle kingdom complex to explain China's tardy and ineffectual response to the West. Though a socialist nation was to arise where a Confucian empire once stood, the old dreams of cultural glory and political dominance in Asia and the traditional hostility toward equal state relations and broad international contacts seemed to live on. Carried down to the mid-twentieth century, this interpretation served to account for the inability of the PRC to stomach Soviet direction, its pretensions to a tutelary role in Asia, and its calculated aloofness from, even contempt for, various forms of international exchange.

Together, these two ideological interpretations provided a plausible explanation for the xenophobic and expansionist strains associated for a time with Chinese communism. Born and raised in the immediate afterglow of the imperial tradition, the first generation of Communist leaders imbibed, perhaps unconsciously, the old sinocentric assumptions associated with the tribute system and carried them into postimperial China. To those assumptions they added the rigid, anti-Western rhetoric of Marxism-Leninism. Viewed in this way, the past became something of an embarrassment, a dead hand holding back China's accommodation to the contemporary international system.

It might be argued, however, that in seeing Chinese foreign relations in historical perspective we face not a single embarrassing tradition but rather an embarrassment of traditions. A moment of meditation on the Chinese past suggests that if we look back beyond the revolutions of the twentieth century, or even past the "middle kingdom" view of the nineteenth, we may find other, older styles of dealing with the world that have also persisted into the modern period.

It could be argued to begin with that the imperial style comes in two forms. The tribute system model described above, with its unshakable sinocentricism, would be one. But the other would be the decidedly more extroverted pattern of the Han (206 B.C.–A.D. 220) and Tang (A.D. 618–907). Those two dynasties and the period between them saw extensive dealings with foreign peoples—Romans, Byzantines, Persians, and Arabs, to name some of the more distant. Foreign goods were widely accepted, indeed avidly sought, within China. A flourishing inland trade and a no less prosperous maritime trade reaching to Korea and Japan and across South and Southeast Asia to the Middle East fed new goods, aesthetic values, and ideas into China. At the same time frontier policy also contributed to the cosmopolitan nature of the age. At moments of Chinese strength it secured the inland trade routes and brought foreign peoples within China's borders. At moments of Chinese weakness, these same people along the periphery would assert themselves, at times claiming political control of parts of China.

The combined effect of long-distance commerce and frontier interaction was a "barbarization" of Chinese culture. It was reflected in clothing, furniture, food, music, dance, technology, mathematics, and, perhaps most strikingly of all, religion. Zoroastrianism, Manichaeism, Nestorian Christianity, and Islam had all penetrated through Central Asia by Tang times. But none left a deeper imprint than Buddhism. Arriving from India in the late Han, it was to grow in influence as China entered a period of political crisis, and in time to become an important part of both elite and popular culture. Cosmopolitan strains persisted beyond the Tang, even down to the supposedly inflexible and introverted Qing. At the outset of the dynasty the Kangxi emperor took great delight in the foreign learning and the command of technology displayed by the Jesuits resident at his court, while the noted scholar of that time, Gu Yanwu, warned against an ethnocentric outlook, noting that "there are some Chinese customs which are inferior to those of foreign countries."[1] The late Qing and Republican periods offer an even more striking example of foreign trade and frontier contacts bringing new material culture, new ideas, and new institutional patterns to a China in crisis. These took hold in urban centers and were absorbed into the cultural mainstream far more rapidly than in the Han-Tang millennia, and with more sweeping consequences for all aspects of Chinese life.

From those periods of political division after the collapse of strong dynastic power comes yet another tradition for us to consider. Described in such classics of Chinese history as the "Chronicle of the Warring States" and in enormously popular historical tales such as the "Romance of the Three Kingdoms," this tradition shows Chinese functioning in an amoral interstate system characterized by constant maneuver and ruthless competition.[2] Its leading figures are not burdened in their decisions by hoary tradition; rather, they repeatedly resort to the classic realist calculus, trying to achieve the desired end by the most economical means. Temporary accommodation, alliances made and abandoned, ambush and treachery, the careful cultivation of domestic resources and morale, psychological warfare,

1. Ssu-yü Teng and John K. Fairbank, *China's Response to the West: A Documentary Survey, 1839–1923* (Cambridge, MA: Harvard University Press, 1954), p. 10.
2. The "Chronicle" (known in Chinese as the *Zhanguoce*) and the "Romance" (*Sanguo yanyi*) are available in translation. See James I. Crump, Jr., *Chan-kuo Ts'e* (San Francisco: Chinese Materials Center, 1979); and Moss Roberts, *Three Kingdoms: China's Epic Drama* (New York: Pantheon, 1976).

and of course raw military power all occupied an important place in the arsenal of the statesmen of these periods of disunity.

The Warring States period (403–221 B.C.) is the original and most frequently consulted version of this model in Chinese history. That period began with seven major states contending for power; it ended with one of them, Qin, imposing centralized control over China for the first time, after having exploited divisions among the six and overcome them one by one. Though Confucian moralists later condemned the "opportunist and deceitful stratagems" that characterized that time, generations of Chinese have nonetheless looked back with admiration to the statesmen of that shadowy era who "knew how to manipulate the situation to their own advantage and inspire complete awe by their prestige."[3] Indeed, Qin has become a byword for hegemonical aspirations, and the man who realized them, the first emperor of the Qin, has long been regarded as the patron of a coercive, legalistic style of government.

The appeal of the Warring States model was particularly strong in the late nineteenth and early twentieth centuries. In the late Qing, Chinese leaders, caught up in a world startlingly similar to that mythic age, engaged in their own effort to "manipulate the situation" and maintain "prestige" against the rebels within and the barbarians (always ready to exploit divisions among Chinese) without. While much of their public rhetoric was couched in terms of condescension toward the intruding foreigners, their private calculations by contrast often employed the vocabulary of strategic interest, balance of power, and diplomatic maneuver. The politically fluid postimperial period between 1916 and 1928—with the Chinese divided against themselves and imperiled by outside powers—constituted an even more direct parallel with the era of the Warring States. During this their heyday, warlords, each a power unto himself, made pacts only to betray them, marched their armies to and fro, and nursed their hegemonic ambitions, while the foreigners stood by ready to fish in troubled waters as the competing internal forces solicited their aid. The extended contest between the Nationalists and the Communists,

3. J. I. Crump, Jr., *Intrigues: Studies of the Chan-kuo Ts'e* (Ann Arbor, MI: University of Michigan Press, 1964), p. 30; and Sima Qian, *War-Lords*, trans. William Dolby and John Scott (Edinburgh, Scotland: Southside, 1974), p. 90.

each group with its ties to a foreign power, might be taken as the last act in a latter-day version of the Warring States drama that ended with the Communists in the role of the ruthlessly centralizing Qin. The similarities would be inescapable to an elite that even in the twentieth century took its history seriously and to a Mao who even at times likened himself to the first emperor of the Qin.

Finally, the Chinese foreign-relations tradition should make room for the unloved collaborator, called forth by foreign invasion and subjugation. When weakness rendered continued resistance imprudent, Chinese have made the best of it. The "barbarians" who established such major dynasties as the Jin (A.D. 265–420), the Yuan (1271–1368), and the Qing could conquer China but not transform it. To rule they needed Chinese assistance. While some members of the Chinese ruling elite would during these periods of subjugation withdraw into moral and intellectual self-cultivation in anticipation of a better day, others traded their services, indispensable to the handful of conquerors, for a share of power. Here, then, is another foreign relations model in which accommodation became the price for peace and administrative continuity.

This tradition, too, has reemerged over the last century. Qing officials entered into a collaborative relationship with the British in the dynamic treaty-port sector. When they realized the foreigners were too powerful to resist, they helped collect the revenue, oppose "native" rebellion and anarchy, and restrain the hotheads in their own ranks. Qing power was thus prolonged and the British were spared the impossible burden of direct rule while enjoying unfettered access to the Chinese economy. The fractured polity during the Republican era made so grand a collaboration impossible, yet in more modest forms it reappeared. The Japanese found disgruntled patriots, wistful monarchists, and thoroughgoing opportunists ready to serve in North and Central China as well as Inner Mongolia. Wang Jingwei, who headed the most infamous of these collaborator regimes, that at Nanjing between 1939 and 1944, articulated the predictable arguments. He wanted to stop the suffering brought on the Chinese people by Japan's 1937 invasion. A negotiated settlement with Tokyo would end the hopeless resistance and at the same time help eliminate the Chinese Communists (whom Wang had long opposed) and discomfit Chiang Kai-shek (who was Wang's long-time rival within the Nationalist party).

This resurgent collaborationist tradition in the modern era has created a fixation among Chinese patriots with the traitors within. The reaction was evident as early as the Opium War (1839–42), when British victories sent Qing authorities looking for scapegoats. The search for *Hanjian*—Chinese traitors—among those associated with foreigners invariably intensified whenever the West threatened during the balance of the dynasty. This preoccupation with countrymen seduced by the foreigners carried over into the twentieth century, as Nationalists and Communists viewed each other as tools of American and Soviet interests respectively. And it remained alive even in a reunified Communist China, where Christian connections, Western training, or foreign employment could at such a time of crisis as the Korean War or the Cultural Revolution evoke deep suspicion and even persecution.

The history of Chinese foreign relations thus consists of not just one or two traditions but a multiplicity of traditions, some dating back over several thousand years. These traditions constitute a rich source of instruction, inspiration, and political discourse. They show a Chinese people who have known the best as well as the worst: virtual political hegemony and cultural supremacy over much of Asia as well as repeated subjugation and internecine strife. They hold up many models of statecraft, from the lofty imperial style to shrewd Machiavellian cunning. They teach the use of brute force, of trade and cultural exchange, of secret diplomacy and alliances, of compromise and even collaboration with conquerors. We have, then, a tapestry of traditional foreign relations that is notable for its breadth and richness, not its narrowness and poverty.

The Quest for Territorial Security

Having made clear that China's foreign relations is influenced by several traditions, we now face the task of dealing with the set of topics laid out at the outset of this essay, beginning with the historically derived definition of security that dominates contemporary Chinese foreign relations. Here we encounter an imperial legacy distinct from the sinocentric outlook associated with the tribute system. The last two dynasties—the Ming (1368–1644) and the Qing—formulated a territorial agenda that is still extant. They controlled a core cultural area that reached an extent roughly comparable to today's, and at the same time identified and, by the middle Qing, secured those peripheral areas whose control was important to the security of the core.

The core cultural area which the Ming and Qing consolidated and to which the PRC fell heir in 1949 was the product of an unbroken historical process going back roughly thirty-five hundred years. Beginning on the North China plain on the lower reaches of the Yellow River, Chinese culture spread outward. By the time of the first major dynastic period (Qin-Han) roughly two thousand years ago, it had reached the northern limit between lands favorable to intensive agriculture and the inhospitable steppe. A "great wall," begun under the Qin, roughly delineated this northern boundary, from Gansu in the west eastward to the sea. The southward march of Chinese culture was to carry it over a longer distance and to require a longer time before reaching geographical barriers—open sea to the east and dense jungles and towering mountains to the south and west. In that march the lower Yangzi River valley was secured by the Han, and the great stretch of southern provinces brought fully under control by Mongol times. The population of this cultural core rose steadily— from 60 million under the Han, to perhaps twice that during the Ming, to 300 million by the late eighteenth century under the Qing. Conquerors might penetrate the geographic barriers that defined the core area, but they could not transform the deeply rooted culture shared by its dense and relatively homogeneous population.

Beyond the solidly Chinese core lay a contested periphery. Parts of it, imperiled and even lost to outside political control in the nineteenth and twentieth centuries, were nonetheless substantially sinicized by the late Qing, thanks in the main to a belated yet nonetheless effective policy of colonization. On Taiwan, migrants from southern coastal Fujian and eastern Guangdong established Chinese cultural dominance following the expulsion of the Dutch in 1662. Despite occasional Qing attempts to halt this population movement, Chinese on the island had come to number 1.9 million by 1811. In

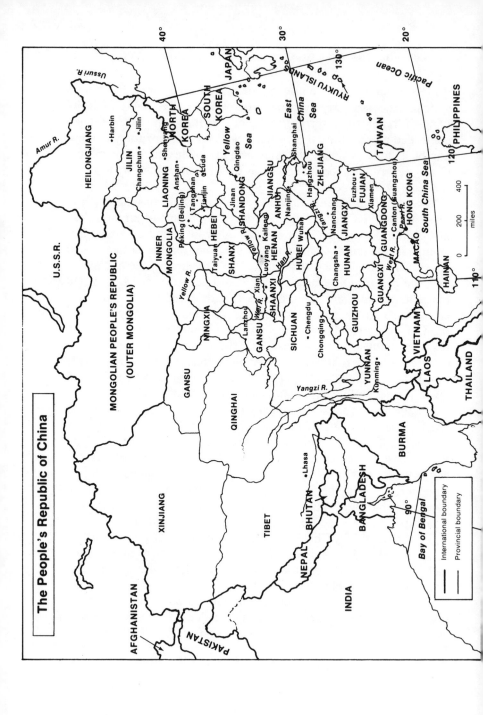

The People's Republic of China

1887, following an official decision to encourage settlement in order to head off Japanese ambitions, the population had climbed to 3.2 million and the island had assumed full provincial status. Though lost a short time later (1895) to Japanese control, the island remained fundamentally Chinese in culture, a fact that contributed to the Allied decision to restore it to China at the end of World War II. In Manchuria, too, migration secured a peripheral territory. By the Ming dynasty southernmost Manchuria had become predominantly Chinese, but beyond that stretched a great sweep of land thinly populated by tribal peoples, notably the Mongols and the Jürcheds. One group of Jürcheds had already conquered China once and ruled as the Jin dynasty, and a second, the Manchus, were to repeat the feat in the mid-seventeenth century. Once established as the Qing, this group quickly moved to define its territorial claims in northern Manchuria against Russia (through the Treaty of Nerchinsk of 1689) and at the same time to limit Chinese settlement in this, the Manchu homeland.

The Manchus slowly and reluctantly retreated from their restrictive settlement policy. Increased Russian pressure, which had led to the cession of the lands north of the Amur and Ussuri rivers by the treaties of 1858 and 1860, had contributed to the policy reversal. Intense population pressures in North China completed the process of undercutting resistance to Chinese migration into this resource-rich but thinly settled region. A policy favorable to new settlement and the incorporation of Manchuria into the regular system of provincial government took shape after the Russo-Japanese War, and the flow of population traveling northward on the recently built railroad along the narrow corridor that connected North China to southern Manchuria became a torrent, overwhelming tribal peoples and filling out the once remote northern regions. By 1911 Manchuria had a population of 15 to 17 million, 90 percent of whom were Chinese—a sharp contrast to the estimated one million inhabitants of the entire area at the end of the eighteenth century. Against this continuing flood of peoples, both Russian and, after 1905, Japanese occupiers were unavailing. Like Taiwan, Manchuria was to be returned to China after World War II on the basis of its unquestioned ethnic identity.

In Mongolia, as in Manchuria, the Qing was driven reluctantly to an active policy of direct rule and promotion of Chinese settlement. A long decline in Mongol power and an effective exploitation by Peking of the differences between the Oirat Mongols in the west from other tribes in the east had at first left the Qing satisfied with indirect control and opposed to Chinese settlement and trade. A buildup of Chinese had nonetheless occurred, setting off sporadic protests throughout Mongolia in the early twentieth century. This unrest, coupled with the lengthening shadow of Russia and Japan, precipitated a sharp reversal of Qing policy in favor of vigorous promotion of colonization, facilitated by railway building into the area. A slow rate of migration and a sharp Mongolian reaction against the growing Chinese presence eventually led to the loss of Outer Mongolia (which is now the Mongolian People's Republic) and a running battle to secure Inner Mongolia (now one of the autonomous regions of China). The prolonged period of internal instability in China following the 1911 revolution gave the Mongols their chance to pursue independence and Outer Mongolia the chance actually to detach itself from China. However, in Inner Mongolia the policy of colonization, carried forward from the Qing by Republican governments, brought an end to local resistance. By the mid-1950s Mongols accounted for only 15 percent of the total population (7.5 million) of that region.

To the west, in Xinjiang and Tibet, Chinese governments, both Qing and Republican, made claim to political control but failed to establish a cultural dominance that would have legitimized and facilitated that control. As early as the Han period Chinese had begun to penetrate through the Gansu corridor into Xinjiang. The Chinese buildup by the nineteenth century (leading to the incorporation of Xinjiang as a regular province in 1884) had been sufficient to stir Uighur and Kazakh resentment but not overwhelm it, and thus the Qing had repeatedly to put down rebellions. The Nationalist government subsequently was unable until after World War II to marshal sufficient power to overcome local pressure for autonomy and establish effective control. Despite the rise of Russian and later Soviet influence, Xinjiang still lay at least marginally in China's orbit.

Tibet, yet another long-time focal point of competition among

Inner Asian powers, came still closer to slipping away from Chinese control. The indirect control exercised by the Qing was challenged early in this century by the British operating out of India, but a 1906 agreement with Britain left China with its claim to suzerainty unimpaired. In its remaining years the Qing sought to consolidate its position in Tibet by implementing reforms favorable to Chinese influence and by strengthening its military presence. Before the collapse of imperial authority in 1911, eastern (or "inner") Tibet had come under Peking's direct control, and in 1928 that region was converted into the provinces of Xikang and Qinghai. But central Tibet, closely supervised before 1911, thereafter eluded China's grasp and remained out of reach until 1950.

Farther out on the contested periphery China was unable to protect its interests during the declining years of the late Qing and the disarray of the Republican period. At the height of Ming-Qing power, Korea, the Ryukyu islands, and much of Southeast Asia fit to one degree or other into the tribute system and were kept there by the promise of trade, the attractions of contact with the advanced Chinese culture, the legitimizing role the Chinese emperor played vis-à-vis lesser rulers, the careful cultivation of personal relations between members of the elite, Chinese patronage of Lamaism and Buddhism (influential in Tibet and Mongolia), and even diplomatic and military support against rebels or invaders. But these methods were to prove unavailing in the last half of the nineteenth century as the European maritime powers, Russia, and Japan not only quickly sheared China of this outermost security zone but also began encroaching on China's peripheral territories, and even intruded on the core of China itself. By 1860 it had become clear to Peking that it faced a crisis of a magnitude unknown since the Mongol conquest, some six hundred years earlier.

Devising a response to this foreign threat on several widely separated fronts was an inherently difficult task; it was rendered impossible at first by the outbreak of several major rebellions, most notably the Taiping. By the time the Qing had restored internal order, Russia had detached the Manchurian territory north of the Amur River and would soon threaten Chinese influence on the entire Inner Asian frontier from Xinjiang to Korea. The European powers had simultaneously imposed their treaty system along the China coast and extinguished Chinese political influence in Southeast Asia, climaxing in the French takeover of Vietnam. China tried to extend its protection but failed in a war against France in 1884–85 and had to renounce all claim to suzerainty. Japan, responding to Qing decline and European intrusion, made good on its claim to the Ryukyus with the help of a simultaneous crisis between Russia and China over the Xinjiang frontier. Peking tried to blunt Japanese ambitions in Korea from the 1860s onward but here too failed and had to abandon all hope of influence following defeat at the hands of the Japanese in 1894. As a result of that defeat, China also lost Taiwan to Japan. One reverse now followed another in quick succession as Russia, Germany, Britain, and France went to work defining their own separate spheres of influence within China proper through a combination of railway, mine, and other concessions. Despite a world war that thereafter distracted and weakened these European powers, Chinese governments were helpless to reassert Chinese interests along the periphery or even to hold back rising Japanese ambitions within China itself.

This decline of Chinese power also spelled the virtual abandonment of pockets of overseas Chinese scattered along the Southeast Asian periphery and beyond (chiefly in Japan and the Americas). Chinese had set off from South China coastal provinces in large numbers beginning in the early nineteenth century in response to the push of economic and social crisis and the pull that overseas capital development exerted on unskilled labor. During the last quarter of the century alone, 4.85 million were counted emigrating, and the number continued to grow into the first decades of the twentieth century. Many returned home, but a substantial residue accumulated overseas. (A 1970 estimate of Chinese in Southeast Asia set the figure at 14.6 million, about 6 percent of the area's total population.)

By the late nineteenth century these overseas Chinese began to encounter a rising tide of sinophobic nationalism. The resulting efforts to eliminate their economic dominance and integrate them into the indigenous culture or see them expelled served in turn to consolidate overseas Chinese communities, to orient the overseas Chinese more than ever toward China as protector and cultural fount, and to make them avid supporters of building a China strong and progressive enough to command respect for its citizens abroad. Against this background the attitude of hostility or studied indifference displayed by Chinese officials toward these emigrants gradually gave way to one of solicitude from the 1870s onward. By establishing diplomatic missions and concluding a number of agreements with host countries, the Qing implemented a new policy of protecting Chinese contract laborers and established Chinese communities abroad against exploitation and abuse. In the end the Qing effort proved unavailing, and the Republic, despite the important contribution of overseas Chinese to its creation, was able to do no better. A China unable to defend itself was in no position to defend its even more vulnerable countrymen abroad.

Even at the nadir of Chinese strength in the 1930s, its leaders insisted that the Muslim peoples, Tibetans, and Mongols (in both Inner and Outer Mongolia) would in some way or other have to be attached to a revived China. Mao Zedong told Edgar Snow in 1936 that these peoples would form "autonomous republics" within a Chinese federation, a position consistent with formal Communist party stands taken as early as 1922. Chiang Kai-shek, in *China's Destiny,* which was published in 1943, compared the three peoples to "clans" united to Han and Manchu by common ancestry. Together all five made up one nation. The map included in a revised edition of that book stretched China's borders into the Soviet Union, into North Burma, and over to the Ryukyu islands.

After 1949, the PRC predictably acted in line with the same compelling strategic logic that had long informed imperial policy. Loss of control on the periphery had repeatedly—both in the Qing and under other dynasties—rendered the cultural core vulnerable to penetration and attack. Most recently, Russian encroachment along the Inner Asian frontier had proven the prelude to meddling at China's expense in Manchuria, Mongolia, and Xinjiang, and it had stimulated a brief flurry of British activity in Tibet. France had used Indochina as a base for securing its influence in South China. Japan had moved from Korea into Manchuria and Mongolia, and from Taiwan it pursued its ambitions in Fujian. Thus for reasons of realpolitik if no other the PRC was quick to align itself with the objectives of the Qing, exerting control directly along the periphery where possible, and cultivating influence in other ways in more remote areas in which intense nationalism among peoples once subordinate to China and more recently subject to colonialism made overt interference costly and even counterproductive.

On both the immediate and the more remote periphery the PRC was to fall back on the repertoire perfected during imperial times. When direct control was the objective, colonization backed by military power still served as the most effective instrument of policy. In 1950 the PRC sent in troops to resecure Tibet. Chinese-imposed reforms followed, setting off resistance in eastern Tibet. The spread of resistance westward and an outburst of popular demonstrations in Lhasa led to forceful Chinese military countermeasures in 1959. In northern Xinjiang the Chinese influx had by the mid-1960s outnumbered the Kazakhs by 2.6 million to .5 million. To keep Kazakhs from combining forces with Uighurs to the south, Peking ruled them apart from each other. The Chinese army played a prominent role in this colonization process, combining garrison duty with agricultural production and conservation, construction of factories, and development of the region's rich mineral resources. Colonization was also the preferred line of policy in Inner Mongolia. During the Great Leap Forward in the late 1950s, and again during the Cultural Revolution in the late 1960s, colonization efforts were generally intensified and an accommodating cultural policy toward the national minorities in Mongolia and elsewhere was replaced by one of enforced sinicization.

On the farther periphery where hostile powers might lodge, the PRC has resorted to the time-honored devices of military expeditions, bestowal of honors, the cultivation of good personal relations with the ruling elite, promotion of trade, and the grant of aid. Thus it has sought, with mixed results, to win a modicum of influence in North Korea, Japan, Vietnam and elsewhere in Southeast Asia, the Himalayan states, and Outer Mongolia. With its limited maritime power the PRC has had the least success in extending a mantle of protection over overseas Chinese and reclaiming political control of Taiwan. Chinese resident in Southeast Asia have remained often unwelcome guests, hostages to the shifts in the politics of the host country and the ups and downs of that country's relations with a resurgent China. The PRC has been able to do little more than to urge on these overseas Chinese a prudent integration into the local culture and, in the wake of major bouts of persecution as in Indonesia and more recently in Vietnam, to bluster and take in some refugees. The Taiwan problem, tightly knotted at the outbreak of the Korean War, persists, with the PRC only marginally closer today than it was then to its objective of political integration. The Sino-American communiqués of 1972, 1978, and 1982 may have reduced China's fears of American support for an independent Taiwan, but they hardly broke U.S. ties to the Nationalist government there. The political and diplomatic obstacles to reunification thus remain substantial while the problems of merging different social and economic systems may be growing greater year by year.

This policy toward the periphery, imperial in its genesis, is also clearly imperial in its fundamental impulse toward exercising control over neighboring peoples consonant with available Chinese power. Like all imperial policies, it thus has had its risks as well as its reasons. It has bred resentment and revolt, opened opportunities for meddling by outside powers, and even led to serious international confrontations. The clash of arms with the United States in Korea, maintenance of an occupation army in Tibet and Xinjiang, the border war with India, and the headache of a Soviet-aligned Vietnam must be counted as but some of the costly by-products of contemporary China's inherited strategic policy.

The Cosmopolitan Response to China's Humiliation

The lessons drawn by Chinese from their country's foreign relations experience constitute the second form in which the past has left its mark on the present. That experience in the modern era, beginning with the Opium War against Britain and ending with the Yalta concessions to the USSR, has been essentially one of humiliation and one-sided struggle. Through the late Qing and the Republican era Chinese witnessed the collapse of their forward position on the periphery, the imposition of unequal treaties, invasion by foreign forces (with the capital falling twice), a carving up of China proper into spheres of influence, and finally occupation by Japan. It should be no cause for wonder that this long string of setbacks made an ever deeper impression on Chinese observers of international affairs. Confronted by a seemingly endless string of reverses, these observers sought to diagnose the nature of the problem afflicting their country in order to prescribe a cure.

Scholars of "China's response to the West" have tended to emphasize the degree to which a creative response to the new foreign challenge was impeded by old outlooks, practices, and institutions. While it would be wrong to insist, in the spirit of contrariness, that the Chinese response was actually flexible, innovative, and sophisticated, it is nonetheless important to note that some Chinese observers were quicker than others to grasp the changed circumstances and act on them. At one extreme, to be sure, a conservative and at times even obscurantist outlook prevailed, reaffirming China's cultural superiority and advocating staunch adherence to neo-Confucian orthodoxy as the key to a successful foreign policy. This view had originally arisen in reaction against the Buddhist intrusion and the barbarian invasions that had brought down the Tang early in the tenth century, overwhelmed the Song in the thirteenth, and immediately thereafter resulted in a century of Mongol dominance. When the Ming restored Chinese political control in the fourteenth century, intellectuals turned introspective, looking for the moral and ethical flaws that might account for China's recent vulnerability to foreign intrusion. The replacement of the Ming by yet another barbarian dynasty, the Manchus, intensified this preoccupation with ideological orthodoxy and laid the basis for a standpat foreign policy position that tended to equate the nineteenth-century "barbarian" challenge with earlier ones. By the turn of the century this outlook, finally discredited by repeated failure, had lost its appeal.

But at the other extreme, there developed a more cosmopolitan line of analysis in the 1830s and 1840s along the South China coast among scholar-officials most intimately involved in dealing with these "sea-going barbarians." Cultivated by successive generations of intellectuals, this outward-looking view was to survive, even flourish. It was to lead to substantial cultural transformation. And, most to the point for our purposes here, it was to contribute significantly to the framework of post-1949 Chinese foreign relations. Thus it deserves attention for this reason as well as to offset the more familiar image of a sleepy China slow to awake to the dramatic changes going on about it.

The term *cosmopolitan* is used here advisedly, to suggest a recurrence of one of those earlier periods of responsiveness to foreign ideas and material culture. To some of the pioneering students of "maritime affairs," not to mention a growing number of their intellectual successors, it became increasingly clear that the problem posed by the West required not just a simple mastery of new armaments but a willingness to encompass new cultural worlds in order to draw instruction from them and to protect the Chinese state against their power. But the resonances from Han and Tang should not keep us from hearing echoes of the Warring States model. Some of these early observers and makers of Chinese policy, no more wide-eyed naifs than hidebound dogmatists, quickly recognized that China had been thrust into a new world system where claims to cultural superiority would count for naught and where a diplomacy of delay and maneuver would be essential to win time to mobilize the power requisite to China's survival and safety. The realistic calculations that had never been far below the surface of the tribute relationship became more pronounced in an international environment that became progressively more threatening. The parallels between a contemporary system described by some Chinese as early as the 1840s in terms of cut-throat competition and the intense struggle among the Warring States must have been striking. Indeed, the implicit conclusions to draw about an appropriate policy must have been unavoidable to leaders with a penchant for seeing current problems in terms of the past.

A search for paternity of the cosmopolitan line might take us to a number of figures, among them Xu Jiyu, an official from land-locked Shanxi who served through the 1840s along the southern coast and ultimately became governor of Fujian. In 1848, in his early fifties, he published a world geography that in penetration and balance compared favorably with contemporary foreign accounts of China. Xu soon fell from imperial favor, and his geography at first wielded little influence. But the Tongzhi restoration in the 1860s proved a better time for both, bringing Xu back into official life and his book into wide circulation as an important, perhaps the single most important, survey of China's new international environment.

Xu built on a foundation of work prepared by other notable coastal officials and their aides, such as Ruan Yuan, Lin Zexu, and Wei Yuan. Like them, he was troubled by the threatening foreign presence and believed that Chinese would have to learn about this threat in order to keep it at bay while China sought, as the neo-Confucians contended it should, to return to the road of virtue from which, as mounting peasant rebellion gave evidence, it had already strayed.

Xu's significance and his achievement owe much to his belief, certainly firm by the time he composed his work, that other cultures deserved study and even emulation where they pointed China back to good practices that had fallen into decay. To be sure, Xu sought not to assault the sensibilities of his readers. He affirmed China's place as the "lord of Asia" and avoided any direct comparisons with the West unfavorable to China.[4] But at the same time he left no doubt that peoples usually referred to contemptuously as "barbarians" (a term nowhere to be found in his survey) might repay study. The European countries boasted ancient cultural roots, efficient domestic organization, and great wealth and technological development. The United States, treated in greater detail than any other country including Britain, presented an even more intriguing picture. Once a colony of Britain, it had patriotically fought for its independence and gone on to enjoy rapid economic development and to lay the basis for a harmonious social and political system strikingly congruent with Confucian ideals. Xu in effect held the United States up to his readers as a potential counterweight that China might use against Britain, as a model that might be followed in developing China's own frontier areas, and as a reminder that Chinese had not lived up to ancient standards of virtue.

As Xu saw it, the growing peril of British hegemony gave China little time to act. Already Africa, India, and Southeast Asia had fallen victim to Britain and the other European powers. China was

4. Fred Drake, *China Charts the World: Hsu Chi-yü and His Geography of 1848* (Cambridge, MA: Harvard University Press, 1975), p. 68.

certainly, as the recent war made clear, the next target. Thus China had been engulfed by a new and dangerous world order which brought to mind—in a comparison Xu made explicit—the Warring States period. Salvation, Xu seemed to say to his readers, lay through careful study of foreign ways so that China could borrow their strengths and exploit their rivalries and weaknesses.

Xu's cosmopolitan conception, incorporated into much late nineteenth-century thinking on foreign affairs, was to undergo an important revision in the hands of Liang Qichao, a central figure in China's intellectual transformation at the turn of the century. A native of the Canton delta, Liang had by the 1890s digested the classics and moved on to "foreign learning" (including Xu's survey). Even more than Xu, Liang had reason to be impressed by the relentless foreign penetration of China. Defeated in war, outmaneuvered in diplomacy, humiliated daily on their own soil, the Chinese were demoralized and uncertain how to fend off total subjugation.

Liang explained this steady deterioration of China's position partly in terms of a long cultural decline from the diversity and vitality enjoyed before the Qin unification. But foreign intrusion had greatly exacerbated this deeply rooted, chronic cultural malaise. In the late 1890s Liang complained bitterly against the unending stream of contempt that Westerners directed against China in hopes of reducing the Chinese to passivity. "When they intend to conquer a country, . . . day after day they will criticize the corruption of that country's government, the disorder of its society, and the tyranny of its officials."[5] Liang also noticed the way the powers divided the Chinese people, securing the service of some against the interests of others. Liang singled out for opprobrium compradors and Christians who shamelessly served the foreigners to advance their own interests.

To account for the foreign contribution to the crisis at hand, Liang and others turned to the concept of economic imperialism, imported from Europe through Japan and easily accepted because of its compatibility with the older, pervasive assumption that foreigners were drawn to China out of greed. By 1904, after residence in Japan

---

5. Chi-yun Chen, "Liang Ch'i-ch'ao's 'Missionary Education': A Case Study of Missionary Influence on the Reformers," *Papers on China* 16 (1962): 104–05.

and travel through the United States, Liang had identified the great industrial trusts that had arisen in the major Western countries as the new motor driving the major powers to compete for effective control of yet untapped markets and sources of raw materials. In some cases they would establish their control through direct rule as the United States had just done following its conquest of the Philippines or as the British had done against the Boers in South Africa. But as he looked at China, Liang saw that control might just as effectively be secured by indirect means, so that economic advantage could be had without the burden of colonial administration.

Liang assigned to "practical statesmanship," best exemplified during the Warring States period, the task of revitalizing China, creating national "wealth and power," and shaping a "new citizen" devoted to the interests of the nation. In making this point Liang made explicit what Xu had only implied: Chinese would need to borrow from abroad. Here the systems of the very states threatening China pointed the way, especially Meiji Japan where another Asian people had succeeded in turning back the foreign threat. Stimulating the capitalist ethic and industrialism in China would produce strength and prosperity. "If our people at this time could collect capital and use Western techniques to seek profit from our cheap labor, the national wealth would rush ahead, and after a decade no one in the world could withstand us."[6] The parliamentary system would secure popular participation; it would bind the ruled to the rulers actively, not passively; and in the final analysis it would strengthen the state in its ability to deal with foreign affairs. Schooling would inculcate new virtues that had served to make the West and Japan vital and dynamic. The new citizen in a new China would, unlike his forebears, be optimistic, active, future-oriented, productive, and, above all else, devoted to the nation.

Liang's conception of the tasks of "practical statesmanship" reveals the degree to which a return to Confucian virtue, which had been so central to Xu, had been overshadowed by 1900 by the question of survival and the appeal of expedience. Liang had none of Xu's

6. Martin Bernal, *Chinese Socialism to 1907* (Ithaca, NY: Cornell University Press, 1976), p. 144.

steadfast loyalty to the dynasty, but after some vacillation he embraced a constitutional monarchy as the most promising vehicle for reform. What was urgently needed, he believed, was a protracted, authoritarian program of economic development, political integration, and popular education that would provide the domestic prerequisites for an effective foreign policy. Revolution, advocated by Sun Yat-sen and others, carried risks Liang was not prepared to run. A political upheaval would open the way for foreign intervention and almost surely lead to popular excesses.

Xu's concern to understand the new world into which China had been precipitously plunged and Liang's search for a programmatic response to imperialism were the intellectual starting points for the generation of intellectuals and political activists that came to maturity in the May Fourth period, so named for the date in 1919 when antigovernment demonstrations exploded in Peking later to spread to other cities. A cosmopolitan outlook that had been the marked exception among the elite in Xu's day had become pervasive in a generation for which Mao Zedong can serve as a useful exemplar. Mao's affinity to that outlook is clear. He had read Liang's writing with intense interest, indeed for a time he "worshiped" Liang and Liang's mentor Kang Youwei, and his early view of the world suggests a close familiarity with Xu's geography or some other work derived from it. By the 1920s Mao had carried another step forward this process of borrowing from abroad.

As with Xu and Liang, the starting point for Mao was a visceral reaction to the foreign danger and a yearning for a restoration of China's greatness. Reading in his youth about China's earlier reverses in Korea, Taiwan, Indochina, and elsewhere, Mao later recalled becoming "depressed about the future of my country and [I] began to realize that it was the duty of all people to help save it."[7] But the "people" were in fact divided, as Liang had already noted. Now Mao, who accepted Liang's essentially economic interpretation of imperialism, would subject to closer analysis this divisive impact of imperialism on Chinese society. On the one hand, the capitalist powers had forged a collaborative relationship with a bloc of one

7. Edgar Snow, *Red Star over China* (New York: Grove Press, 1961), p. 131.

million Chinese—the warlords, the bureaucrats, the comprador capi-
talists (or big bourgeoisie), reactionary intellectuals, and the big
landlords. Arrayed against them were the true "people"—workers,
peasants, and the petty bourgeoisie—in all, 395 million strong. Some
4 million middle bourgeoisie were caught in between, swinging un-
steadily from one side to the other, Mao contended.

Mao also accepted Liang's call for a people endowed with new
virtues and a state with strong powers. But whereas Liang had hoped
that a reformist approach would be sufficient to deal with China's
cultural and political malaise, Mao saw the need for a more drastic
course of action. In this he was in keeping with the May Fourth
spirit—intensely critical of the traditional elite culture, absolutely
persuaded of the need to purge it, and receptive to an unprecedented
degree to foreign models and solutions. Mao himself converted to
Marxism in 1920 (though he did not acquire a firm theoretical grasp
of it until the late 1930s). It helped him analyze the impact of
imperialism on China, as clearly reflected in his attempt at class
analysis noted above. And its application within the Soviet Union
gave hope and direction to him and other radicals in search of a
strategy to transform China.

Mao's commitment to eliminating the contradictions within Chinese society created by imperialism and to building a totally new
China led him to adopt a revolutionary and populist outlook that
Liang had been loath to embrace. Only open and sustained struggle
would free China from its neocolonial status, make the body politic
whole, and ensure the renewal of Chinese culture. The Bolshevik
revolution and the Soviet model thus appeared as one natural source
of inspiration. But clearly no less important was an indigenous
populist tradition, which made the people the embodiment of Chinese strength and virtue. Mao's early populist proclivities are easy to
document. He had read with great interest the writings of Wang
Fuzhi, a Ming loyalist well known in the late Qing for his insistence
that preserving the people and their culture was the primary duty of
the ruler. Mao admired the antiforeign, antifeudal struggles of the
Taiping rebels and the Boxers, and agreed with the charges that the
Manchus had sacrificed the interests of the Chinese people to the
powers in order to save themselves. By overthrowing the Manchus,

the Chinese would reclaim their patrimony and demonstrate to the world they could no longer be dominated. And so he had served briefly in the revolutionary forces in 1911–12. The failure of the Republican revolution to live up to its promise did not destroy his dream that an aroused and united Chinese people might yet become masters of their own fate.

A popular revolution loomed ever more prominently in Mao's thinking as the means to realizing the foreign no less than the domestic side of his vision. As revolution eliminated the exploitative relations within China sustained by imperialism and its native allies, the Chinese people would be unshackled, and, conversely, popular liberation would strengthen the anti-imperialist forces within China. In 1927, during an investigation of rural unrest in Hunan, Mao rounded out his populist view when he discovered a revolutionary force of enormous potential. The peasantry, he reported, "will rise like a tornado or tempest—a force so extraordinarily swift and violent that no power, however great, will be able to suppress it."[8]

Thus by the late 1920s Mao, though still far from the levers of party power, had laid the conceptual foundations for Chinese Communist foreign policy and its correlative, a revolutionary domestic policy. His conception of foreign policy was like the works that inspired and were yet to influence it—Stalinist tracts and pre-Qin philosophical texts, histories of the Taiping and Boxer risings as well as Marx's account of the Paris commune, May Fourth journals together with Chinese historical romances—a striking study in eclecticism and syncretism. But at its core was a broad international outlook mixed with a populist faith.

The Conflict between Dependency and Autonomy

Mao's compounding of cosmopolitan and populist impulses sustained rather than resolved a notable tension earlier evident in Chinese foreign relations. Since the mid-nineteenth century, those with a more cosmopolitan outlook had preferred to transcend China's weak

8. Stuart Schram, ed., *The Political Thought of Mao Tse-tung* (New York: Praeger, 1963), p. 180.

international position by playing the powers off against each other
while borrowing foreign techniques that would make China less
vulnerable. Populists had responded that self-strengthening and unequal alliances were pernicious in their effect. China would have to
draw on popular strength, contended this alternative view, as a
substitute for inadequate conventional power and a debilitating
dependence on foreign techniques.

This conflict between those disturbed by the high costs of autonomy and those anxious over the perils of dependency had dominated
China's foreign policy debates from the 1840s to the end of the
dynasty. The xenophobic variety of populism that prevailed in this
period was rooted ideologically in a Confucian view of the people as
the sole source of the mandate to rule and the prime object of
solicitude on the part of good officials. A close bond between ruler
and ruled not only reflected and ensured harmony and virtue but also
strengthened the state against external challenge. Socially, early
populism sprang from a concern that foreign contacts would create
demoralization, economic disruption, and lawlessness. Populists
worked up and employed with considerable effect a long list of
foreign-associated evils. Early trade had brought the opium curse and
a deflationary outflow of silver as Chinese imports exceeded exports.
The Taiping Rebellion, a pseudo-Christian movement that engulfed
Central China at midcentury and nearly brought the dynasty down,
had highlighted the missionary menace. The treaty ports filled up
with Chinese—merchants, translators, converts, and even officials
—dependent on foreign protection and largesse and in awe of foreign
power.

To drive out the foreigners and punish Chinese seduced by foreign
money and deluded by foreign ideas, populists wanted to rely on the
righteous wrath of the people. While patriotic provincial and metro-
politan officials would sternly refuse further diplomatic concessions,
the local elite would organize militia units to drive out the barbarian
intruders and inspire local efforts to put straying countrymen in their
place. Ye Mingchen, the governor-general who held the British at
bay outside Canton in the 1850s, epitomized this early populist
outlook. Ye preached to the court, with considerable effect, on the
need to deal with foreigners only on Chinese terms. Inscrutable and

unreasonable, barbarians could not be accommodated in safety. Those who rebelled against the imperial benevolence would have to be punished and expelled. If it came to a conventional test of strength, regular forces might fail, but not the inexhaustible strength of the common people. In a long war of attrition popular forces would wear down foreign troops and eventually drive them home. The Emperor and his officials had only to cultivate popular loyalty, avoid even a hint of appeasement, and snuff out heterodoxy in order to see tranquillity restored.

By the end of the second Anglo-Chinese conflict (1858–60) the populist prescription, with its impulse toward an autonomous foreign policy, had been tested and found wanting, with Ye borne off in chains by the British. The simultaneous spread of rebellion raised further doubts about a populist line; the people were now plainly of dubious loyalty to the imperial cause. While popular loyalist demonstrations under gentry direction might possibly serve to hold foreign aggression at bay, mass movements that escaped gentry control and took on a heterodox cast would on the contrary certainly divide China, weaken resistance, and open the way to subjugation. After 1860 a more cosmopolitan policy alternative for the first time got a sustained try at the hands of officials alert to the technological dynamism and skill of the West and their disturbing strategic and political implications for China. Foreign ships and troops had already twice bested China in warfare along the coast. Foreign trade connected the coastal provinces to global markets on an unprecedented scale, with consequences virtually impossible for officialdom to control or even channel. Foreign ideas, disseminated through missionary writings and Chinese translations, were about to have a profoundly unsettling effect on the urban elite. On the horizon were railways which would penetrate the frontier from several points, making once safely remote regions dangerously accessible.

More than any other late Qing official, Li Hongzhang embodied that effort to shape an outward-looking foreign policy. Recent experience had convinced Li that China's weakness relative to other powers made immediate armed resistance self-defeating. Thus China would have to accept the status quo defined by the recently imposed treaties, use those treaties to bind the powers against further demands, and in the chief tribute states along the periphery try to preserve China's influence by playing the powers one against the other. But that was at best a short-run solution. To achieve safety China needed an armed force and navy up to Western standards, needed its own system of modern communications (railroads, steamships, and telegraphs), needed modern arsenals to equip Chinese forces, and needed schools to train Chinese in Western science, law, and languages. As Li was quite free to admit, his was a vision profoundly legalist in its emphasis on power as the foundation of the Chinese state and informed to a degree by the example of the Warring States.

But the consensus in which Li participated was rent from the beginning by disputes over strategic priorities and the appropriate responses to specific foreign challenges. A classic debate of this sort occurred in 1874 between Li and another self-strengthener, Zuo Zongtang, who was fighting Muslim rebels in Northwest China. Li made a claim on China's limited funds to build up a fleet and improve coastal defenses generally. Li regarded Japan, "right on our threshold" and covetous of Taiwan, as a major threat necessitating a sharp increase of maritime power.[9] Zuo responded that unless he received the resources needed to hold the Northwest, the Emperor would have to watch the achievements of his imperial predecessors undone and the way open for invasions that had traditionally come from Central Asia. It is less important to note that Zuo won the debate than to recognize the difficulties that conscientious officials faced in trying to determine at which endangered point along an extensive frontier China should develop and apply its strength.

By the late 1890s, official sentiment for a return to a populist policy, never far beneath the surface, was sharply on the rise. Populists had kept up a steady sniping at Li's self-strengthening measures. They argued that foreign influences were undermining the foundations of the Confucian society and state without improving China's security. The French had devastated the new southern fleet

9. Immanuel C. Y. Hsü, "The Great Policy Debate in China, 1874: Maritime Defense vs. Frontier Defense," *Harvard Journal of Asiatic Studies* 25 (1964–65): 215.

in 1884, and the Japanese had ridden roughshod over Li's carefully nurtured naval and military units in the north a decade later. Populists had also been at the forefront of opposition to Li's diplomacy and were the first to decry its consequences. Diplomatic maneuver had failed to save the Ryukyus, Vietnam, or Korea. After the powers had picked them off one by one, Li desperately sought to secure China proper against assault by forming an alliance with Russia in 1896, but that strategy too failed in short order. No sooner had the powers begun the scramble for concessions in 1897 than Russia joined in, adding new concessions in Manchuria to the ones Li had already made to purchase the alliance. Elsewhere France, Germany, and Britain staked out their own comparable claims.

By 1899 a conjuncture of events dramatically restored the populists to power and then convulsed China's foreign relations into still deeper crisis. The advance of the powers to a point only a short step away from the formal partition of China gave rise to unsettling rumors of imminent foreign invasion. A series of natural disasters between 1898 and 1900, including severe drought and a shift in the course of the Yellow River, increased the unrest along the northern coast. In Peking the Empress Dowager came out of retirement to snuff out a reform program which drew part of its inspiration from abroad. She locked the Emperor away and hunted down his advisers. In their place rose xenophobic populists, assuming a prominence unknown since the 1850s. Under the new dispensation the court quickly made its choice: to bring an immediate halt to diplomatic appeasement and to stifle the anti-Manchu impulse evident in the popular unrest in the north. Now the Boxers with their promise to "exert our energy for the nation in order to bring peace to the land" became imperial allies, and "secondary devils" (Chinese with foreign training or connections) fell victim to mob violence and official persecution.[10]

By the autumn of 1900 the Boxer experiment in popular resistance had failed (though it may have served as more of a deterrent to the extension of formal foreign control than was appreciated at the time).

10. Teng and Fairbank, *China's Response*, p. 189.

The court was put to flight and Li called back to service to negotiate in the last year of his life the price for the withdrawal of foreign forces from North China and Manchuria. Officials with a more cosmopolitan outlook returned to ascendance through the last decade of the Qing. They resurrected and expanded on Li's early policy, while xenophobic populism fell into permanent eclipse as a policy alternative.

But populism was not dead; it was only undergoing a transition from a xenophobic to a nationalist outlook, which would begin to override the centrifugal forces of class, linguistic, and regional differences at work in China. This transition was clearly under way by the last decade of the Qing when a series of urban protest movements developed against foreign mistreatment of overseas Chinese and foreign demands against China. Already these urban protests had acquired their defining characteristics, which were to persist into the Republican period. They were spearheaded by students, with officials, merchants, and journalists joining in. They encountered an ambivalent if not hostile government response, and after an initial outburst of fervor they died away with their specific goals usually unmet. They were slow to evoke—or even to seek—peasant support, a serious failing in a country overwhelmingly agrarian. Students fancied themselves successors to the gentry, the self-appointed spokesmen for China's interests and the natural leaders of the Chinese people. But when the students took to the street, the "people" were nowhere to be seen.

For a brief time in the mid-twenties—during the Northern Expedition led by the Nationalists and Communists in alliance against the northern warlords—the promises of nationalistic populism were fulfilled, as peasants as well as workers were drawn into the cause. The result was a crescendo of anti-imperialist activity. The decade had begun with students denouncing mission work as a source of superstition and a form of cultural imperialism. Demonstrations, boycotts, and strikes paralyzed Shanghai and spread to other cities in 1925, and in 1927 Nationalist forces entering Nanjing turned on foreigners there, looting their property, killing six, and forcing the rest to seek safety on gunboats lying offshore. The Nationalist party, itself in step with this popular anti-imperialism, demanded an end to the unequal treaties. No longer would foreign troops be stationed on Chinese soil, nor would foreign gunboats patrol Chinese waters, and foreign residents would be brought under the jurisdiction of China's legal and fiscal system.

The collapse in 1927 of the unstable Nationalist-Communist united front marked the beginning of a steady drift away from the popular mobilization and sweeping anti-imperialism on which Chiang Kai-shek had risen to power. Thereafter he clamped down on student-led anti-Japanese demonstrations, which he regarded with almost as much alarm as peasant unrest in the countryside. To deal with these domestic problems Chiang launched the "new life movement" in an attempt to create his own version of the "new citizen" dreamt of earlier by Liang Qichao—a citizen responsive to state authority and resistant to the siren call of social revolution and political dissent. On the foreign policy front, Chiang struck a series of short-term compromises with the Japanese and then retreated to defensive positions in the interior, while flirting with their major nemeses, first the Soviet Union and then the United States. Chiang's strategy gained him enough time, materiel, and diplomatic support to carry him successfully through the Pacific war, but left him facing the Communists with his regime's popular prestige impaired and his economic base in shambles.

As noted above, the Communists followed from the mid-twenties a different path, one that combined populist and cosmopolitan strains. Their populism was reflected in their resort to mobilizing the peasantry by appeals to patriotic resistance to Japan and by the promise of a new order in the countryside. It was also reflected in their determination to turn back foreign cultural penetration and economic exploitation and to reintegrate into the nation those Chinese who had unwittingly served foreign interests. On the other hand, the Communists looked abroad—to the Soviet Union—for ideological inspiration. To be sure, imported Marxist-Leninist doctrine underwent a self-conscious process of sinicization. But this was precisely, as one of Mao's aides with a sense of perspective pointed out, what Chinese had always been good at doing—taking foreign ideologies "to embellish and develop . . . , thus rendering them particular creations of our nation."[11] Marxism, not Buddhism, was the topic under discussion, but the parallels between the cases were—and still are—hard to miss.

The populist and cosmopolitan strains remained in uneasy juxtaposition after 1949, creating in subsequent Chinese Communist policy an unresolved tension that accounts for some of the recurrent debates and major shifts in PRC foreign relations. Here again we have the familiar set of problems: How was a weak China to maintain true independence and security if it did not locate reliable outside diplomatic support and draw on appropriate developmental models and foreign technology to become strong? But might not such a course entangle China in a one-sided, neocolonial relationship with militarily and economically stronger powers, dividing and demoralizing the nation? Was not dependence on the genius, industry, and patriotism of the Chinese people a surer path to independence and strength? These questions have echoed in the debates over whether to align with the United States, the USSR, or neither; over whether economic development should follow the Soviet model (as in the First Five Year Plan), concentrate on tapping popular energies (as in the Great Leap Forward), or emphasize importation of capitalist technology and techniques (as under the Four Modernizations); over whether to rely on a mass guerrilla-style military strategy or develop a conventionally equipped and trained army; and even over how many and what kinds of foreign transplants should be tolerated in the people's garden of art and literature.

These questions were already at the heart of Chinese policy in 1949 and 1950, at the time of the establishment of the PRC. While Mao journeyed to Moscow to secure economic assistance and strategic guarantees from the USSR, he condemned the United States for meddling in Chinese affairs, put on notice those Chinese "democratic individualists" thought to be tools of the Americans, and laid down restrictions on foreign merchants, missionaries, and diplomats. Three decades later the United States and the USSR had changed places,

11. Chen Boda, quoted in Raymond F. Wylie, *The Emergence of Maoism: Mao Tse-tung, Ch'en Po-ta, and the Search for Chinese Theory, 1935–1945* (Stanford, CA: Stanford University Press, 1980), p. 21.

but the tension in Chinese foreign policy was no closer to a resolution. Only recently, Deng Xiaoping reminded us of this when he pointed out both the danger of becoming "corrupted and seduced by capitalism" and the countervailing need to take advantage of technological and scientific "cross-fertilization among different peoples."[12]

This persistent tension between the temptations of dependency and the quest for autonomy is hardly unique to China. Indeed modern communications, transportation, and weaponry have made all national boundaries more tenuous. The particular experience of foreign domination has made many countries of Asia and Africa, not just China, peculiarly sensitive in this regard. Yet for the Chinese the tension has seemed unusually acute, perhaps because of the broad sweep of land that the Chinese have come to occupy. It confronts them with the massive difficulties of securing it and adjacent territory against unfriendly powers. Even today the Inner Asian border remains a zone of conflict, and a part of the core, Taiwan, goes unredeemed. To the northeast in Korea and to the south in Vietnam, major powers are lodged much as they were a century ago, while the overseas Chinese are as much as ever the captives of sinophobic nationalism. That acute tension may also derive from the lively memory of an unusually long and powerful tradition of imperial greatness. That memory goads the Chinese, whose nation is today by their own admission still poor, weak, and in many respects backward, to "stand up" so that in a world of nationalism their greatness will at last receive recognition. This urge has most commonly been translated into the often reiterated hope that China's liberation would "have a deep influence on the revolutions in the East and throughout the world."[13]

Finally, the conflict between dependency and autonomy has been accentuated by the events of the last two centuries, which serve as a constant reminder of the perils no less than the inescapability of involvement in international affairs. From the vantage point of the

12. Deng quoted in Richard Bush, "Deng Xiaoping: China's Old Man in a Hurry," in Robert Oxnam and Richard Bush, eds., *China Briefing, 1980* (Boulder, CO: Westview, 1980), p. 10.
13. Mao in 1936 in Takeuchi Minori, comp., *Mao Zedong ji* [Collected works of Mao Zedong] (Tokyo: Hokubōsha, 1970–1972), 5:102.

late twentieth century, a Chinese could not help but be impressed with the repeated problems created by borrowing technology and models of development that are burdened down with unwanted cultural baggage. Nor could our observer brush away China's long and sorry experience with foreign allies beginning with the Russian betrayal in the late 1890s, continuing through the sellouts at Versailles and Yalta after coming out of the two world wars on the winning side, and culminating in the metamorphosis of the Soviet Union from chief friend to the primary enemy. But that same observer would also have to acknowledge that China's episodic attempts at self-isolation, from the Boxer Rebellion to the Cultural Revolution, have been costly and ultimately futile.

The Future of the Past

Viewed in historical perspective, then, China's foreign relations is perhaps most notable for its long cumulative record, its repertoire of traditions and models, and its enduring tension between populism and cosmopolitanism and between dependency and autonomy. In short, it impresses us with its complexity and the inadequacy of simple explanations. Set in this context, the incorporation of Marxist-Leninist ideas into Chinese thinking (once made so much about) seems not so much a case of inappropriate or unfortunate borrowing as a demonstration of the staying power of cosmopolitan instincts, while the transformation of Marxism-Leninism into "Mao Zedong Thought" illustrates the countervailing influence of an indigenous populist tradition. Similarly, the middle kingdom world view (also once of broad interpretive appeal) may not satisfactorily account for China's obsession with some of its former tributaries and its ambivalence toward intimate cultural and political relations with other states. We might do better if we trace these same characteristics of Chinese foreign relations back to the persistence of the power-oriented approach to international policy handed down from the Warring States period, to a sound appreciation of the potent economic and cultural pull of the major capitalist powers, and to the hard lessons drawn from alliances that backfired.

We may by this point take it as a given that the study of China's complex past sheds important light on some of the central patterns and problems of China's contemporary foreign relations and serves as an antidote to simplistic conclusions. But is it safe to take the next step and assume that the past will remain a force to be reckoned with in Chinese foreign relations in the years ahead? Does the past, in other words, have a future as a source of insight into China's external relations? In broad terms the answer is an assured yes, though surely some aspects of that past will prove more influential than others and hence more deserving of our attention in the years ahead. Which ones? The very multiplicity of ways in which China's past influences its outlook and behavior and the depth and subtlety of that influence rules out a single simple or authoritative answer. Even so, a few informed guesses are not only in order but possible.[14]

History seems to have left its deepest mark by setting a demanding security agenda that will continue to guide Chinese leaders against challenges from intrusive superpowers, resentful and nationalistic neighbors, and restive ethnic groups. For Peking to turn its back on that agenda would be not just to surrender the practical advantages of defense in depth but—an even more weighty consideration—to repudiate a heritage in which all Chinese take considerable pride.

A close second in the potency of its influence would seem to be that unresolved tension between the temptations of dependency and the impulse toward autonomy that affects development policy and security calculations. As Kenneth Lieberthal's contribution to this volume suggests, Chinese leaders in the years ahead are likely to draw on outside technology, models, and resources, and yet they will surely watch with concern the unintended and unwanted social and economic changes produced by the multiplication of foreign contacts. Much as their predecessors did, those leaders will nervously look for—and have difficulty finding—a straight and open road, avoiding on the one side the wasteland of self-reliance that leaves China poor and weak and on the other the swamp of international diplomatic and economic involvement that compromises the ideal of self-determination.

14. The corollary to this set of observations is, of course, that the history of Chinese foreign relations deserves continued study and support if we wish at least to maintain our level of insight. My impression unfortunately is that little fresh work is appearing and that the pool of specialists in the field has not been sustained.

The third area of historical influence, the place of the past in the Chinese consciousness, poses the most formidable and intricate challenge to the powers of prediction. Which of the remembered pasts, we want to know, is likely to have the liveliest influence on policy? Chinese commentators with official standing answer that the only past that is meaningful to policy today and for the foreseeable future is the recent one, defined by them in terms of oppression and struggle over the last century and a half. Built into mythic proportions, this orthodoxy traces the rise of a revolutionary spirit, the triumph over Chinese collaborators who had shamefully capitulated to imperialism, the eradication of imperialist influence within China, and the emergence of a post-1949 foreign policy built on the principles of full and formal reciprocity and equality in dealing with others and of opposition to great power dominion whether expressed in the form of hegemonism or imperialism. This officially sanctioned history is bound to retain an important place in the thinking of Chinese concerned with foreign policy, though it is conceivable that its emotional power will drain away as the years pass and the drama of the pre-1949 period gradually looms less large on the broad canvas of Chinese history.

There are some grounds for arguing—contrary to the claims of the exponents of historical orthodoxy in the PRC—that the century of humiliation and the lessons drawn from it do not even now have a monopoly claim as the relevant past. Rather it seems fair to say that the century of humiliation which constitutes the negative pole of Chinese experience is inextricably joined to a positive pole defined by recollections of the imperial past, especially in the guise of its great dynasties of Han and Tang. It is also conceivable that as the negative pole loses strength, the appeal of the positive pole will concomitantly increase. This rise in appeal of the imperial past seems likely to happen in any case, for it offers the only indigenous benchmark for measuring progress toward a position of restored national power and pride. To the extent that this long and rich imperial past defines the future for which Chinese strive, it is not in the crude sense some would have it—as a system of middle kingdom arrogance to be revived—but rather as a standard (or perhaps more accurately a national myth) of cultural achievement and international power and influence to live up to. The distinction could end up as an excessively fine one, however, for a restoration of China to a position of greatness is likely to lead inexorably though not by design to increasing dominance over adjoining peoples and states and to sharpen still-lively fears of the middle kingdom in the minds of neighbors. Other aspects of the past are likely to be of lesser influence in the future. The romantic past identified with the Warring States and Three Kingdoms periods has served its purpose as a compass for China's coming to terms with the new Western-imposed international order. To the degree it remains important, it will be as a source of inspiration for Machiavellian stratagems and maneuvers particularly appropriate to a relatively weak country with great ambition. It will, in short, influence style. But it is doubtful that it has today or will have in the immediate future an impact on the basic goals of policymakers.

Perhaps the most problematic component of this set of historical influences to appraise is the Marxist-Leninist-Maoist one. A revolutionary ideology would clearly seem to play a role in the way policymakers see the world, and thus to a very sizable extent it should be expected to influence behavior. Yet the major strategic crises through which the PRC has passed—in Korea in 1950, along the Taiwan straits in 1958, along the Indian border in 1962, in Vietnam in 1965, and along the Soviet border in 1969—would seem essentially to have less to do with Communist ideology and more to do with the maintenance of historical boundaries and influence along the periphery.

Undoubtedly for the foreseeable future, condemnation of imperialism and praise of proletariat internationalism will remain an important part of Peking's rhetoric. But it is doubtful that in the future, any more than in the past, a weak China will risk scarce resources on translating that sometimes fervent rhetoric into action. And even when the time comes when growing strength will give Peking the luxury of putting aside its cautious, low-risk foreign policy, action is far more likely to come in nearby areas of strategic concerns than at distant points beyond China's established horizon. The tempting conclusion to reach is that Communist ideology has done little to transform in any fundamental sense China's inherited strategic calculations and concerns, nor is the rise of a more assertive China in the future likely to change dramatically that state of affairs.

The reader should take this attempt to read the future with the tentativeness and caution with which it is offered, for as any historian knows one of the greatest lessons of the past is the danger of projecting recent experience into the years ahead. There is always, we must keep in mind, the possibility of some kaleidoscopic re-arrangement of China's foreign relations along altogether new lines and consequently of historical forces and memories playing roles previously unimagined. To be sure, history can serve as a basis of prophecy, and if in this case Chinese foreign relations moves steadily along anticipated lines, then Clio's high priests will be vindicated. But even if the future betrays and confronts us with dramatically altered circumstances, a sense of the past will remain important in banishing momentary bewilderment and providing new bearings.

Americans, it would seem, have a special and even urgent need for this sensitivity to the persistent and complex role the past plays in Chinese foreign relations. We are locked for better or worse in a complex relationship with a people for whom history remains impor-tant and whose way of life is profoundly foreign to us. Yet we may be peculiarly resistant to acquiring the requisite insight. We are, it has often been noted, an insular and forward-looking people, insensitive to historical forces and prone to see others through the distorting lens of our own cultural values.

These tendencies are clearly reflected in our China policy. When the Chinese have concentrated on borrowing from Western culture and relying on Western allies for defense of home territory, then Americans have responded warmly, invoking (as in President Car-ter's announcement of restored diplomatic relations) their own spe-cial myth of "a long history of friendship" between the peoples of the two countries and expressing (to take Secretary of State Alexander Haig's phrase) their own "great affection and respect" for China.[15] At times such as these we imagine ourselves locked in a special relation-ship with the Chinese, whose apparent moderation and pragmatism

15. *New York Times*, 16 December 1978, p. 8; and *Christian Science Monitor*, 15 June 1981, p. 10.

mirror our own most prized attributes and validate our own longings for a world made over in our own image. If China with its old and radically different culture can be won, where can we not prevail? Conversely, when China has turned its back on the world or gone to the "wrong" foreigners for direction and support, then Americans have reacted with dismay, decrying the rise of radicalism and xenophobia and trotting out simple generalizations, such as the legacy of the middle kingdom or the impact of Marxism, to account for these deviations from the path of "normal development." Our own immoderate expectations of China's fitting the American mold and our surprise and overreaction to China going her own way have thus contributed to the general instability that has characterized our bilateral relations. The lesson seems clear. Our dealings with China need to take account of not just our own preferences and experience but China's as well.

If our sentimental impulses and concomitant susceptibility to disillusionment deserve to be neutralized by historical perspective, the same can be said of an American approach to China that develops along purely power-oriented lines. We may wish to use China to strengthen our geopolitical position, guarantee access to strategic raw materials, and ensure regional stability, but wishing it will not make it so. To assume a Chinese outlook either fundamentally parallel with our own or at least susceptible to our persuasion in regard to important points of divergence is to indulge in a kind of wishful and unrealistic "realism." It would be convenient for American policymakers to think of Chinese leaders as mere mechanical gauges accurately registering the international forces impinging on them or as computers impersonally assessing their alternatives by the program of power politics. No doubt Chinese leaders, like those of any other country, perform both functions to some degree. But like their counterparts in other lands, they also act on inherited outlooks and goals and are subject either personally or politically to fixations and ambivalences rooted in the experience of their culture. Their behavior may be perfectly explicable and in a sense rational in the Chinese context at the same time that it seems puzzling and even irrational from the perspective of an American practitioner of power politics.

Both the sentimental approach and the power approach tend to confuse the world as it has been and is with the world as we would like it to be. To try to find room for both approaches is to make a worse hash of what has usually been a bad situation. Washington has of late done precisely this, letting sentiment guide its dealings with Taiwan and power calculations its approach to the PRC. It thus not only compounds error but also multiplies the chances for misunderstanding and instability in our relations with Peking.

To argue for a public and policymakers with greater historical perspective is nothing new, but there seems an abundance of daily evidence to suggest that such a perspective is still in short supply. The strain between dependency and autonomy in Chinese foreign relations complicates our relations to begin with. Why then compound the difficulty with an American policy informed by our own needs and experience but out of touch with those of the Chinese? In a broader and deeper historical perspective we may at least hope to find a basis for greater empathy, a more measured American China policy, and in the end a more stable Sino-American relationship than has prevailed in the past.

2 Domestic Politics and Foreign Policy   KENNETH LIEBERTHAL

No country's foreign relations can be understood without reference to its domestic affairs. In large part, of course, foreign policies reflect challenges and opportunities in the international arena. Every country must be sensitive to developments beyond its borders. But domestic factors such as the level of economic development, the success of economic programs, the emergence of new leaders, and the attitudes of the populace toward the outside world combine with international circumstances to create a nation's foreign policy.

These propositions are as true of China as they are of liberal democratic systems. To be sure, much of the PRC's foreign policy since 1949 has been shaped by developments in the international arena: the emergence of the Cold War between the Soviet Union and the United States, the U.S. policy of containing Communist regimes, the desire of the Soviet Union to maintain leadership over the international Communist movement, the rise of the Third World as a major factor in international affairs, the shifting military balance between Washington and Moscow, and so on. But Chinese foreign policy has also been molded by domestic forces. Each of China's principal domestic strategies—from the First Five Year Plan (FFYP) and the Great Leap Forward (GLF) of the 1950s, through the Cultural Revolution of the 1960s and 1970s, to the Four Modernizations of the 1980s—has had clear and direct implications for its posture toward the rest of the world.

China's experience since 1949 has involved two basic connections between its domestic affairs and its foreign policy. To begin with, China has adopted both domestic and foreign policies that deal in an integrated way with a common problem: How can China preserve its cultural integrity while developing the resources that will provide security and prosperity in the modern world? In this regard, Peking's leaders resemble those of other late-developing countries confronted with the challenge of the West. They feel they must maintain their national identity in a world undergoing rampant westernization, and at the same time they seek some way of catching up with the Western countries in national strength and prestige. Given the importance of these problems, and given China's fascination with its ancient civilization and rich culture, differences among its leaders over the proper mix of values and strategies to deal with these problems have become political issues of the greatest importance.

China's leaders have developed no single answer to these dilemmas. Indeed, they can be divided into three clusters of opinion on the basis of their attitudes toward their country's history and culture and their preferred strategies of economic modernization. Those whom we will call *nativists* draw deeply from the outlook of the imperial era in defining their own world view. Fundamentally, nativists see power both internationally and domestically more in political and moral than in material and physical terms. They stress the identity of China as a moral civilization in which contamination by less cultured forces is one of the greatest dangers. They thus encourage a closed-door foreign policy and a reign of virtue domestically. They disparage concepts of individual liberty and legal restraints and condemn all those who reflect the alien values of the bourgeois West. The second group, the *eclectic modernizers,* are more tolerant toward foreign things but still want China to preserve a unique and superior indigenous culture. (Some wish to maintain Chinese traditions, whereas others reject tradition almost completely but still fear "corruption" by the West.) They want to strengthen China by using foreign technology while at the same time shielding the country from the cultural influences that accompany these technological imports. The third group, the *all-around modernizers,* make the most complete break with China's past, viewing it as the chief explanation for the country's continued inability to march in the front ranks of the world. While they do not seek uncritical westernization, they do want to alter fundamental elements of the culture that impede rapid economic development and scientific progress. This group is more willing than the others to expose China to the tensions of contact with foreign culture in its quest for a transformation of Chinese culture.

In post-1949 politics, the balance has shifted among these three positions, with none of them ever achieving complete dominance. During the early and middle fifties the regime had an eclectic to all-around modernizer cast, although the major foreign influence was the Soviet Union rather than the West. In the late 1950s a more nativist approach prevailed, as reflected in the criticism of Western-trained intellectuals and in the Great Leap Forward. During the early 1960s there was a movement back toward the all-around modernizer position, but this tendency was overwhelmed by the nativist fanaticism of the Cultural Revolution. The early 1970s were highly polarized, with nativists battling a coalition of modernizers, and since Mao's death pure nativism has been at its lowest ebb ever in the Peking leadership. The basic point, however, is that fundamental concepts that connect an analysis of China's past to imperatives for its current domestic and foreign policy have informed the thinking of all major decision makers since 1949, and Peking's leadership still has not achieved a full consensus on these fundamental issues.

The second link between domestic affairs and foreign policy is that any package of such policies—whether that of the nativists, the eclectic modernizers, or the all-around modernizers—strongly influences the distribution of power, status, and wealth among different institutions, leaders, and regions. The groups and individuals that prosper under one package may suffer under the others.

In the early and mid-1950s, for example, the strategy of learning from the Soviet model placed enormous power in the hands of a central planning apparatus and the heavy industry and defense ministries that it served. Mao's shift to a more nativist policy during the Great Leap Forward stripped power from these ministries and shifted it to Communist party cadres. During the recovery period of the early 1960s the pre-Leap ministerial system again emerged, but it then was destroyed—with the army moving in to fill the resulting power vacuum—during the Cultural Revolution. The new open-door approach toward the international arena since Mao's death has again brought the government organs to center stage, at the expense of both the Party and the army. But this time there have been strong (albeit diminishing) pressures to draw power away from the central planning apparatus and vest it in other government organs.

In each of these cases, the major impetus for change came from within the system, but the international arena also influenced the strategy adopted. It was easiest for the Chinese to deal on an intimate basis with the Soviet Union in the 1950s by adopting a system that bureaucratically matched Moscow's own. In the 1980s, however, this centralized bureaucratic system has itself become an impediment to smooth interaction with individual firms in the capitalist West. Different development strategies have thus been shaped by both domestic forces and international opportunities, and these in turn have exerted a strong influence on the distribution of power among the country's major ruling bureaucracies.

Which individuals and regions prosper has been determined by the same set of forces. In overly simple terms, bureaucrats fare best under the Soviet system, antibureaucratic and anti-intellectual individuals experience upward mobility when nativists are in power, and intellectuals and entrepreneurs thrive under a more Western-oriented open door policy. In parallel fashion, China's interior cities grew fastest under the Soviet system, as this system was best suited to transferring the country's wealth to the interior. By contrast, a more Western and market-oriented open door strategy inevitably favors the coastal cities, which have the infrastructure and human capital to take advantage of it. The current policy of foreign-assisted offshore oil development will, for example, pump enormous wealth into coastal southeast China, markedly increasing the differences between that region and the interior.

In sum, different development strategies both reflect conflicting views about how to solve the problems stemming from the century of humiliation before 1949 and seriously affect the distribution of power, resources, and opportunities within the country. The losers, naturally, have tried to keep these issues actively on the political agenda, as we shall see.

The Maoist Era

China made three fundamental foreign policy choices after 1949: to ally with the Soviet Union in 1950; to adopt a position of hostility toward both the United States and the USSR during the 1960s; and to include the United States in an anti-Soviet "united front" in the 1970s. In each case, the decision reflected careful consideration of the international arena and the prospects and dangers that it held. All three decisions, however, also both were influenced by and in turn reacted on China's domestic situation and prospects.

In October 1949, Mao Zedong and his colleagues had few resources to deal with a seemingly threatening international environment. They commanded a guerrilla army that lacked modern weapons. The country itself was in a shambles following decades of warlordism, civil war, and conflict with the Japanese. Tensions among different sectors of the population ran high, and the political agenda was full. The United States, moreover, had tilted heavily toward the Nationalists in the civil war, and the Chinese were uncertain whether America would try to prevent the ultimate victory of the Communist revolution. The Chinese therefore decided to "lean to one side"—that is, to look toward the Soviet Union rather than toward the West. Mao traveled to Moscow for three months of negotiation just two months after the founding of the PRC. The length of the negotiation undoubtedly reflected disagreements over substantive issues between the two sides. It also reflected the fact that the agenda included far-reaching cooperation in both domestic and foreign affairs.

A thirty-year treaty of friendship and alliance emerged. The Soviet Union extended a protective military umbrella over the PRC, and the two countries' foreign policies marched in virtual lockstep during the following half decade. But in many ways the bilateral domestic interaction was even more impressive.

Under the Sino-Soviet treaty the Chinese almost literally imported the Soviet system for building socialism. Despite their years of control over rural base areas before 1949, the Communists fully recognized that they lacked the experience necessary to rule China from its cities and to bring about rapid, planned, socialist construction. They therefore turned to the USSR for advice on their state organizational structure, on setting up an economic planning system, on priorities in industrial development, on curricula for their educational system, and so forth. Soviet advisers staffed the major ministries, especially those related to national defense. Moscow also sent thousands of blueprints for new factories, and the years 1950–57 witnessed what is one of the largest scale transfers of technology from one country to another in history. To be sure, Moscow kept its actual financial aid to a minimum and sought some economic advantages in return for its assistance. But overall there is little doubt that the PRC's impressive record of growth and political development from 1950 to 1957 could not have been achieved without Soviet assistance. Even after Mao Zedong had launched a bitter polemic against Moscow years later, he still acknowledged the importance of Soviet aid in the early years, arguing that as of 1949 the Chinese simply did not know how to build socialism on their own.[1]

Thus, their domestic as much as their international needs pushed the Chinese into the arms of the Soviets in 1950, and the Soviet embrace proved strong indeed. In the latter half of the 1950s and the early 1960s, ironically, a combination of domestic and international factors would again shape Sino-Soviet relations, but this time it would drive them in the direction of bitter enmity.

On the international side, once the Soviets had launched a satellite in late 1957, Khrushchev calculated that for the first time the USSR had the power to bargain on an equal basis with the United States. Therefore, the Soviet Union could at last feel confident enough to enter into serious talks with Washington to establish a stable postwar world. Khrushchev's subsequent rollercoaster relationship with the United States peaked at Camp David in 1959 and hit its nadir during the Cuban missile crisis of 1962. But Khrushchev's fixation with the United States remained a constant of his foreign policy, and evidently by the late 1950s he was willing to try to gain extra bargaining leverage by promising that he could prevent Chinese development of

---

1. See Mao's speech of 30 January 1962 to 7,000 cadres in Stuart Schram, ed., *Chairman Mao Talks to the People* (New York: Pantheon, 1974), p. 178.

nuclear weapons, if necessary.[2] Peking remained profoundly suspicious of Khrushchev's willingness to deal with Washington, fearing always that the Russians might seek some advantage at Peking's expense. When Peking actually put its relationship with Moscow to the test, as in the Taiwan straits crisis of 1958, the Soviet response consistently failed to reassure Moscow's Chinese allies. Fundamentally, by the late 1950s the Soviet Union had achieved its territorial ambitions and sought a *modus vivendi* with America. To the Chinese, the United States still prevented the completion of their own civil war by standing in the way of the unification of Taiwan with the Mainland and protecting the Nationalist government that still claimed to be the sole legal government of all of China. A Soviet accommodation with the United States would thus inevitably have left the Chinese short of their key international goals—and because of this basic difference in perspective, Sino-Soviet relations grew increasingly strained.

China's domestic affairs also contributed significantly to the dissolution of Sino-Soviet friendship in the late 1950s and its transformation into bitter enmity in the early 1960s. The Soviet model channeled scarce resources and power into the hands of some and not others, and by 1956 this imported system had produced a domestic political and social situation that Mao Zedong found profoundly distasteful. The centralized planning system generated huge, top-heavy bureaucracies that in turn bred elitism and privilege. Given the focus on rapid, planned economic growth, the key staff of these bureaucracies at the center typically consisted of educated urban officials rather than the peasant cadres who had carried on the revolution during the years in the wilderness. The Soviet model's utilization of economic incentives was creating an increasingly stratified urban society. And the priority on heavy industry built into the model was robbing the countryside of the resources it would need to grow. Mao's antibureaucratic, egalitarian, and somewhat anti-intellectual and anti-urban sensitivities were deeply offended.

During 1955–57 Mao struggled to devise a more uniquely Chinese path to rapid economic development. He may have been motivated in part by a perception that the centralized, specialized bureaucracies

2. Adam Ulam, *Expansion and Coexistence,* 2d ed. (New York: Praeger, 1973).

so important to the Soviet model robbed him of some of his personal political power. Indeed, when he turned toward the radically different Great Leap strategy of development, he commented that for the previous few years he had understood little in the position papers the government had sent him and thus had had to approve them in virtually total ignorance.[3] Mao's personal power had always resided more in the Party than in the Government, and he had always felt more confidence in his understanding of the rural rather than the urban areas.

Mao wrestled with these tensions at a time when China had to devise its sequel to the Soviet-inspired First Five Year Plan. It would have been difficult to repeat the strategy of the First Plan, as the agricultural sector had become a major drag on the economy and agricultural production seemed unlikely to increase fast enough without greater resources than the plan's strategy allowed. Mao decided by the spring of 1958 to launch the Great Leap Forward, a program that sought simultaneous rapid growth in both the cities and the countryside through total mobilization of the labor force. The nativist impulses in this near-utopian strategy were strong: The strategy relied on summoning the moral and political reserves of China's peasants and workers to provide the country with a means of escaping (and ignoring) the imperatives of the more technologically oriented development strategy that Peking had imported from the Soviet Union.

The Great Leap shifted power from the government toward the Party and from bureaucratic planners toward Mao. It also, however, cast aside the Soviet model and de facto made China a challenger to Soviet ideological supremacy in the international Communist movement. Ideological movements rarely handle pluralism gracefully, and this dramatic Chinese departure from Soviet orthodoxy further poisoned the relations between the two countries. Indeed, in mid-1959 Mao purged Peng Dehuai, the Chinese minister of defense, at least in part because he had allegedly communicated to Khrushchev his own doubts about the wisdom of the Great Leap strategy. And in 1960

3. *Miscellany of Mao Tse-tung Thought,* Joint Publications Research Service No. 612691 (20 February 1974), pp. 77–84.

Khrushchev made a heavy-handed attempt to force the Chinese to abandon the Leap by suddenly withdrawing all Soviet aid and advisers. Thus, Mao's experimentation with an alternative development strategy after having utilized so fully Soviet experience in the early 1950s heavily contributed to the deterioration of Sino-Soviet relations. The fact that the Great Leap failed disastrously, with the deaths of more than 10 million people, did nothing to mitigate the bitter aftertaste it left in Sino-Soviet relations.

Indeed, when the catastrophic results of the Leap had severely damaged Mao's prestige and eroded his domestic power, the Chairman decided to utilize Sino-Soviet relations as one of his tools for making his comeback in Peking politics. This strategy severely affected Chinese's ties with the USSR during 1962–65. Essentially, Mao began a polemic in which he accused Moscow of having turned revisionist. He then used this polemic to gain wide publicity in China for what was in reality Mao's critique of the domestic policies being followed by his colleagues against his wishes. Ultimately, in 1965–66, Mao turned against his colleagues and accused them of precisely the kind of political and ideological errors for which he had been castigating Moscow. Thus, Mao's chief target Liu Shaoqi became "China's Khrushchev," and Soviet-style "revisionism" became the bogeyman of Chinese politics. The Cultural Revolution took as a leitmotif the need to keep from developing along the lines of the Soviet Union, with (not surprisingly) severe adverse consequences for Sino-Soviet relations.

The Cultural Revolution, indeed, marked an attempt to purify the society at the same time that it was supposed to bring Mao back into a position of prominence. It thus drew from deep nativist currents, identifying ideological purity and militant xenophobia with national strength. In pursuit of this cleansing of the system, Mao proved astonishingly willing to cut the country off from the corrupting influence of contact with the rest of the world, to the degree that at one point, for example, the PRC had only one ambassador in residence abroad. This domestic political implosion proved deleterious to China's overall foreign policy, damaging its relations with governments virtually across the ideological and economic spectrums. Domestically, the Cultural Revolution reduced the power of both the party and government apparatuses, creating a vacuum into which the army soon moved. It at the same time marked the nadir of the influence on policy of urban-educated cadres and the intelligentsia in general.

Just as the Cultural Revolution ended any cooperation between Peking and Moscow, the 1968 Soviet invasion of Czechoslovakia, followed by Sino-Soviet border clashes in 1969, contributed to the decision to bring the Cultural Revolution to a close, lest internal turmoil invite Soviet aggression. During 1969–71 Peking sought to impose order on the country and mobilize its resources in preparation for possible war. These efforts created both opportunity and danger for Lin Biao, the defense minister, who had become Mao's official heir apparent in 1969.

Lin, as head of the military, could obviously use the war scare to expand and consolidate his power, and the army indeed virtually took over administration of urban China in the wake of the Soviet conquest of Czechoslovakia. But the movement away from the Cultural Revolution, with which Lin had been closely identified, also spelled potential danger for him. His concerns grew as Premier Zhou Enlai persuaded Mao to support both a more pragmatic economic development strategy and a possible rapprochement with the United States to counter the Soviet threat. Lin opposed the U.S. option, which portended the removal of the military from its dominant position in the civilian administrative apparatus. These issues were decided only with Lin's sudden death in September 1971, two months after Henry Kissinger's dramatic secret visit to Peking. The Chinese claim that Lin died while trying to flee to the USSR after an unsuccessful attempt to assassinate Chairman Mao and seize the succession for himself.

Lin's death left two major groups contending for the succession to an aged and ailing Mao. The Cultural Revolution had polarized Chinese politics to the point where each of these factions articulated strikingly different packages of domestic and foreign policy views. In schematic terms, the nativists, under Mao's wife Jiang Qing, argued that China should maintain a relatively "closed-door" foreign policy, restricting contact with the outside world to a minimum. Only in this way could the country preserve the social and political purity essential for its strength and dignity. If this concentration on domestic purification and rejection of foreign contacts impeded economic development, that would be preferable to rapid industrial growth whose result would simply be to put the country in the hands of "revisionist" leaders like those who had led the Soviet Union astray over the previous decades.

The modernizers (both the eclectic and all-around varieties) united under Zhou Enlai and, after 1973, Deng Xiaoping. They placed priority on economic development, which they felt could be rapidly accomplished only with greater ties to the international community. These ties could not be established and sustained, however, without more pragmatic domestic policies that would, among other things, create confidence among foreign businessmen in China's economy and provide a framework for ongoing economic relations with the West that would transcend specific trade deals. Zhou and Deng had many other economic and political reasons for wanting these changes in domestic policy, but the beneficent effects on China's international economic position remained an important concern.

A military and diplomatic strategy also underlay each of these policy stances. The nativists felt that security ultimately lay in the ability to project an image of militant unity so that any potential aggressor would see the country as ultimately too difficult to occupy. They may also have believed that leftism, with its attendant fixation on secrecy in internal affairs, would hide some of China's serious physical weaknesses from its enemies. The modernizers, by contrast, believed that security demanded that China develop the economic base necessary to a strong military, and also that the PRC take diplomatic advantage of the cleavages among its potential enemies to lessen the threat it faced. These views forced the modernizers to advocate a more open-door foreign policy diplomatically as well as economically, and encouraged the nativists to oppose them in all these spheres.

In broad terms, power seesawed between nativists and moderniz-ers during Mao's last years, with the aging chairman trying to balance off the two groups while the factions themselves refused to accept a permanent division of power. When the nativists enjoyed increasing influence, as in late 1973 and early 1974 and again for much of 1976 (until Mao died in September), both domestic and foreign policy reflected their preferences. These were months of domestic political mobilization, antiforeign propaganda, and increasing restraint in foreign trade. By contrast, when the modernizers were on the rise, as from mid-1974 through most of 1975, they shifted domestic priorities toward pragmatic economic growth, reduced the level of political mobilization, and sought to expand economic and political contacts abroad. Events in the domestic arena largely tilted the power balance back and forth between nativists and modernizers during these years, but the repercussions were felt in China's foreign affairs as well.

Thus, under Mao Zedong's aegis Chinese politics eventually became highly polarized. In his final decade in power—a decade of murderous political infighting—personal enmities became closely bound up with different perspectives on the best path for the revolution to follow. Given the breakdown in political norms during these years, factionalism ran rampant and complicated the situation still further.

It should be clear from the above that the close interaction between domestic and foreign policy was not limited to the final frenzied years of the Maoist era but was also reflected in the creation of the Sino-Soviet alliance in the 1950s, in its decline and collapse in the early 1960s, and in the controversies over the rapprochement with the United States and the opening to the West in the 1970s. Consistently, from 1949 until the death of Mao Zedong in 1976, domestic and foreign policy were seen as parts of a single, comprehensive, integrated policy package.

The center of gravity during most of the first fifteen years of the People's Republic—from 1949 to the Cultural Revolution (excluding the Great Leap Forward)—was what we have called eclectic modernism, a policy which favored international economic and political ties that would enable China to obtain capital and technology from abroad but also attempted to keep China's modernization on a socialist course under the control of the Communist party. The realities of international affairs during these years demanded that the PRC deal primarily with the Soviet Union and its allies. During Mao's later years, however, he increasingly rejected the domestic distribution of power and resources that this strategy produced. He finally chose to swim with more nativist currents and support a policy of more limited ties with the developed world, emphasizing (at least rhetorically) the promotion of revolution abroad and at home the modernization of China through indigenous methods, notably mass mobilization. Mao never backed the nativists to the exclusion of the modernizers, but his interventions did shift the balance among the three groups during the Cultural Revolution decade.

The Post-Mao Era

The leading nativists, such as the Gang of Four, were purged in the month after Mao Zedong died, but the Maoist era itself left a legacy of severe economic problems and of factionalism and intrigue throughout the political system. Under Deng Xiaoping, a wide-ranging post-Mao strategy was gradually developed and tested, one aimed at moving the country toward rapid economic growth while reforming the political system so as to prevent a return to Maoist-type policies. Deng's strategy, like the strategies of his predecessors, is a package of domestic and foreign policies. It too remains controversial, although the present lines of cleavage differ from those of the period before 1976.

With the continuing elimination of nativists from positions of power, the remaining antagonists are the eclectic modernizers and the all-around modernizers. These groups, as we have seen, had united to oppose the nativists in Mao's last years, but they nevertheless disagree in their answers to two crucial questions: How much should China reform its internal system in order to spur its economic growth? How much foreign influence should be permitted in the country, both economically and in social and ideological matters? While both groups agree on the importance of economic development, they disagree about the degree to which foreigners should be allowed to penetrate China, and thus about the degree to which the internal system should be reformed to facilitate China's interaction with the international community. In this connection, Deng Xiaoping's efforts have remained controversial precisely because they would, if not modified, produce substantial changes in the distribution of domestic power and resources, and these changes would be linked directly to the PRC's efforts to derive increasing benefits from the international community. Foreign and domestic policy thus remain closely connected in Chinese politics.

The economic situation that Deng and his colleagues confront seems a maze of contradictions. Eighty percent of the people live in villages, yet China boasts the world's largest urban population. The PRC is a poor country, but it has the world's fifth largest industrial plant. And whereas China has extraordinarily low per capita foreign trade figures, it conducts an overall foreign trade of more than U.S. $40 billion per year, higher than all but one or two non-OECD countries. These contrasts reflect the fact that China contains more than a fifth of the world's total population. They also highlight the great complexity of the economic imperatives the country faces.

What is more, the Maoist strategy of economic development had left the country facing critical economic problems. With some 800 million Chinese living in the countryside, agricultural production remained inefficient, acting as a drag on the rest of the economy. The most fundamental problem in agriculture is a severely adverse ratio of population to arable land, but flawed policies have contributed to the difficulties. For example, in 1958–60 and again during Mao's last decade Chinese peasants were ordered to "take grain as the key link," which meant in many cases to concentrate, in a highly inefficient fashion, on grain production to the neglect of other crops. Also, ideologically based objections to free markets, private plots, and other "vestiges of capitalism" combined with egalitarian elements in the distribution system in the collective sector to rob peasants of much of the incentive for hard individual labor. Mass mobilization of labor to build irrigation works and other major undertakings was often carried out with such a disregard for technical requirements that the results proved more harmful than helpful. And finally, national priorities in general kept the countryside starved for the funds necessary to carry out a significant technological upgrading of agricultural production.

In the urban economy, heavy industry received the lion's share of capital investment funds, leaving the consumer goods industries unable to provide the commodities necessary to spur workers to greater efforts. Within heavy industry itself, moreover, attention was paid to expanding the gross value of output more than to making output mesh with demand. Thus, for example, in the mid-1970s increasing quantities of specialized steel had to be imported from Japan even as the PRC steel industry was stockpiling large quantities of its own finished products that did not meet market demands. Even more importantly, in making investment decisions inadequate attention was paid to the needs of certain critical sectors, thus creating severe bottlenecks. In the energy sector, disproportionate investment went to a few large petroleum fields, with consequent underfunding both of additional petroleum exploration and of development of coal and hydroelectric power. By the late 1970s China's energy shortage had become so severe that it was holding down the rate of industrial growth to well below the post-1949 average. Transportation, especially railroads, is another critical bottleneck, as is communications. In all these areas it will take a number of years, and massive capital commitments, to make up for the earlier decades of neglect.

The Maoist policy toward human capital was also harmful. During the Cultural Revolution people with higher education and technical skills were attacked with special vengeance, and for more than a decade the country's educational system was rendered almost incapable of training technical specialists. Thus, those who had already acquired their expertise before 1966 lost some of their skills through a decade of political struggles, when most were barred from practicing their professions. At the same time, new talent was not developed to replace older specialists. Given the wide-ranging attack on experts and expertise, moreover, it appears that the Communist party took over substantial responsibility for management of the economy after the military was edged out in the wake of the Lin Biao affair in 1971. The government apparatus, by contrast, was seen as too "bourgeois" to be entrusted with as much responsibility as it had enjoyed during 1953–57 and 1962–65. And along a different dimension, Chinese policy toward remuneration in urban enterprises provided virtually no reward for greater efforts nor any punishment for inadequate performance. The result, unsurprisingly, was a general degradation of skills and slackening of enthusiasm for work.

Finally, a strong xenophobia characterized China during Mao's last decade, although it became somewhat less virulent after 1970. Foreign trade remained at extremely low levels, and the country's expertise concerning the international economy atrophied badly. Thus, by 1977 Peking had to devote major efforts to developing the skills necessary to make use of the international economic system as a source of capital, technology, and managerial expertise for China's economic growth.

Any effort to reform the economic system to make it more compatible with the need to absorb foreign capital and technology would have potentially far-reaching implications for the political institutional structure in the PRC. For more than two decades people with technical expertise had been discriminated against in job assignments. Those in key administrative positions throughout the bureaucracies often lacked education[4] and the requisite technical skills. In the Communist party apparatus especially, many people held critical posts by virtue of political background and loyalty rather than administrative or technical skills. And the lines of authority in the administrative system remained ill-defined, allowing Party cadres to exercise control over their counterparts in the government organs charged with running the economy.

The Cultural Revolution had thus created enormous tensions in the political system and had encouraged the resolution of these tensions through factional struggles. After a decade of recurring turmoil, many bureaucrats had learned that the way to survive was to be as outwardly compliant and noncommittal as possible, while in fact never working hard to implement any particular set of policies. Experience showed that policies were likely to be reversed within the foreseeable future—with serious consequences for those who had become identified with them. The general inattention to specific economic results displaced the systems of responsibility that previously had held people accountable for their performance, and the incessant political infighting eroded organizational discipline in favor of personal, factional political loyalties. Moreover, roughly half the 38 million members of the Chinese Communist Party had joined the CCP

4. As of 1982, 40–50 percent of China's administrative cadres had not completed junior high school education: *Renmin ribao,* 14 May 1982—in *Foreign Broadcast Information Service Daily Report: People's Republic of China* [hereafter cited as *FBIS*], 18 May 1982, p. K1.

during 1966–76, and these people retained a commitment to the recruitment and promotion practices that characterized those tumultuous years.

Deng's initial strategy tackled this myriad of problems in an integrated way. He calculated that China would need rapid economic growth and a rising standard of living both to protect its security and to continue to hold the loyalty of the populace now that Mao's overwhelming presence was no longer there. To achieve this growth, he decided that the country could draw substantial resources from the international community through astute diplomacy combined with the proper reforms in domestic policy. At the same time, he gave technical specialists a central role in optimizing the use of resources in domestic affairs, and he based the rest of his domestic program on the premise that people would work hard only if given clear responsibility and material rewards for good performance. Given the Maoist legacy, these new principles were potentially revolutionary in their implications, and the policies designed to implement them were thus highly controversial.

Specifically, Deng sought to strengthen the international united front against the Soviet Union and its allies, thus more closely identifying China with the strategic objectives of the United States, Japan, and Western Europe. By so doing, Deng calculated that the PRC would confront fewer obstacles to acquiring foreign capital and technology. Sino-U.S. relations would perforce be the linchpin of this approach, given America's strong ties with Japan and its critical role in NATO. This strategy would also, of course, benefit Peking by providing additional security against Soviet pressure, as long as Peking did not go so far in its strategic identification with the West that it provoked Moscow into some counter action.

Domestically, Deng launched a wide range of initiatives. Over a period of several years he rehabilitated most of the victims of Mao's political campaigns going back to the 1950s. Many of these people were urban, educated specialists. Deng also sought to place specialists in positions where their skills could be used and concomitantly to remove persons lacking expertise from positions that required it. This effort removed an increasing share of economic decision making from the hands of the Party apparatus and transferred it either to the government or to the enterprises themselves. It also demanded that efforts be made to clarify the locus of responsibility for tasks and that mechanisms be devised to link performance with reward. The potential effects, both on the distribution of power between the Party, the government, and the enterprises and on which types of people would advance in the system, were profound. In Deng's program, the Party apparatus, staffed by the somewhat less educated, more rural oriented, and more xenophobic cadres, stood to lose the most.

Other aspects of Deng's program also rankled members of the Party. His advocacy of greater use of material incentives in both urban and rural production, along with his other initiatives, ran counter to the Maoist dogma of the past decade and required a direct retreat from Maoist orthodoxy and a downgrading of the role of politics in the society in general. The related increase in China's international exposure also reduced the regime's power to control the populace's exposure to ideas. But since the Party had had responsibility for ideological education and the enforcement of political criteria in policy implementation, the Party apparatus had again borne the brunt of Deng's reforms.

Deng's program also had implications for the military. Had Deng and his colleagues been willing to give priority to military modernization, the People's Liberation Army (PLA) might well have strongly supported his other reforms in order to gain access to the West's advanced weapons systems and related technology. But the military has remained low on the priority list for resources under Deng, and the domestic aspects of his program have increased the military's dissatisfaction. For example, many officers continue to regard Mao Zedong highly. Many of them also are relatively xenophobic and believe that the importation of foreign ideas is bad for China's morale—and thus potentially dangerous to its security. Deng's policies have shifted investment toward the consumer goods industries, to the detriment of the heavy industrial sector on which the military depends. And rural reforms have made farm work sufficiently attractive to peasant youths that for the first time in memory the PLA has encountered recruitment problems in the countryside. Perhaps most fundamentally, however, the PLA is, like most militaries, ardently nationalistic, and thus it contains many people who are extremely sensitive to any possible compromises of China's sovereignty. Some argue that Deng's efforts, both in the economy (for example, inviting in foreign experts, encouraging direct foreign investment, selling China's natural resources, etc.) and in other areas (such as adjustments of policy toward Taiwan to cement U.S.-PRC relations, as noted below) have involved precisely such compromises.

Summing up, Deng has seen the solution to China's problems in terms of a strategy encompassing major domestic and foreign initiatives. These initiatives have the potential to recast the distribution of resources, prestige, and privilege quite dramatically in China. They have also subjected the country to a barrage of foreign ideas and influences unequaled since the heyday of the Sino-Soviet relationship in the early to middle 1950s. The logic of these policies, moreover, portends even more far-reaching changes, for Deng has pulled Chinese politics closer to the all-around modernizer position than has any previous Chinese leader. Foreign investors require a legal framework within which to work, only part of which is in place. Joint equity ventures combine with other forces in the economy to argue for a more rational price structure, which would be a change of profound dimensions in the PRC.

With these and other pressures, not surprisingly many have begun to advocate some pulling back from the initiatives launched in 1978, and considerable backtracking has in fact occurred. Thus China is finding once again, as it has found repeatedly since the 1870s, that a decision to import technology and expertise selectively from abroad and introduce it into the Chinese system triggers an almost insidious multiplication of changes that eventually become so upsetting that they produce a backlash of significant dimensions. That this has again been occurring in recent years is shown by the sequence of changes in Chinese policy since 1978, which have been mapped out at a number of major central work conferences.[5]

5. Central work conferences are meetings that bring together the elite to review the current situation and determine the broad outlines of policy for the coming months. Sometimes these decisions are then ratified by a formal meeting of the Central Committee or a Party Congress, but often they are not. Central work conferences typically discuss and decide on a range of issues. Not infrequently, they last for weeks and even months at a time. There is no regular schedule for convening these important meetings, but usually there is at least one each winter and one each summer. On

The central work conference of November–December 1978 marked a turning point in post-Mao China. At this meeting, Deng Xiaoping culminated his effort to make economic development—encapsulated in the phrase Four Modernizations—*the* goal for all activity in China. This effort entailed attacking the more pro-Maoist members remaining in the leadership, demanding that more resources be funneled into the agricultural sector, declaring the completion of the campaign that had been waged to root out the ideological influence of the nativist Gang of Four, and positing that in the future even the Communist party's work would be judged according to whether or not it promoted a pragmatic strategy of economic development.

Deng's domestic strategy as of late 1978 assumed that substantial foreign assistance could be obtained both in the form of technological transfers and through direct capital acquisition. Deng saw the United States as key to this program for several reasons. First, as noted above, he assigned last priority to military spending in the allocation of funds, but this in turn presumed a relationship with the United States that would afford additional protection against Soviet pressure. Second, Deng believed close Sino-U.S. relations would give all foreign businessmen the confidence to make substantial investments in the PRC. In a more diffuse sense, also, Deng was preaching an outward-looking strategy, and it would undoubtedly add to his political momentum to be able to demonstrate payoffs in Sino-U.S. relations from his efforts.

A concern dealing more strictly with foreign policy also influenced Deng's approach to the United States in late 1978. Sino-Vietnamese relations had deteriorated rapidly throughout 1978, as Peking backed the Pol Pot regime in Kampuchea against an increasingly Moscow-oriented government in Hanoi. In the early winter the Soviet Union and Vietnam signed a pact that gave Hanoi the confidence it needed to launch an invasion of Kampuchea without fear of a Chinese counterattack. Deng strongly advocated a retaliatory strike against the Vietnamese but wanted to establish full diplomatic relations with

---

central work conferences in general, see Kenneth Lieberthal, *A Research Guide to Central Party and Government Meetings in China, 1949–1975* (White Plains, NY: International Arts and Sciences Press, 1976).

Washington first so as to gain additional protection against Soviet pressure during the PRC's action against Hanoi.

For reasons of both domestic and foreign policy, therefore, Deng Xiaoping sought normalization of relations with the United States at the end of 1978, and indeed the key negotiations to reach this goal occurred during the November–December central work conference. His success in the negotiation created a sense of euphoria that helped carry through his domestic agenda at the same conference. For the first time since 1949, all major powers now recognized Peking as the sole legal government of all of China. Deng's new strategy thus seemed to have accomplished quickly what neither Mao nor Zhou Enlai had been able to complete in their lifetimes. But Deng's normalization of relations with the United States included a compromise over Taiwan which many of his colleagues would find distasteful: He had agreed to normalize relations even though the United States asserted that it would continue to sell weapons to Taiwan. Essentially, he left China with few options to exercise to bring Taiwan to heel, and if any future U.S. administration should dramatize this by adopting a two-China policy, Deng would shoulder the blame. Thus, the political outcome of this central work conference left Deng with a major victory but also with major potential vulnerabilities.[6]

While the decisions of late 1978 had an enormous impact on China during the following two years, significant problems arose with some of the key elements of the package adopted by the 1978 conference. The Chinese attack on Vietnam in February–March 1979 went badly, and thus insofar as Deng had justified the Taiwan compromise on the basis of the need for this retaliatory strike his judgment looked questionable. The Four Modernizations program involved efforts in so many areas that the central authorities feared a loss of control. The economy began to overheat and produce the first serious infla-

6. The decisions of the November–December central work conference were embodied in the communiqué of the Third Plenum of the Eleventh Central Committee, which met in the wake of this conference. Participants in the negotiations on normalization of Sino-U.S. relations have indicated that Deng Xiaoping personally carried on the key negotiations with Ambassador Woodcock and that Deng agreed to the compromise on Taiwan on the spot at one session, without first consulting his colleagues.

tion in many years. And, ominously, the American presidential election of 1980 produced a new incumbent who favored establishing official relations with Taiwan and who had previously declared that normalization of relations with Peking had been a bad deal for the United States.

These developments, domestic and international, coalesced in December 1980, when the Chinese leadership convened another central work conference to make far-reaching decisions on both domestic and foreign policy.[7] Specifically, the December 1980 meeting cut the central budget by 20 percent to help curb inflation. It also halted many of the economic reforms then underway. Politically, this conference decided to give the Party a stronger role than it had had since the late 1978 decisions that gave absolute priority to rapid economic development. This same meeting adopted measures to curb the spread of foreign ideas and foreign influence and decided to cancel or reduce some major projects that involved substantial foreign participation. Lastly, at precisely this time the Chinese seized on the sale by the Netherlands of two submarines to Taiwan as a pretext to issue uncompromising statements that "no country, [not] even a superpower" could expect to maintain normal diplomatic relations with the PRC if it also made significant arms sales to Taiwan or adopted what amounted to a two-China policy.

Thus, the December 1980 central work conference hardened China's stances on the Taiwan issue and on preserving the country's economic and cultural integrity, while downplaying economic development somewhat and arguing that China could maintain its own security even if relations with the United States should sour. It thus dealt in an integrated way with the mutual influences of domestic and foreign policy as of late 1980. These decisions were made in response both to Ronald Reagan's election and to the mounting domestic pressures of the previous months.

During 1981 China's domestic economy began to get back on track and under control. By the end of the year, Deng's central concern was with managing a succession to a younger leadership committed at least in broad outline to his programs. But U.S.-China relations

7. Central work conferences also met in between these two meetings.

remained unsettled. The Reagan administration still had not made clear its full position on Taiwan and related matters, and thus the Taiwan issue remained a vulnerable spot for Deng. By January 1982, indications of political stress increased. Vice Premier Li Xiannian made startling statements on foreign affairs,[8] Deng Xiaoping conspicuously dropped out of sight for about a month, and other leaders did not appear at functions that they normally would have attended. But in early February a central work conference convened and a new set of policies was worked out.

The issues among which a balance was struck at this meeting evidently included the following: a commitment (but without providing name lists) to a major restructuring of the State Council, a program that potentially would allow Deng and his protégé Zhao Ziyang to put many of "their" people in place in the government ministries;[9] a new, and very hard-line, position on future U.S. weapons sales to Taiwan; a greater stress on economic planning, as opposed to use of the market, and greater emphasis on heavy industry than previously indicated (both of which marked some retrenchment from reforms implemented over the previous three years); a tough line against cadre corruption; and an open-door economic policy, combined with a hard line on the kinds of ideological contamination that contacts with the outside world inevitably produced. The issue that was probably the most important to Deng was the reform of the State Council, and the decision there at least sanctioned the reform effort and made it possible (although not certain) that Deng Xiaoping and Zhao Ziyang would be able to use the reform to put their own people in key slots. China's response to the Taiwan arms sales issue figured in as well, however, as did the PRC's foreign economic posture and the treatment of foreigners in China. The decisions made on each of these issues reflected the need to achieve a balance on the entire agenda.

8. For example, Li commented to an Italian reporter that "it is said that there are close relations between China and the United States. It is not true. We know very well that the United States is still an imperialist country." *L'UNITA,* 8 January 1982—*FBIS,* 19 January 1982, pp. G1–3. Other strong statements by Li on Sino-U.S. and Sino-Soviet affairs during January 1982 are available in *FBIS,* 5 January 1982, p. B1; and *FBIS,* 8 January 1982, p. C1.

9. Zhao would head the commission charged with carrying out this restructuring.

Decision making since Mao's death and the purge of his nativist followers thus still makes events in the domestic arena indirectly affect decisions in foreign policy, and vice versa. These interrelationships are neither mechanical nor precise, but in the give and take of Chinese politics they provide for ongoing interaction between the country's domestic and foreign policies.

Reforms and the Future

Recasting the system to maximize efficiency and technical proficiency while devolving necessary administrative power to lower levels entails fundamental changes in who wields power throughout the country. In broad terms, as noted above, the Communist party has been asked to yield control over specific economic decisions to its government counterpart. And within the government, the less educated cadres are being replaced by younger and better educated candidates. This process is proceeding slowly and fitfully, but the trends are both clear and ominous for millions of the cadres who wielded power over the last two decades of Mao's tenure. Not surprisingly, more than a few of them have been quick to find fault with the implementation of this new economic strategy—and because of the overall dearth of experience in this area, there is more than a little fault to be found.

It is in this context that the continuing differences between eclectic modernizers and all-around modernizers assume importance. The former accept the importance of importing technology and expanding foreign trade, but they oppose major political changes. The latter, by contrast, stress the importance of importing foreign technology as well, but would also modify the country's institutional structure and practices in order to achieve modernization.

The tensions between the two groups have been exacerbated by the spillover from other aspects of the modernization program. Peking's decision to raise standards of living has quite naturally made many Chinese increasingly concerned with material goods. A part of the strategy for improving the quality of life has been to expand rapidly the number of television sets available to the populace and to upgrade the quality of television programming. But television has taught peasants about the higher standards of living in China's major cities, and it gives people throughout the country a glimpse of standards of living abroad. The shock from what they have seen has been enormous, for most of the world (and especially China's non-Communist neighbors in East Asia) has experienced unprecedented rates of growth during precisely the two decades when all but heavy industry in China on a per capita basis grew modestly, if at all. Foreign tourists, welcomed because of the foreign exchange that they bring into the economy, have also added to this awareness of the country's relative economic backwardness. Somewhat predictably, this situation has produced varying combinations of rampant materialism and cynicism among many people, especially youths living in the cities. Their desire to emulate foreign living styles and their distaste for political involvement have in turn alarmed both the eclectic modernizers and the remaining nativists among their elders in the upper echelons of the political system.

In sum, China in the 1980s faces economic constraints that force it to look to expert-led growth and significant interaction with the international community in order to develop its economy at reasonable speed over the final two decades of this century. A vast population, limited energy resources, an inadequate transportation infrastructure, and massive underdevelopment of the educational and scientific establishments have taken their toll. The government now has little choice; it can turn away from an open-door economic policy only if it is willing again to sacrifice economic growth and improvements in the standard of living by imposing an ideologically charged mobilization regime on the population. While this turn of events cannot be completely ruled out, it seems very unlikely. Nevertheless, the modes of interaction with the international community and the attendant changes that it will bring in China remain hotly debated issues. Even the efforts by the leadership to develop a decision-making process based on consensus rather than on political warfare have not severed the connection between domestic political decisions and China's international policy.

What, then, does the future portend? The answer lies in a combination of domestic and international forces already at work. First, even though many Chinese recognize the need for economic and political reforms there remains little chance that the current reform effort can be brought to completion. This somewhat gloomy assessment results partly from the fate of similar movements in other Communist countries—to date China seems to be following the same pattern. In the short term, the reforms create new problems without fully resolving the previous difficulties. The widening set of interests affected adversely by the reform program begins to mobilize in opposition. Since the program's results do not immediately justify the disruption it is causing, a strong leader is required to keep it on track until, years hence, the full system is in place and improvements can be seen. In China, however, part of the impetus for the reform effort is recognition of the enormous problems created when Mao Zedong arrogated power to himself during the Cultural Revolution. Ironically, without a figure of Mao's towering authority in the rest of the 1980s, the reform effort probably will generate too much opposition to be sustained. For some time, therefore, significant tensions about the best way to proceed will trouble China and the scope of the reform effort will remain a matter of continuing controversy.

Second and relatedly, China has already passed its heroic stage of development. Revolutionary fervor has waned. The intense battles of the Cultural Revolution era introduced a self-protective factionalism that remains strong in the ruling party, government, and military bureaucracies, despite the best efforts of Deng and his colleagues to get rid of it. It will be extremely difficult to eradicate factionalism completely without an overriding commitment to a revolutionary cause. The factionalism certainly need not mean that murderous political battles will be a fact of life for the PRC in the 1980s, but a sustained, unified commitment to any program may be difficult to generate, as each faction bends some of its efforts toward looking for vulnerabilities in whatever program another faction puts forward.

And third, whatever China's performance during the coming decade, it seems certain (barring a cataclysm among its international rivals) that the PRC will make little progress in closing the gaps that currently separate it from its competitors. Should the PRC choose to focus its energies on specific sectors of the economy, the country could make substantial progress, but only at major cost to other sectors. Factional politics in Peking may, in any case, not permit such sustained concentration on a few selected goals. At the same time, throughout the remainder of the 1980s the country will face energy shortages that by themselves will put a cap on growth. Necessary infrastructure investment required for all-around development involves spending staggering sums; concentration on this problem will hold down standards of living for most of this decade. The sheer size of China's population means, in addition, that average per capita increases in the standard of living will come only with extreme difficulty.

Thus, the domestic reform program will probably run into political difficulties because it appears to produce inadequate economic results, especially when China is compared with other East Asian countries. Under these conditions, the reform effort might be largely stymied over the next five years or more, as bureaucratic interests reassert themselves. The likely result—barring some major catastrophe in the economy or a dramatic shock such as military conflict with the Soviet Union—would be the reemergence of an administratively dominated economy. A commitment to economic development would remain, but there would be an unwillingness to pursue development in ways that undercut the prerogatives of the bureaucrats who run the system.

In all probability, this type of system would tilt more toward the eclectic modernizers and thus be somewhat more conservative on a broad range of issues that they identify with sovereignty than would its reformist counterpart. Reassertion of the power of the national bureaucracies would reduce the direct access that foreign firms are now beginning to enjoy to Chinese firms. It would also produce a more restrictive cultural policy, one designed to enable China to obtain technical and scientific knowledge from abroad while screening out broader foreign cultural influences. The military and a strengthened central planning apparatus might succeed in shifting economic strategy back toward increased priority for the machine building and metallurgical interests. Changes along these lines—as well as possible new restrictions on Chinese emigration—would sap some of the energy from relations with many developed countries.

None of these shifts would require that China change its strategic orientation of cooperating with the West and Japan in order to develop the country and protect itself against the Soviet Union. But the strength of these bonds and the degree of mutual influence among the societies concerned would probably fall short of what would otherwise have developed, and there would thus be less good feeling and mutual understanding to cushion the shocks to these relationships that unforeseen events would inevitably produce. In sum, in the 1980s domestic political interests, unresolved questions about institutional roles and prerogatives, and ongoing debates over economic development strategy remain salient elements in the determination of China's foreign policy.

3 China in the International Economy

BRUCE REYNOLDS

In 1970, the year that it began to emerge from the chaos of the Cultural Revolution, China exported just over $2 billion worth of goods. Forty-seven percent of these were agricultural products, nearly one-quarter were destined for other Communist countries, and about 90 percent left Chinese harbors on ships flying foreign flags. By 1979, a remarkable transformation had occurred. China's exports now totaled about $14 billion. Less than 30 percent were agricultural products, and less than 15 percent were sold to other members of the Communist camp. What is more, even though China's foreign trade had increased nearly sevenfold over the previous ten years, Chinese flag vessels now carried three-quarters of it. China's merchant marine comprised 680 ships, making it the second largest fleet in Asia.

This is indeed a new China. Long isolated from Western trade and commerce, China today has become an active participant in the international economy. Not only is the People's Republic now trading more with the rest of the world than at any point in its history, but its trading partners, the composition of its trade, and the range of its international undertakings are all very different than in the past.

In this chapter, I explore China's role, past, present, and future, in the world economy. I begin by reviewing the fundamental characteristics of China's domestic economy, which help determine China's pattern of interaction with the international economic order. I look next at China's response over the years to various opportunities offered by the international economy. I focus in particular on China's participation in grain trade, in trade in technology, and in international capital flows, as well as China's level of trade, choice of trading partners, and attitude toward the creation of a New International Economic Order. In the process, I will discuss the kinds of considerations—strategic, ideological, or strictly economic—that have been most important in shaping Chinese economic policy in the past. A concluding section considers possible futures. Here I will speculate that China will become increasingly integrated in a dynamic East Asian regional economy, but that the growth of China's trade will depend on the future of the economic reforms that Peking has undertaken since the death of Mao Zedong.

The Domestic Economy and Its Effect on China's Trade

Any analysis of China's role in the international economy must begin with the distinctive features of China's domestic economy. These can be grouped into three sets. First, there are what I will call *structural characteristics*: China's resource endowment, technology, and ideology. These features change very slowly, and they will condition Chinese policy choices for a long time to come. Second are the *central economic goals* of the Chinese leadership, as manifested over the past three decades: growth, stability, equity, and self-sufficiency. China pursues these goals subject to the constraints imposed by its structural features. Third are the *institutions* through which the Chinese government tries to implement its goals: in particular, state or collective ownership of industrial enterprises, centralized directive planning, and state monopoly of foreign trade. While somewhat inflexible, goals and institutions are obviously more amenable to change than such fundamental characteristics as land/labor/capital ratios. Indeed, one conclusion that can be reached from a survey of China's recent economic history is that the institutional structure of the PRC is no longer compatible with its economic goals, particularly growth, and that those institutions must be reformed in the coming decades if China wishes to achieve maximum growth rates and to participate fully in the international economy.

STRUCTURAL CHARACTERISTICS   Let us begin by placing four labels on China: less-developed country (LDC), continental economy, East

Asian resource endowment, and Leninist political structure. Each of these reflects a part of the Chinese reality, giving some insight into why China does what it does. Granted, the reality is a synthesis of all four labels, and more; but to analyze is always to dissect.

China is an LDC by virtue of its per capita income, somewhere between $250 and $500, which places it somewhat above India, but below, say, the Philippines, and far below South Korea. Despite the industrialization of the last thirty years, China remains largely an agricultural country: Agriculture provides 35 percent of its gross national product (GNP), and 70 percent of the labor force still works the land.

Accordingly, China faces a set of problems common to all LDCs. And its solutions are seldom unique. Every large LDC, for example, has a technically backward, low-income rural sector supplying food to an industrial, urban sector. Virtually every LDC government tries to control the price at which that transfer of food occurs. Unless rural purchase prices are generous, the urban-rural income disparity will precipitate unmanageable migration to cities. But raising the urban sale price arouses opposition from the politically powerful city population. What to do? In 1979 China chose to please both sides. It sharply increased agricultural purchase prices, with no corresponding increase in urban sale prices. This sleight of hand was made possible by a subsidy to urban consumers which, in 1980, totaled $12 billion. This was certainly a large figure, but it was still a familiar story to, say, the Egyptians, whose $1.8 billion subsidy in 1980 was more than three times as large as China's when reckoned on a per capita basis.

Unlike Egypt, however, China has a continental economy. This has two major implications for its participation in world trade. First, China is much more likely to find, within its own borders, the entire range of resources which its economy requires. Thus the ratio of foreign trade to GNP will tend to be small. Smaller countries, in contrast, find it much more difficult to be self-sufficient, and must import a greater array of goods from abroad. Thus the fifty-three countries of Africa, with a total population one-tenth of China's, carry on twice as much trade as the PRC. Similarly, if China's twenty-nine provinces were independent nations, their total foreign trade would be far higher than that of a unified China. But the PRC is a single country, not an amalgam of independent states, and thus it illustrates the simple but powerful rule: Large countries trade less than small ones.

A second consequence of China's size works in the opposite direction, facilitating certain kinds of exports. China's large domestic market enables it to develop, behind implicit or explicit tariff walls, industrial products such as agricultural machinery which require mass production to achieve low unit costs. Then, after the new technology has been mastered through domestic sales, China can plunge into the colder waters of the international marketplace. In this sense, China resembles India, another poor continental economy, which is the seventh largest exporter among LDCs of capital goods, in the unlikely company of far richer countries like Brazil, Argentina, and Korea.

But unlike India, China is not only a large developing country but also an East Asian economy. Like Korea, Japan, and Taiwan, it is burdened with extraordinary population density. This demographic fact of life has created a distinctive East Asian technology: wet-rice agriculture, which makes land extremely productive, but only through enormous infusions of labor. Every hectare of arable land in China feeds ten people, compared to four in India and one in the United States. In China, every hectare demands the attention of seven peasants, whereas in India two suffice. Wet-rice agriculture, in its turn, has modified the course of agricultural modernization in East Asian countries. Modern agricultural technology is especially productive there. And because the dense population has made for less unequal land distribution, in East Asia the Green Revolution has brought with it a much milder exacerbation of rural income inequality than in other countries. Some proponents of a distinctive "East Asian development model" would go further and note other features that China shares with the rest of the region, such as a relatively high literacy rate and, in consequence, an easily trained labor force. Such a labor force facilitated the development of skill-intensive manufacturing, which fueled export-led growth in Korea and Taiwan and could conceivably have a similar impact on China's trade patterns.

In addition to these economic characteristics, China's Leninist ideology conditions the way her economy functions. Leninism requires state ownership of industry, central planning of the economy, and the concentration of power in the hands of a vanguard Communist party. Since 1978, Peking has sought to reduce its commitment to the economic side of Leninism, attempting to reduce the power that central and provincial governments wield over the economy. But economic power and political power are closely intermingled; economic decentralization can quickly breed political pluralism. Thus, an ideology which stresses the importance of the Party's vanguard role breeds stiff resistance to economic decentralization. Russia and Eastern Europe have been wrestling with this contradiction for a quarter century, with resistance getting the better of reform. Their experience sheds light on China's dilemma.

GOALS   In its particular mix of these four structural characteristics—underdevelopment, continental size, East Asian factor ratios, and Leninist politics—China is similar to many countries and yet identical to none. Much the same can be said of its goals. China's goals—rapid growth, price stability, income equality, and national self-sufficiency—are the aims of every LDC, but China has pursued them in a combination that is distinctive.

China's accomplishments in each area are impressive. China has achieved annual growth rates in industry and agriculture since 1952 of around 10 percent and 3 percent respectively, and an overall growth rate of GNP of 5–6 percent per year. Prices for consumer goods rose only 30 percent over the years 1950–79, or less than 0.5 percent per year—an enviable record of price stability. Income equality has been pursued vigorously, and in urban areas the results are obvious: China has avoided the glaring juxtaposition of wealth and squalor prominent in many other LDCs. Still, the degree of inequality within the rural sector is no different than in comparable countries, and the same is true for the urban-rural income gap (urban incomes in China are roughly twice as high as rural incomes). Lastly, China's goal of self-reliance (a policy which faded over time, and especially in the late 1970s) has clearly constricted trade. Imports in 1977–78 averaged only 4.6 percent of GNP, well below the levels of other large countries such as the United States (7.5 percent), India (6.5 percent), or even the USSR (5.4 percent).

China's performance in these four areas is all the more remarkable when one recognizes that the first goal—growth—runs counter to the other three. Consider price stability. China's thirty-year price freeze has badly eroded the incentive to produce. In the coal industry, for example, costs have risen as mines were forced to exploit increasingly poor deposits, but the price of coal has remained constant. Even after the belated 1979 price changes, many Chinese coal producers continue to operate at a loss. The more they produce, the more they lose. Agriculture, too, experienced rising costs pushing against frozen prices. As the incentive for voluntary production and marketing diminished, the state was forced to intervene ever more directly (and clumsily) in the production process and in agricultural production, through higher levels of collectivization and compulsory requisition of grain.

The pursuit of income equality also conflicts with growth, for it erodes incentives even more directly than does price stability. In the past, a peasant household or production team which worked especially hard, and generated extra output, saw most of that income redistributed to the larger collective through the commune accumulation fund. In the same way, under the system of lifetime employment known as the "iron rice bowl," workers in Chinese industry were shielded from dismissal or demotion no matter how sluggish their work. Some of the success in agriculture in 1978–79 (when grain output rose by an astonishing 19.5 percent in two years) reflects the dismantling of this system. Similar gains are now being sought in industry through mechanisms linking wages to individual productivity.

Lastly, insistence on national self-sufficiency also undermines rapid economic growth, since it sacrifices the potential gains that could be achieved through importing advanced technology and through the international specialization of labor. China's philosophy of foreign trade has been to export only what is needed to import, and to import only what China cannot produce itself. Until now, Chinese leaders have explicitly rejected the idea that their country could benefit if it deliberately abstained from attempting to produce goods that other nations could manufacture more efficiently.

Despite these internal contradictions, China, as we noted above, has performed well in all four areas. This can be traced to a leadership which, compared to that in many other LDCs, has an unusual commitment to all four goals and a rare ability to mobilize the Chinese people in their pursuit. Despite irrational and inefficient prices, an absence of strong material incentives, and minimal levels of foreign trade, China has been able to achieve its growth targets, but only at a steadily rising cost in terms of forgone consumption. China's rate of savings and investment has consistently been over 30 percent since 1970, reaching the unprecedented level of 36.5 percent in 1978. By way of comparison, few other countries except Japan claim a savings rate of 30 percent, and, at a higher level of per capita income, Japan can afford such a rate far more easily than China can.

This rising investment rate reflects the growing tension between the goals of growth, on the one hand, and price stability, income equality, and trade autarky on the other. A given amount of investment was yielding an ever smaller amount of growth, in part because of inefficiencies stemming from pursuit of the other three goals. Sustaining China's high growth rate required that a higher and higher proportion of GNP be devoted to investment—with a correspondingly lower proportion remaining for consumption. In the years after 1976, China relaxed its ambitions for equality, price stability, and autarky, hoping that the resulting increases in efficiency would enable it both to maintain a high growth rate and to permit a higher rate of consumption. Trade autarky gave way to a keen interest in comparative advantage and the "international division of labor." Income differentials were accepted as necessary to "develop the initiative" of workers, peasants, and production units. In 1980, some price flexibility emerged, although a surge of inflation soon led to renewed price controls.

In principle, China should be able to trade income equality and trade autarky for higher growth, while still insisting on the third goal of price stability. But in practice these three goals form a seamless web. Without a powerful set of monetary or fiscal controls with which to regulate the economy, Chinese leaders can stabilize prices only by freezing them—that is, by making only occasional and limited use of market-generated prices. But without price flexibility, the trade-off between equality and autarky, on the one hand, and growth on the other becomes very expensive. To understand just why this is true, we must look more closely at domestic economic institutions.

INSTITUTIONS   China's current economic dilemma, and the direction of future policy, is intimately tied up with the central planning system through which the economy is run. Under that system, more than two-thirds of industrial output is produced by state-owned industrial enterprises. A small number of key plants are directly controlled by the central government, while the rest are run by provincial industrial departments. But all are subject to tight restrictions by government planning agencies, which set the enterprises' annual production plans, control the size of their labor force, directly allocate key inputs, appropriate and distribute their output, and determine their prices.

Such a system has inherent inefficiencies. Key production decisions are made by government bureaucrats, most of whom lack training in economic techniques, and all of whom have imperfect information about market conditions and enterprise potentialities. What is more, the process forges an intimate connection between politics and economics that virtually guarantees planning decisions that are irrational from an economic point of view. The economic activities of enterprises, for example, are often structured to correspond to arbitrary administrative boundaries, rather than being allowed to find natural markets. Transportation patterns, too, parallel the administrative hierarchy, so that trade between two neighboring county seats must often pass through the provincial capital hundreds of miles away. Investment decisions are based on political criteria rather than economic efficiency. Capital is transferred through outright government grants that need never be repaid, rather than through bank loans that require regular payments of principal and interest.

In effect, this set of institutions has distributed China's largest industrial plants among administrative kingdoms, dukedoms, and baronies. The system bestows very palpable assets on local authorities: jobs to parcel out, local control over the distribution of output, a flow of profits into local budgets. Predictably, over the past thirty years, local governments have learned how to protect these vested interests against external interference. It is no exaggeration to say that, today, the twenty-nine Chinese provinces are less economically integrated than the nations of the European Economic Community (EEC). Annual planning meetings in Peking take on much the same character as an EEC Council of Ministers' discussion on reducing steel quotas or raising farm subsidies. One anecdotal instance of this protectionist mentality: When an Anhui commune ignored its backward county tractor plant and instead bought higher-quality, cheaper tractors from another province, the local county government was incensed. "Those tractors will never run," it declared, and refused to allocate the necessary diesel fuel.

The foreign trade sector is run in the same fashion. Enterprises or other units which wish to import foreign goods must work through administrative channels, receiving permission from the foreign trade bureaucracy in Peking. Exporters do not interact directly with foreign markets; they are insulated from their customers by the state trading corporations through which all foreign buyers must work. And the same factors which generate protectionism by Chinese provinces and counties work for the nation as a whole. The First Ministry of Machine-Building, for example, is rumored to have an Office of Equipment Approval which has veto power over the importation of any machinery which, in its judgment, could be built by Chinese industry itself.

These kinds of economic institutions are a powerful tool for developing heavy industry in the early stages of growth. During such periods, economic development is basically *extensive*: It results from adding more factors of production (especially capital) to the economy, without using them any more efficiently than before. At later stages of development, however, growth must become *intensive*. It must be based, that is, on a continuing process of technological and managerial innovation, such that each factor of production becomes more efficient and more productive.

The switch to intensive growth in an economy such as China's requires three kinds of institutional reforms. First, it requires that central economic power be dispersed to individual enterprises so as to permit innovation. Second, it demands that incentives and rewards be adjusted so that producers are encouraged to use the resources at their disposal more efficiently. And third, the reforms must see to it that, over the long haul, extra resources flow to producers who have achieved high rates of efficiency, and that fewer resources flow to the rest.

Since the end of 1978, Chinese planners have pursued these goals through a set of reforms that combine the tools of decentralization, material incentives, and profit. To begin with, they have relaxed many of the provisions of central planning, allowing for more local initiative and leaving detailed decision making in the hands of each enterprise. Next, they have linked the incomes of both workers and managers to the profitability of each factory, thus providing a power-ful stimulus to greater efficiency. And finally, by allowing enterprises to reinvest a portion of their profits, and by reducing the amount of investment capital that is provided directly to enterprises by the state, planners can ensure that only efficient enterprises have funds for expansion.

These reforms were put into place in China in 1979 and 1980, under State Council directives issued in July 1979. But they quickly encountered both political and economic obstacles. Politically, the reforms threatened the power and perquisites of a wide range of groups and institutions which had benefited under the old order. Bureaucrats who had administered the economy saw their sphere of authority shrink. Managers who had been appointed and promoted on the basis of political considerations were now told that they would have to learn technical and administrative skills. Inefficient factories, which had been protected by state subsidies, were now instructed to become profitable. Party *apparatchiks,* who had lived by the dictum that profit was morally wrong, were now supposed to implement reforms that enshrined it.

Moreover, the new system also threatened the goals of income equality and price stability. Under the reforms, some enterprises would retain fewer profits per worker than others—and thus be able to pay higher bonuses and make more investments—and for reasons which were arguably not their fault. As noted earlier, the price of coal, for example, is unrealistically low. The cost has risen as extrac-tion has grown more difficult, but the price paid to producers has not been adjusted accordingly. The price of petroleum, in contrast, is unrealistically high. As a "new product" in the 1960s petroleum was priced to reflect the initially high production costs, and that price was never readjusted as the cost of production fell. Thus, under the current reforms, an oil enterprise would earn and retain unfairly high profits, while a coal mine would earn and retain much less.

Rather than adjust the whole set of prices, the Chinese chose to address this problem by varying the profit retention rate, industry by industry. But even this was not enough. Soon, varying profit retention rates appeared within each industry, to make allowances for inefficient producers. In the end, China had a crazy-quilt pattern of special profit retention ratios and subsidies, designed to limit income inequality. Any intelligent producer soon realizes the true rules of this game: If greater efficiency raises your profit margin sharply above that of your peers, the state will lower your profit retention ratio. Over the long run, therefore, there is little incentive to lower costs or increase productivity.

Despite Chinese reassurances that the restructuring of the industrial economy will proceed, the lack of price flexibility vitiates every area of their reforms. The only way to generate a fair and rational set of prices is to unfreeze the system and let producers interact, bidding prices up or down to market-clearing levels. Without prices which provide for uniform profit rates, the new provisions for profit retention and the new tax system will remain arbitrary and unjust. And as long as prices do not balance supply and demand for industrial inputs, state rationing will have to balance them instead. This means that even though efficiency may bring an enterprise greater profit, and thus greater investment capital, that money will not assure access to the rationed resources needed to expand. Instead, the same administrative procedures—application to the Materials Supply Bureau, and allocation based on political criteria rather than efficiency—will remain in place. Without price reform, in other words, the "new" system will still look very much like the old one.

To summarize the main points of this section: China's economy possesses four structural characteristics which are not amenable to rapid change: low per capita income, continental size, an East Asian population density and agricultural technique, and a Leninist ideology. The mix of goals pursued by the leadership—rapid growth, price stability, income equality, and national self-sufficiency—is somewhat more flexible. In the past, heavy and equal stress has been placed on all four, with good results. But the first goal, growth, now conflicts with the other three, as China passes from the stage of extensive growth to that of intensive development. As growth becomes more difficult in the 1980s, some lowering of ambitions in all four areas will be inevitable. In addition, since the inefficiency of the economy is rooted in the way in which it is run, some institutional reform also seems desirable and likely. China must give producers incentives to work hard and use resources well, and it must also reshape the channels through which investment funds are allocated. At the same time, it must somehow break down the pervasive trade barriers that freeze the economy into inefficient patterns of production. These reforms, despite the political and economic obstacles they encounter, are necessary not just to raise domestic productivity but also to create a climate within which liberalization in foreign trade policy will be possible.

China's Role in the International Economy

All nations, if only by default, make policy responses to the opportunities presented by the international economic environment. To what extent shall we engage in trade? With which nations should we trade most extensively? What sorts of goods should we import and export? What kinds of economic relationships—trade, trade plus credits, trade plus credits plus foreign investment—should we agree to? What posture should be taken toward the growing demands for a new international economic order? In this section, I will summarize China's role in the international economy over the last thirty years by considering each of these questions in turn, with particular attention to two areas of trade that have been of special importance to Peking: agricultural products and technology.

Three different sorts of considerations work on Chinese policymakers as they confront these issues. One set are issues of *economic efficiency*. Which course of action will be most profitable to China in real terms and in the short run? The second consideration, which often moves policy in the opposite direction, is *ideology*. What decision conforms most closely to the reigning set of ideas about how societies and politics evolve and interact? Last, and standing midway between these two, is *strategy*. What decision would produce the most favorable political relations with particular countries? Are there long-run economic considerations which short-run profit maximization might overlook?

As we consider China's role in the international economy since 1949, we will look especially for behavior which goes against the prevailing pattern in comparable countries, or against the prevailing wisdom of economists. We will seek to explain such anomalies in terms of the interplay of these three considerations: economics, ideology, and strategy.

Level and Direction of Trade /

China's attitude toward international trade grew out of the circumstances it faced in the 1950s. It sought rapid industrialization for reasons both of nationalism and defense, but in so doing Peking found itself faced with a trade embargo by the Western nations. Not surprisingly, China adopted a policy of strong import-substitution: that is, to develop at home industries whose output would substitute for imports. (Such a policy is sometimes called autarky, or, by the Chinese, self-reliance.)

This policy could be summed up in the phrase "import whatever is needed to reduce imports, and export only what is needed to pay for imports." Through a sequence of backward linkages, it leads a country from import-substitution in consumer goods to import-substitution in producer goods. To take textiles as an example, a policy of import-substitution in China initially meant producing textiles at home instead of buying them abroad. But new textile plants require new textile machinery. At first, this machinery had to be imported. But this opened up a new area for import-substitution: developing the domestic machine-building industry. As that industry grew, it in turn precipitated imports of specialty steels and other intermediate goods, and hence, a need to develop domestic production capacity in raw and processed steel to replace imported varieties.

Under the influence of this policy, Chinese foreign trade atrophied, falling from a world share of 1.4 percent in the 1950s, to

1.1 percent in the 1960s, and 0.8 percent in the 1970s.[1] In the years after 1970, to be sure, trade grew rapidly, increasing sixfold in money terms by 1978 and nearly quadrupling in real terms. Yet even in 1977 and 1978, China's foreign trade ratio was still only 9.2 percent. This compares with 32 percent for all developed countries, and 23 percent for low-income developing countries. Even a continental-sized country like India had a higher foreign trade ratio.

Import-substitution makes some sense when restricted to consumer nondurables—textiles, processed foods, and so forth. These products are labor-intensive, and thus appropriate to the labor-rich developing countries. By extending the policy to intermediate and final producer goods, however, the Chinese have gone against their comparative advantage. It seems unlikely that these capital-intensive goods can be produced more cheaply in the PRC than in the industrial countries. By ignoring the possibilities for international specialization, China was producing at home everything which could be produced, regardless of the cost.

Other developing countries, particularly in South America, also pursued an extended import-substitution policy after World War II. In general, they have fared badly, and the most successful of the lot have been those, such as Brazil, who abandoned the policy earliest. In China's own backyard are a group of economies—Korea, Taiwan, the Philippines, Hong Kong, Singapore—which are reaping the fruits of the opposite policy. They pursued import-substitution only briefly to foster domestic production on nondurable consumer goods. Thereafter they concentrated their efforts on promoting exports of those same consumer nondurables to the industrialized countries. Under this export-promotion policy, the developing Pacific economies grew at an average annual rate of 7.9 percent in the 1960s and 8.6 percent between 1970 and 1978, compared with 4 percent for the South Asian countries and 5.5 percent for developing countries as a whole. Furthermore, because their expanding industries were labor-intensive rather than capital-intensive,

1. These statistics, and many others in the following pages, are drawn from the monumental study by A. Doak Barnett, *China's Economy in Global Perspective* (Washington, DC: The Brookings Institution, 1981).

industrial employment grew rapidly, spreading the benefits of economic growth more widely through the population.

Does China's policy of import-substitution flow out of economic considerations, or strategy, or ideology? From a purely economic point of view, to maximize the gains from trade at any one point in time, China should produce according to her comparative advantage, welcoming capital-intensive imports instead of trying to produce such goods at home. But military strategy argues for having one's own source of steel, fuel, and the other prerequisites of a modern army. There are also some economists who argue that maximizing gains from trade at each point in time through comparative advantage may reduce long-run growth and violate a more strategic conception of optimal economic policy. Strategy, then, favors import-substitution, while short-term economic interest opposes it. Ideology—as well as Chinese nationalism—also vigorously favors import-substitution, arguing that China can learn to do anything which foreigners do, and do it better.

Ideology also would dictate that China should trade more with other Communist nations than with capitalist economies. But the evidence suggests that ideological considerations have had little influence on the direction of China's trade. Instead, strategic factors (rewarding friends, punishing enemies, and maintaining initiative) seem to have been much more important than either economic criteria (seeking the best customers and suppliers) or ideological considerations (trading with other socialist economies) in determining China's selection of trading partners.

Only in the 1950s, at the height of the Sino-Soviet alliance, did China trade more with the socialist bloc than with the West. But China's economic tilt toward the East was influenced more by the embargo that the United States imposed on trade with China than by Peking's own ideological predispositions. Indeed, China did all it could to break through the American embargo and establish economic relations with the West, both because it wanted access to European and American technology and markets, and because it felt that if economic ties could be forged, political recognition might well follow.

China achieved initial success in this area in the early 1960s, when

Japan and major Western European countries began to dissociate themselves from the U.S. embargo. Once that occurred, China's trade with the Communist camp began to decline, both in absolute terms and as a percentage of China's foreign trade. By 1970, the Soviet bloc accounted for only 20 percent of China's total trade volume; by 1980, that ratio had fallen to 10 percent.

If ideological considerations fail as an explanation of the direction of Chinese trade, purely economic factors fare little better. The Soviet Union, for example, is one of China's natural trading partners, offering raw materials (such as wood) and industrial equipment in exchange for China's agricultural products and light manufactures. But for more than twenty years, China has chosen to forgo this opportunity. Once the Sino-Soviet split occurred, China deliberately ignored the potential advantages of trading with Moscow. Even the increase in Sino-Soviet trade in the early 1980s seemed to be inspired by strategic considerations rather than economic motives. Peking seemed to see trade with the USSR as a way of symbolizing a more independent posture between Moscow and Washington, rather than as an avenue to mutual economic advantage.

China's trade with the market economies also reveals the influence of strategic considerations on the pattern of trade. As China's relations with the United States rose and fell in the 1970s, trade followed along closely. Grain purchases, in particular, have shifted toward or away from the United States depending on the political climate. When Sino-American relations appeared stalled in the mid-1970s, China reduced its grain purchases from the United States and increased those from Canada and Australia. The Sino-American grain trade resumed in 1978 as political relations began once again to improve.

The role of strategy is evident, too, in Sino-Japanese trade. Although Japan, like the USSR, is a natural trading partner of the PRC, Peking seems wary of becoming too dependent on Tokyo. Thus Deng Xiaoping, in talks with U.S. secretary of commerce Juanita Kreps in 1979, stressed that America's trade with China "must come equal to Japan's," and in fact the subsequent years witnessed a sharp increase in the American share of Chinese imports, at the expense of both Japan and Western Europe. By the early

1980s, the United States and Europe together were supplying about 35 percent of China's needs, while Japan was held to providing about one-quarter.

Agricultural Trade and Grain Imports

In what ways would we expect China to participate in one particular part of world trade, the trade in agricultural products? Classical economic theory predicts that a country will tend to export those products which make intensive use of the factor(s) abundant to that economy. Since China is rich in land, relative to capital, one would expect that China would export agricultural products in exchange for capital goods. And this was the pattern in the early 1950s, when agricultural products accounted for about half of its exports.

Over time, however, two considerations have changed this pattern. First, China's capital stock has grown rapidly, increasing twentyfold in the two decades after 1953. Because of this, light and even some heavy manufactures have become exports in which China enjoys a comparative advantage. Second, while land in China is abundant relative to capital, it is scarce when compared to labor. This is particularly evident when China's land-labor ratio is compared with that of the United States, Australia, or Canada—all grain-exporting nations. These two facts help to explain the decline in agriculture's share of total Chinese exports: from about 50 percent in the early 1950s, to 37 percent in 1969, and 23 percent in 1979. In the early 1980s, a watershed was reached: China became a net importer of agricultural products, importing roughly $1 billion more than it exported.

Grain imports have been a major part of this transition. Imports began in the 1960s, but were held at modest levels, never rising above 3 percent of domestic production. In the 1970s, too, grain imports remained very iow, not reaching 2 percent of domestic production until 1977. Then in the following years, policy shifted. Grain imports climbed past 4 percent of domestic production in the early 1980s.

This sustained rise in imports has occurred in a period when agriculture was doing relatively well. Growth rates in 1970–77 were higher than for 1957–70, largely due to added applications of chemical fertilizer and other modern inputs. These gains will be harder to sustain in the 1980s, although reforms in the organization of agriculture and in the pricing system may have some payoffs in the mid-1980s. Thus it seems likely that grain imports in the range of 10–20 million tons will continue through the decade.

China's increasing grain trade mirrors the postwar trend for the world as a whole. Grain began to enter world trade in the 1950s, with three major exporters, the United States, Canada, and Australia, accounting for 60 percent of it. The developing world, which imported only 20 million tons in the early 1960s, was buying 90 million tons in the early 1980s, and is predicted to purchase 180 million tons by the year 2000. India and Indonesia in the mid-1970s imported 5 to 8 percent of their grain needs. And even a relatively developed country, the USSR, has imported up to 20 percent of its grain in recent years.

In making the decision to increase their grain imports, what relative weights have the Chinese given to economic, strategic, and ideological considerations? While the fact that China imports 4 to 5 percent of its domestic grain production may seem like a modest proportion, this level actually represents a distinct degree of dependence for China. We must bear in mind that most of China's harvest stays in the hands of the peasant producers; only about 50 million tons is procured by the state. A good portion of this is absorbed by transfers to grain-deficit rural areas; the rest supplies the major cities. Thus imports of 12 or 15 million tons of grain represent a large proportion of the total grain consumption of urban China.

When we review China's trade in agricultural products, then, we are led to conclude that, at least in recent years, economic considerations of comparative advantage have weighed heavily in the trade decisions. Official policy still stresses the ideological desirability of self-reliance and the strategic dangers of excessive grain imports. But China's practice does not appear to differ markedly from that of any other land-scarce LDC. If anything, China's level of grain imports seems distinctly higher than in most of the rest of the developing world.

Technology Trade

Another area where economic and strategic imperatives seem to pull in opposite directions is the import of technology. In the 1950s,

Chinese imports of machinery and equipment were massive, constituting 33 percent of total imports. Because of China's close relations with the USSR, and the American embargo against the PRC, most of China's technology imports came from the Soviet bloc. The Sino-Soviet rift at the end of that decade was, consequently, extremely costly to Chinese industrialization. In the 1960s, with restricted access to technology from either East or West, trade in this category diminished, dropping to only 14 percent of total imports. In the 1970s, as relations with the West grew closer, and as economic growth began to dominate political considerations, the ratio rose to 22 percent, and it exceeded 30 percent once again in the early 1980s. The impact of this technology flow on Chinese growth has been significant; some studies suggest that growth in the 1950s would have been 20 to 50 percent lower, and in the 1970s 15 percent lower, without it.

Does China engage in technology imports more, or less, than economic interest alone might dictate? One possible baseline is the share of imported machinery in each year's total investment in new machinery. For the USSR, a mature and trade-averse economy, this proportion was about 5 percent in the 1970s. For the United States, another mature, but less trade-averse, continental economy, the ratio was slightly above 10 percent. In the case of the PRC, the 1970s ratio was roughly 10 percent. Setting aside strategic and ideological considerations, one might expect the PRC, with a smaller industrial sector and a technology gap to overcome, to exhibit a higher propensity than the United States to import new machinery. In fact, during the 1950s, fully 40 percent of China's new machinery came from abroad. But this dropped to 4 or 5 percent in the 1960s, returned to no more than 10 percent in the 1970s, and rose somewhat above 10 percent during the buying spree of the early 1980s.

Why has China purchased so little abroad? The Chinese themselves point to a number of external factors, such as the embargo that the United States imposed on them in the 1950s and 1960s, and the continued controls, even today, on the export of advanced American technology to China. Western observers, in contrast, frequently emphasize the limits on China's ability to absorb advanced technology, due to a shortage of skilled personnel, high-quality raw materials, and energy.

But the most persuasive explanation can be found in strategic and ideological considerations. China's financial conservatism—its reluctance to become indebted to a stronger industrial power—has, until recently, held its level of imports to that which could be paid for directly by exports. What is more, the ideological principle of self-reliance has been particularly restrictive in the area of technology. During the Cultural Revolution, radical leaders insisted that those who wished to purchase equipment from abroad were displaying their contempt for China's own abilities and expressing an unseemly adulation of foreign things. Even today, Premier Zhao Ziyang has stressed that "the aim of our foreign economic and technological exchange is of course to raise our capacity for self-reliance. . . . Under no circumstances should we waver on this point."[2]

Foreign Capital

On the basis of economic considerations alone, what use would we expect China to make of world capital markets and foreign credits? Would we expect China to take advantage of the international capital flows from which other LDCs had borrowed over $600 billion by 1983? As a large developing country, China's economy is relatively short of capital, in the physical sense. This means that capital—machinery and equipment, plus the technological know-how to put them to use—should be very productive in the Chinese setting. Thus the potential rate of return is high, perhaps 7 to 15 percent. In the industrialized economies, where capital is relatively abundant, the true rate of return on capital, and thus the normal long-term interest rate, is much lower—in the range of 2 to 5 percent. One would thus predict that physical capital would flow to China and other LDCs, and that lenders in the capital-rich countries would extend financial credit to make that physical investment possible. This flow, both physical and financial, would continue until the rate of return on capital, as well as the market rate of interest, was equal in both areas.

One reason that this theory cannot be applied uncritically to China is the size of the country. It would require a very large transfer of

2. "Report on the Sixth Five-Year Plan," *Beijing Review,* 20 December 1982, p. 18.

capital to equalize rates of return. But at any one point in time, there are limitations on the number of investment projects (dams, factories, and so forth) that are truly feasible. Problems of identifying appropriate development projects, and shortages of entrepreneurship and skilled labor, mean that beyond a certain point, additional investment projects will have a low rate of return—less than the cost of borrowing capital abroad.

Still, one would expect any country to wish to be "borrowed up"—to have undertaken investment projects, using foreign credits, up to the point at which the rate of return had fallen to the cost of capital. (Of course, such a country must also bear in mind that the rate of return must be expressible in foreign exchange, and that it must generate an adequate flow of foreign exchange to fulfill its debt service obligations.) Thus classical economic theory looks with approbation at the proclivity of market LDCs to take on medium- and long-term foreign debt, while viewing with some concern the liquidity crises generated by fluctuations in the price of oil.

In the case of China, the use of foreign capital markets in this way presents some particular difficulties. First, identifying and ranking the projects with the highest rate of return is not easy: China has weak statistical and accounting systems, and Chinese prices are not always valid indexes with which to calculate rates of return. Second, in a state-run economy, politics can easily override both rate-of-return calculations and considerations of repayment capacity. Poland's experience in the 1970s, for example, illustrates that a government favoring projects with low payoffs will jeopardize its ability to service its debt.

On balance, however, strictly economic considerations would suggest that China, with a ratio of labor to capital perhaps twenty to forty times as large as in the Western industrialized countries, would profit greatly from availing itself of the opportunity for international capital flows. And yet for nearly thirty years, until 1978, China was unique among developing countries in its refusal to enter into long-term funding arrangements. Indeed, China engaged in very little medium-term (from one to five years) or short-term (less than one-year) debt. Total credits from the USSR in the 1950s were probably below $1 billion (excluding military aid provided during the

Korean War) and were all relatively short-term. China began repaying its debt to the Soviet Union in 1954 and had essentially completed the process a decade later. Short medium-term commercial credits in the early 1960s, to the tune of $900 million, facilitated the early grain purchases; and medium-term credits in the 1970s, again in the hundreds of millions, financed the import of complete plants. But China's total indebtedness at any one time did not pass $1 billion until the mid-1970s, and none of the debt was long-term until China began drawing from the IMF in 1978–79. These amounts are extremely small for an economy of China's size. By way of contrast, Mexico, Brazil, and the Eastern European countries all piled up debts in the tens of billions during the 1970s.

Both ideological and strategic considerations help to explain this conservative behavior. China's experience with expensive foreign loans in the late nineteenth and early twentieth centuries, populist antagonism to moneylending, and its Marxist-Leninist aversion to market processes in general all undoubtedly combined to make borrowing abroad politically costly and perhaps genuinely distasteful to China's leadership. And from a strategic standpoint, a large foreign debt must be rolled over or renewed periodically, at which time foreign lenders can exercise political leverage through the threat, implicit or explicit, not to renew credit. If the country's repayment capacity has fallen below the demands of debt service, that threat can in principle be very real (although Western bankers might question the range of options open to them during the Polish financial crisis).

While both considerations argue against foreign borrowing, the implications of each are slightly different. The dictates of ideology are simple: Don't borrow. Strategy sets a subtler rule: Don't borrow too much. On the basis of this distinction, one could argue that while both strategy and ideology affected China's borrowing behavior in the past, after 1977 the ideological constraint was relaxed. Net indebtedness rose sharply in the post-Mao era, reaching $2.5 billion in 1980. Policy statements on using foreign funds stressed the importance of keeping debt service well below repayment capacity. But ideology was bent or stretched to the extent necessary to rationalize the new flow of funds.

Despite this new flexibility, China's use of the opportunities presented by the international capital market and international lending agencies is still quite subdued. In the four years up to December 1982, China absorbed roughly 30 million *yuan* in foreign loans and direct investment. Total investment in fixed capital was about 320 million *yuan* during that period. Thus less than 10 percent of China's investment was foreign-funded; the rest was generated internally. In terms of ownership, at the end of 1981 direct foreign investment in China totaled $2.85 billion. Although this is a large number in absolute terms, it is small relative to the total value of China's modern sector capital stock. That stock of capital generates upward of $100 billion in industrial output each year and its value is some multiple of that. Thus, we can conclude that foreigners own considerably less than 1 percent of China's modern sector.

China and the New International Economic Order

A final area where economic, ideological, and strategic considerations conflict is Chinese policy toward Third World demands for a "new international economic order." The creation of informal mechanisms for discussing such issues began in the mid-1950s. By the 1980s, the process had been institutionalized. The Group of Seventy-seven, formed within the context of the United Nations Conference on Trade and Development (UNCTAD), now includes over 100 countries. It focuses principally on economic issues, and midwifed the 1974 United Nations resolution calling for a New International Economic Order. The Nonaligned Movement, dealing with broader political issues, also numbered over 100 countries at the time of its 1983 meeting in New Delhi. Below these umbrella organizations, twenty-five regional groupings (such as ASEAN) have been formed, as well as more than twenty organizations of raw materials exporters (such as OPEC) seeking improved terms of trade. Marshaling their forces within this framework, the developing countries confront the industrialized world, both in broad arenas such as the 1981 Cancun Conference or the 1978 UNCTAD talks on commodity prices, and in a host of more focused forums aimed at reaching multilateral trade pacts such as the Multi-fiber Agreement.

Ironically, China's economic interests, in this area, lie more with the developed than with the developing world. Like many developed countries, China is a large net importer of primary products, including cotton, rubber, and wood. Its large merchant marine gives Peking a common interest with the United States and Japan in defending the freedom of the seas. Its offshore oil deposits promote an interest in extended territorial limits, rather than an internationalized seabed. China's sheer size enables Peking to seek benefits through unilateral action which other LDCs can obtain only through unity. Textile exports—a growing part of China's foreign trade—are the sole major area where China, in terms of strictly economic interests, seems a natural member of the Third World.

Strategic considerations have ambiguous implications for China's role in the Third World movement. On the one hand, the developed world is where power and wealth lie. Surely China profits more by finding a *modus vivendi* with Japan and Europe than by siding with India and Indonesia. On the other hand, there may be those in China who feel that the future lies with the developing world—that the industrial West is in decline and disarray—and that Peking should align itself with that emerging center of power.

Only ideological factors clearly impel China to support Third World calls for a New International Economic Order. China's experience with Western imperialism, and its Marxist-Leninist analysis of the economic forces guiding world history, dictate siding with the poor nations of the world against the rich. These ideological considerations could influence Peking's policy positions either because Chinese leaders accepted them, or because their legitimacy rested on adherence to them, or both. Even here, however, the dictates of ideology are often vague. During radical periods, China has fulfilled its ideological obligations by supporting revolutionary movements within the Third World; while at more moderate times it has done so by encouraging opposition to geopolitical expansion by the superpowers. Only occasionally has it placed emphasis on the creation of a new international economic order.

Judging by Chinese behavior, economic and strategic interests seem to have dominated ideological imperatives in this area, for China has never been an active champion of the Third World. At meetings where nuts-and-bolts issues are discussed, such as the 1978

UNCTAD talks on international commodity agreements, China has taken pragmatic positions based on self-interest. Significantly, China is not a member of either the Group of Seventy-seven or the Non-aligned Movement. To be sure, Chinese rhetoric has been supportive. At the Cancun summit, for example, Premier Zhao Ziyang said many things that his Third World colleagues wanted to hear. But even there, his remarks were by no means militant. He called only for modest "improvement" in the terms of capital transfers, for "step by step" change in the structure of the world financial system, and in general for a "gradual reform" in existing international economic relations. One senior Chinese foreign policy specialist, speaking privately, put the North-South conflict in an East-West context. The United States, he argued, should be more forthcoming at Cancun, in order to deprive the USSR of opportunities for political penetration in areas such as Central America.

To some extent, China's aloofness from the Third World movement reflects the views of those nations themselves. As the Egyptian chairman of a 1978 Third World forum put it: "We think it would be inappropriate to include China in the Third World. The size of the country, the variety of its resources, the permanent seat on the Security Council, and its real weight in world politics make China a big power."[3] And in 1979 Julius Nyerere, one of the fathers of the Third World movement, listed "the three Third World Giants" as India, Indonesia, and Brazil.[4] Thus to some extent, the Chinese make a virtue of necessity when they declare that "the Third World needs no leader." But it seems likely that China has also recognized that its real interests lie elsewhere.

We have examined Chinese choices in six areas: the level of trade, the direction of trade, agricultural trade, technology trade, the use of foreign capital, and the North-South conflict. What can be observed about the interplay of ideological, strategic, and economic considerations in shaping China's policy in these areas?

The first conclusion to draw is that ideology is a weak constraint.

3. Anwar Aqbal, ed., *Report on the New International Economic Order* (Bombay: New India, 1974), p. 22.
4. Ibid., p. 85.

Consider the three areas where ideology conflicts with strategy: the direction of trade (where ideological considerations drive China toward the socialist camp, but strategic factors impel it toward the West); the use of foreign credit (where ideology says not to borrow at all, while strategy urges Peking to borrow within limits); and the North-South conflict (where ideology suggests identification with the Third World, while strategic calculations are much more ambivalent). Strategy dominates ideology in each case.

Ideology, in turn, conflicts with economic interest in all six policy areas, and here the box score is 3–3. Compared to ideology, economic factors seem to have shaped Peking's decisions on agricultural imports, the direction of trade, and North-South issues. Ideology, on the other hand, appears dominant in influencing the level of trade, the import of technology, and the use of foreign credits. But ideology rules only when it acts in concert with strategic considerations. When those strategic calculations change, as they have in all three of these areas after 1977, Chinese leaders either ignore ideology or redefine it.

A second conclusion is that strategic considerations dominate economic ones. The two conflict in every area but the last (North-South issues), although the contradiction between them is sometimes only a mild one. But only in the case of grain imports can a compelling argument be made that economic necessity is leading China to adopt a course of action that may be strategically unwise. In all other areas—the choice of trading partners and the decisions to adopt policies of import substitution, to limit borrowing from foreigners, and to restrict imports of foreign technology—China has allowed long-term strategic calculations to override short-term economic interests.

We come away from this review, then, concluding that China, particularly in recent years, has not hesitated to place its short-term economic interest above ideological considerations. Nonetheless, it is long-term strategic calculation, and not ideology or economics, that seems to control China's foreign economic policy.

The Future of China's Role in the World Economy

How will China's relationship to the world economy evolve over the coming decade? What use will China make of trade? With what partners, and in what commodities, will the greatest growth in trade be evident?

Some answers to these questions can be found in the circumstances facing all trading nations in the 1980s: in particular, the decline in world trade and the growth of protectionism. World trade fell 5.3 percent in 1982, for the second straight year, after thirty-five years of uninterrupted expansion. Unemployment in the developed countries reached 35 million in 1983. The developing countries faced the burden of $630 billion in external debt, with annual service of $130 billion, reducing their capacity to import. Meanwhile, the prices they received for raw materials were at their lowest level in fifty years. Pressure for protectionist measures suggested that a return to the restrictions of the 1930s might not be far away. Anyone discussing China's trading future would be foolish not to take this context into account.

But these conditions confront all trading nations. As we try to predict China's more specific situation, let us return to the unique characteristics that we listed at the outset of the chapter: low per capita income, continental size, East Asian resource endowment, and Leninist ideology and polity. As the presumably least mutable aspects of the country, they should be the most reliable predictors of the future. We will argue that the first three of these all suggest a larger role for trade, and in particular for East Asian trade, in China's future economy. The fourth, to the extent that it dictates maintaining a centrally planned trade machinery, threatens to inhibit that evolution.

China's continental size, its low per capita income, and its location at the center of Asia all suggest that the PRC may come to occupy a major position in East Asian trade in the next ten years. In particular, China's size, level of development, and resources point toward three major areas of export expansion for the PRC: textiles, machinery, and energy (especially coal and oil). As China's trade increases, Peking will inevitably experience some frictions with its neighbors. On balance, however, there is every reason to believe that China will be able to develop a cooperative, rather than a competitive, relationship with most of its East Asian neighbors.

The accompanying table shows the composition of exports of six

Commodity Composition of Exports in East Asia, 1978

Commodity	PRC	Japan	Taiwan	Korea	Hong Kong	Singapore
Primary products	52.9	8.6	16.1	13.9	3.9	51.2
Foodstuffs (0, 1)	22.5	1.2	10.2	8.2	1.9	6.9
Crude Material (2, 3)	25.7	1.5	4.0	2.9	1.1	38.3
Chemicals (4, 5)	4.7	5.9	1.9	2.8	0.9	6.0
Labor-intensive manufactures	24.4	12.3	23.0	32.3	47.2	5.5
Yarn & Fabrics (65)	17.2	4.8	9.2	12.1	7.5	2.7
Clothing (84)	7.2	7.5	13.8	20.2	39.7	2.8
Capital-intensive manufactures	22.2	79.1	60.9	53.8	48.9	43.3
Machinery (7, 86)	2.8	61.3	25.6	21.9	22.2	26.7
Other (6, 8, 9)	19.4	17.8	35.3	31.9	26.7	16.6
TOTAL (%)	99.5	100.0	100.0	100.0	100.0	100.0
TOTAL (value)	9.9	103.0	468.5	12.7	35.0	23.0
Units	$US	$US	$NT	$US	$HK	$SP

SOURCES: PRC: National Foreign Assessment Center, *China: International Trade Quarterly Review,* 2d quarter 1979; other countries: Miyohei Shinohara, "Trade and Industrial Adjustments in the Asia and Pacific Region and Japan," paper delivered at Rutgers University, April 1981. (Numbers in parentheses refer to Standard International Trade Classification categories.)

major trading economies of East Asia in 1978, dividing them into three categories: land- and labor-intensive primary products, labor-intensive manufactures, and capital-intensive manufactures. As classical economic theory would predict, Chinese exports are found at the lower end of this spectrum. As a relatively poor country, fully half of China's exports are primary products, including both agricultural products and petroleum. Hong Kong relies heavily on textiles, which account for nearly half its exports. Taiwan and Korea have moved sharply into consumer durables and other capital-intensive manufactures, and Singapore even more so. (Singapore's profile is distorted by its re-export of refined petroleum, listed in the table as a "crude material.") At the far end of the spectrum comes Japan, nearly 80 percent of whose exports are capital-intensive manufactures.

We find, in other words, that a country's ability to export capital-intensive goods is closely related to its per capita income, which in turn reflects the abundance of capital in its economy. China will move up this spectrum only as fast as its per capita income rises. And, as it does so, the other economies of the region are likely to be advancing as well. This implies that China will never become a competitor of Japan. But what of the "newly industrialized countries" (NICs) of East Asia: Korea, Taiwan, Hong Kong, and Singapore? And what about the less-developed nations of Southeast Asia, such as Thailand, Indonesia, and the Philippines?

Textiles, a rapidly expanding Chinese export, are bringing China into competition with the newly industrialized countries of East Asia. But textiles are a declining source of exports for the NICs. As their per capita incomes and their labor costs rise, they are moving into what economists call "higher–value added areas," particularly in such skill-intensive and technology-intensive areas as semiconductors and electronics. Encouraging this transition is the fact that both the EEC and the United States have removed the NICs from eligibility for tariff reductions under the Generalized System of Preferences. This means that their exports of textiles and footwear—as well as steel, ships, machinery, and electrical goods—no longer enjoy duty-free status in Western Europe or the United States.

Thus, in the area of labor-intensive manufactures, China will be competing not with the NICs, but with the less advanced economies of Southeast Asia. The textile exports of Thailand, Indonesia, and the Philippines all grew rapidly in the late 1970s, and China will be seeking a larger share of the same markets. Even so, many Southeast Asians believe that they can meet the Chinese challenge. They doubt that China will be able to organize its export sector rapidly or smoothly enough to pose a major threat to Southeast Asian exporters in the early 1980s. What is more, Southeast Asians also expect that there may develop an informal division of labor between China and the less-developed nations of the region, so that China may prove to be an important market for Southeast Asian exports, and not simply a competitor.

A similar possibility for a division of labor exists in the second area in which Chinese exports are likely to expand: machinery. As I suggested earlier, China's large domestic market has justified the development of a relatively mature industrial base even at a low level of per capita income. China now has the capacity to engineer, design, and produce machine tools, making it a viable competitor in world markets for small-scale processing plants and electrical machinery, agricultural equipment, general-purpose lathes, and textile machinery.

China's competitive potential is enhanced by its low industrial wage rate. One harbinger of this trend is China's joint venture with American Motors Corporation to produce up to forty thousand four-wheel drive vehicles a year, using Chinese labor priced at sixty cents an hour. Some of these vehicles will remain in China, but many others will be exported, competing with Japan in an East Asian market where 100,000 such vehicles are purchased each year.

As China increases its export of machinery, it will thus begin to compete with the more advanced economies of Asia, including both Japan and the newly industrialized countries. But even here, there are prospects for cooperation as well as conflict. As Professor Miyohei Shinohara has shown, a "horizontal division of labor" has begun to emerge in East Asia among Korea, Taiwan, and Japan.[5] Instead of the traditional vertical division of labor, in which Japan would import primary products from Korea and Taiwan and export manufactured items in return, Japan now cooperates with those second-echelon countries in the production of capital-intensive manufactures. In electronics, for example, Japan exports high technology parts to Korea or Taiwan, where they are assembled together with locally produced components. In shipbuilding, Japan finds itself exporting engines to Korean or Taiwanese shipyards, which are building ships for Japanese clients.

5. Miyohei Shinohara, "Trade and Industrial Adjustments in the Asia and Pacific Region and Japan," paper delivered at Rutgers University, April 1981.

Because China's continental size has enabled it to develop a comprehensive industrial sector, the potential for a similar kind of interaction between China and these countries clearly exists—especially during the 1980s, when Peking's changing domestic priorities are expected to leave slack capacity in the Chinese machine-building industry. The major obstacle to this sort of arrangement, however, is that China's output of machinery must meet precise specifications, meshing with foreign imported parts. Thus far, quality control has not been one of the highlights of China's industry. But if ways can be found to overcome this problem, the share of industrial products in China's total exports may grow sharply in the coming years. Indeed, one study by Peking's Ministry of Foreign Trade has predicted that the share of such products might double between 1980 and 1990, from 12 percent to over 20 percent.[6]

The third, and best-known, potential source of export growth for China is the energy sector. Like grain, energy is a commodity which entered world trade on a large scale only after World War II. In 1920, only one-seventh of total world energy, principally coal, was supplied through world trade. In 1950, the proportion was still only 20 percent, and the industrialized countries had only a modest energy deficit. But in the next quarter century, oil entered international commerce in large quantities, surpassing coal as the primary source of energy in 1967. By 1975 nearly 40 percent of the commercial energy used in the world was traded among countries, and 72 percent of the energy traded was oil. The developed countries were importing the majority of their energy, especially Europe (75 percent) and Japan (91 percent).

China entered the world energy trade relatively early, although on a small scale. China was a net exporter of coal well before 1949 and has remained so down to the present. In contrast, it has been a net importer of petroleum for most of this century, purchasing it from the West before 1949, from the Soviet Union in the 1950s, and from Eastern Europe in the late 1950s and early 1960s. But as China developed its own oil fields, it gradually became self-sufficient in petroleum. By the mid-1960s, China's purchases of foreign oil had

6. Interview with Ministry of Foreign Trade officials, Beijing, August 1981.

fallen off dramatically. In essence, Peking was importing only special types of refined petroleum products, and producing the rest at home. By 1973, China was a net exporter of petroleum. And by 1980, oil exports, almost all to Japan, accounted for 14 percent of the PRC's export earnings.

What are the realistic prospects for the further growth of China's oil production and petroleum exports? Much will depend on the future of China's offshore oil fields—now just beginning production—since China's onshore wells are facing stagnant or declining production. As a basis for prediction, we can examine the experience of other countries that have recently begun exploitation of offshore oil reserves.

North Sea oil production reached a level of over 2 million barrels per day (MBD) in less than ten years. Mexican production from the Gulf of Campeche rose even more quickly, to 1.3 MBD in the space of twenty months. Clearly, rapid growth rates for new offshore fields are not unprecedented. Let us suppose, therefore, that oil production grows overall in China by 7 percent a year, from the current level of two MBD—a scenario that assumes little or no additional output from onshore wells but offshore growth of North Sea magnitudes. Assume further that domestic consumption, currently taking 90 percent of what China produces, grows at only 5 percent. This would enable China by 1990 to join the small club of countries exporting over one million barrels per day, or $11 billion per year at $30 per barrel.

The impact of such a projection on China's trade picture is modest, however. If total trade in the same period grows at 6 percent, then in 1990 oil exports will account for perhaps 35 percent of foreign exchange earnings, compared with 14 percent in the 1980s. But this assumes that oil prices keep pace with inflation, and it also overlooks the fact that future oil exports will consume foreign exchange (in repayment for the high foreign capital cost of extraction) as well as produce it. It is also likely that oil exports will decline (or even disappear) in the mid-1980s, when onshore production slackens but before offshore oil begins to flow. Still, the promise of Chinese oil is clearly not illusory. It will cover domestic consumption, avoiding the drain on foreign exchange that imports would entail, and will probably provide a modest increase in foreign exchange earnings. If the offshore wells prove very productive, oil could significantly relax China's foreign exchange constraint.

To the extent that China does succeed in expanding energy exports, it is likely that the share of its exports going to Japan will increase, because Japan is a major and adjacent energy consumer. Even though it purchased almost all of China's oil exports, Japan in the early 1980s was still buying more than 90 percent of its petroleum elsewhere. Thus, China should find a ready market for any offshore oil that is found. Moreover, Japan hopes to reduce oil's share in its energy diet from 75 percent in 1980 to 50 percent in 1990, with much of the displacement coming from liquified and gasified coal. Here again, China has substantial reserves, which foreign corporations have already begun to develop.

Thus, in some ways, the 1980s appear to be a unique opportunity for China to capitalize on its resource endowment, its income level, and its geography to cement a strong trade relationship with its East Asian neighbors. But economic reforms will play a critical role in that process. In particular, a horizontal division of labor implies close coordination between Chinese enterprises and others elsewhere in the region. This can occur only to the extent that these enterprises are given the sort of autonomous decision-making power discussed earlier. What is the likelihood of sustained and rapid movement in this direction, given China's Marxist-Leninist roots?

A series of formidable barriers stand in the way of fundamental economic reform. Market-oriented reforms threaten two policy goals that have been espoused by every Chinese leader since 1949: price stability and equity of income distribution. Reforms also threaten ministerial privilege and Party control. The Party would lose some legitimacy, to the extent that production rather than political transformation would become the central social task. And allowing markets to make decisions would take that decision-making power out of Party hands.

Nor does the precedent of Eastern Europe and the USSR bode well for reforms. The USSR promulgated reform decrees with much fanfare in 1965, but little has changed. At best, the Soviet Union can be said to have followed the East German model, creating smaller bureaucratic pyramids from larger ones. Yugoslavia is not a relevant model for China because it never fully adopted the system of ministerial planning which China must now revise. In any event, Yugoslavia's rates of inflation and unemployment do not encourage emulation. Hungary is the most successful precedent: a country which abolished ministries, eliminated cumbersome annual plans, and encouraged enterprises to reorient themselves toward foreign trade using world market prices as a guide. However, this process consumed many years (the usual dating is 1968, but some specialists identify preparatory measures as early as 1958). Furthermore, Hungary is a small economy for which the potential gains from world trade were a strong inducement to reform. This is less true for China, with its low foreign trade ratio.

Thus, when one examines the course of economic reform in China after 1979, one sees the same "one step forward, two steps back" syndrome that has marked the reform process in the USSR and Eastern Europe. Price and profit levers which were supposed to apply uniformly to all enterprises gave way quickly to piecemeal, compensating arrangements for this or that enterprise, until in effect the web of administrative controls was largely reestablished. The need to let prices move toward market-clearing levels bowed to the political reality that prices must be kept stable. All these considerations make it difficult to be an optimist about the prospects for sustained and rapid introduction of the decentralizing measures that might permit Chinese industry to integrate itself into an East Asian system of production.

If China continues to back away from reform, what will this augur for China's economic future, and more particularly, for its participation in the international economy? First, it means reduced economic growth. Rather than the very rapid export-led growth of South Korea or Taiwan, China will have to settle for perhaps 6 percent annual industrial growth. Coupled with a 3 percent growth rate in agriculture, this would result in a 5 percent growth rate in GNP. This of course is a very respectable figure, but over a ten-year period, 5 percent growth instead of, say, 8 percent means that per capita GNP increases by half instead of doubling (assuming 1 percent population growth).

Second, reduced domestic growth and the retention of an administered economy would mean a reduced role for foreign trade. The bureaucratic foreign trade machinery is particularly constraining in an area where China is strong—"low-technology" machinery and equipment. In this area, it is often necessary for domestic and foreign enterprises to cooperate in producing a single product or a set of related products. With little autonomy, exporting enterprises will be unable to respond to foreign coproducers and foreign markets. Furthermore, stalled price reforms may make it difficult for China to gauge what its natural exports are. Unless international prices are used to guide China's export policy, it is conceivable that China could end up exporting goods that, on balance, cost more in terms of real resources than the value of the goods imported.

Nonetheless, there remain some grounds for optimism about China. First, one sees in Peking an ideological flexibility which far exceeds that in the Soviet bloc. China's willingness to establish special economic zones, patterned after the export-processing zones of Taiwan and Korea, is a case in point. At least in these limited pieces of Chinese territory, the market mechanism seems to hold no terror for Chinese planners. What is more, the Chinese are clearly entertaining the idea that the reforms begun in the special economic zones may later be applied to other parts of the country. As one article put it, the zones are considered to be "experimental units in economic structural reform and schools for learning the law of value and the regulation of production according to market demands."[7]

One can also point to a very rapid and successful reform in the agricultural sector. This was the first area of the economy to be reorganized, and it is there that the reforms have been extended the furthest. In early 1979, collective land began to be assigned to individual peasant families who, after meeting their obligations to the state, were permitted to keep or sell the rest of their output. Then, in 1983, peasants received the right to own tractors, engage in long-distance trade, hire employees, and invest in cooperative enterprises. Although most of the prices encountered by the peasants are still set

7. Xu Dixin, "China's Special Economic Zones," *Beijing Review,* 14 December 1981, pp. 14–17.

by the state, the market has been given a major role in agriculture as a result of these reforms. And their success in increasing agricultural output may embolden Chinese leaders to embark on similar reforms in the industrial and foreign trade sectors.

In addition to ideological flexibility and the recent successes in agricultural reform, one is also struck by the commitment of China's top leaders to the process. One well-informed Chinese, asked why one should expect China to reform rapidly when the Soviet Union proved unable to do so, replied crisply: "Because Deng Xiaoping is a reformer, and Brezhnev is not." The same contrast could also be drawn between Zhao Ziyang and Konstantin Chernenko. If China can maintain a strong, stable leadership committed to restructuring the economy, perhaps the barriers to reform can be overcome.

And if the reforms succeed, then perhaps China will join Japan in developing an alternative to both market economies and command economies. Japan, with its system of private ownership, its minimal explicit government control, and its relatively unequal distribution of income, has its roots in the market economy. Yet its 30 percent investment rate, and the success of the government in guiding the allocation of that investment, would make any Eastern European planner envious. If China joins Japan in developing such an East Asian alternative—somewhere in the narrow strip of water separating the capitalist, industrialized world from the shores of socialist, peasant economies—then surely the future belongs to them.

4 China in Asia: The PRC as a Regional Power

STEVEN I. LEVINE

China is outgrowing Asia and trying the world on for size. In the post-Mao era, China has multiplied its political and cultural relations with both the developed countries and the Third World, expanded its participation in the international economic system, and played a more active role in the United Nations and other international organizations.

Yet even as the People's Republic grows into the role of a global political actor, its foreign policy is still concerned predominantly with Asia. China's security concerns focus on Asia, and its military power does not extend beyond the region. Its political and cultural influence have been strongest in Asia, and the largest proportion of its foreign trade is conducted with its Asian neighbors.

China's somewhat ambiguous position in international affairs—more than merely a regional actor, but still less than a global power—has introduced a fundamental paradox into its relations with the rest of Asia. Although much, if not most, of China's foreign policy is focused on Asia, at the conceptual level the Chinese rarely think in regional terms at all. Chinese leaders approach their relations with their neighbors either on a purely bilateral basis, or else with reference to a set of global policies that they attempt to apply to all countries in a universalistic fashion. If China's actual international undertakings—be they support for revolutionary movements or diplomatic interactions with established governments—have been directed primarily toward Asia, this has been dictated by logistics rather than doctrine. To a significant degree, China has been a regional power without a regional policy.

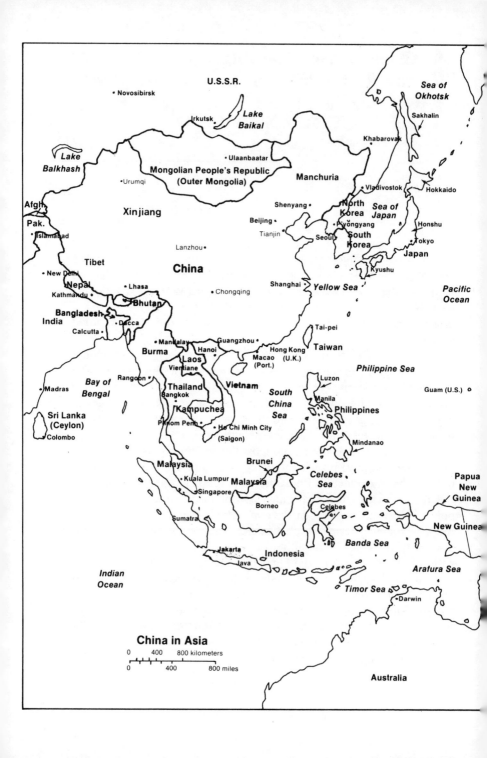

I address in this chapter several aspects of China's role in Asia. First, I examine the implications of this fundamental contradiction between China's status as an Asian power and its ambition to be a major force on a world scale. Second, I offer an overview of China's goals and policies in Asia from 1949 to the present. Third, I consider the major issues in China's Asian policy today and the assets and liabilities China brings to the pursuit of its goals. Fourth, I explore the varying perceptions of China's present role and future prospects that are held by China's Asian neighbors. Finally, I consider what the future may hold for China in Asia. Will the PRC, as some of its neighbors suspect, tread the path of expansionism and regional hegemony, perhaps by renewing its support for revolutionary movements in the region? Will it turn inward, ceding predominant influence in Asia to other powers? Or will China remain on the course charted during the last decade, actively involved in Asia but contributing to peace and stability in the region?

A Regional Power with Global Ambitions

On coming to power in 1949, China's new leaders inherited the task of defining a new role for their country in Asian and world politics. This proved to be an exceedingly difficult enterprise. It was neither feasible nor appropriate for China's new rulers simply to resurrect, even in updated form, a foreign policy based on the middle kingdom concept of late imperial China. As Michael Hunt's essay in this volume has demonstrated, this traditional world view—hierarchical rather than egalitarian, cultural rather than political, and imbued with condescension rather than mutual respect—had been eroded by the events of the late nineteenth century. It was replaced by an image of international politics that was at once more cosmopolitan and less harmonious: an image of the world as a struggle for national survival against Western pressure.

Nor was it possible for China's Communist leaders to follow in the footsteps of Japan. When Japan defined its role in Asia in the late nineteenth century, it had little difficulty in deciding to become a kind of Asian England, replete with an imperial ideology, a powerful navy, overseas colonies, international alliances, and a proclivity toward war. Half a century later, China's revolutionary ideology, as well as its limited power, precluded the pursuit of a similar course—a course that, in any event, would have been a futile anachronism in an age of Asian nationalism.

But while the PRC has not behaved like a traditional expansionist power in Asia or sought to recreate its earlier cultural hegemony over "all under heaven," neither has it been willing to turn its back on the world and simply cultivate its own garden. Underlying the various permutations of its foreign relations since 1949 has been the conviction of China's leaders that their country, by virtue of its location, size, population, resources, and overall potential, is, and by rights ought to be, a major actor in both Asia and the world. Yet in traditional terms, China's power is still quite limited. Outside Asia, China's role in contemporary politics is determined more by what China may become than by what it already is. Within Asia, however, and particularly within contiguous Asia, China's power is by no means insignificant, and the PRC is respected by most and feared by some.

This duality shapes China's relationship with the rest of Asia. As a regional power at present, most of China's interests are centered in Asia. China's foreign policy agenda is dominated not by the general problems of North-South, or even East-West, relations, but rather by issues close to home: the security of its borders, its desire to recover what it considers to be lost lands, its assertion of maritime territorial claims along its eastern coast and in the South China Sea, its concern for ethnic Chinese in Southeast Asia, its fluctuating support for revolutionary insurgencies in the non-Communist states on its periphery, and, above all, its desire to prevent any other major power from establishing hegemony in Asia.

But as a putative and potential global power, China insists on defining these regional concerns with an eye to developments in the rest of the world. For example, China has regarded its conflict with Vietnam as a microcosm of a global struggle against Soviet expansionism. It sees its support of Malaysia's and Indonesia's claims to the Straits of Malacca as part of a broader pattern of Third World opposition to the maritime hegemonism of the superpowers. It portrays its policies toward Taiwan and South Korea as examples of a worldwide resistance against American imperialism. It depicts its trade with ASEAN as an instance of South-South economic cooperation.

The tension between China's regional stature and its global ambitions is also reflected in its ambivalence toward the rest of the region. As an arena for action Asia may be said to be China's destiny, but it is a destiny that China has often tried to elude if not to escape entirely. Few Chinese leaders—whether in the intellectual or the political realm—have identified themselves and their country with the rest of Asia or propounded pan-Asianist ideologies. In fact, for more than a century, most modern-minded Chinese have been oriented more toward the West than toward Asia. To be sure, they have often seemed insecure, hypersensitive, and jealous toward the West, seeing it in large part as a threat to China's dominant values and institutions. But they have also regarded the advanced nations of Western Europe and America as the source of the dynamism and progress from which China must draw inspiration and guidance.

Toward much of Asia, in contrast, China has exhibited a kind of cultural complacency bordering on arrogance, which has expressed itself from time to time in attempts to manipulate, overawe, or intimidate other Asian states, or more often simply meddle in their affairs. China has tended until quite recently to view the countries of Asia—with the exception of modernized Japan—as either backward, subservient, or burdened with outmoded social and political systems in dire need of change. At best, Asia has been seen as the potential setting for a revolutionary transmutation in which China might play a catalytic role. Only in recent years have China's leaders, reflecting a chastened post-Mao political mood and a sober awareness of their country's backwardness, approached their fellow Asians in a spirit of greater equality and manifested a greater willingness to confront issues of common interest with a view to finding mutually satisfactory solutions through pragmatic means.

There has also been a wide gap between Chinese perceptions of themselves and Asian perceptions of China. From the global perspective adopted by Chinese leaders the PRC remains relatively weak in many of the measurable indicators of power, and it is committed to an ideology that makes domination of others unthinkable. It is quite feasible, therefore, for Chinese sincerely to consider themselves to be merely a developing socialist country, belonging to the Third World, which poses no threat to its Asian neighbors. From a regional perspective, however, particularly as viewed from the vantage point of some of the smaller countries of Asia, China is seen not as a less-developed country but as a great power—a large and powerful nation with considerable military, diplomatic, and economic capabilities, and with a long historical record of cultural and political domination of the region.

This fundamental incongruence in perception is an underlying cause of misunderstandings and frictions which arise in the relations between China and its Asian neighbors. China, viewing itself in global terms, does not always realize how strong it is when placed in regional context. The rest of Asia, viewing China in a regional perspective, does not always realize how weak it is on a global scale.

Yet another difficulty for China stems from the fact that, for a very long time, its leaders' views of Asia were based on a set of assumptions derived from the 1940s and early 1950s—assumptions that have long since ceased to be valid. It is an irony of contemporary history that China, a self-consciously revolutionary state, has been so slow to take notice of the multifaceted revolution that has been transforming the face of Asia for a full generation. The Asia of the 1980s—dynamic, developing, and increasingly at the center of world affairs—is a far cry from the war-devastated, poverty-stricken, and tumultuous continent Chinese Communist leaders knew in the late 1940s. At that time, the tides of Western imperialism were just receding from Asian shores. Communal strife, ethnic conflict, endemic poverty, and internal rebellions wracked the newly independent states of South and Southeast Asia. Divided Korea was drifting into civil war and a defeated Japan was occupied by U.S. troops. Neither political independence nor nationalist ideology sufficed to mark a channel leading toward economic development. In short, the Asia of the late 1940s bore a startling resemblance to the chaotic and often desperate condition of China itself in the first half of the twentieth century. No wonder, then, that Chinese Communist leaders believed their prescriptions for China might attain a wider currency throughout Asia. Revolutionary hubris reinforced the traditional pride in the worth of Chinese values and institutions.

By the early 1980s, the momentum of political and economic development had transformed much of Asia, although a marked unevenness has characterized this change. Japan's combination of stable political democracy and high standard of living makes it unique. Taiwan and South Korea have been replicating Japan's economic success but are ruled by authoritarian regimes which invoke internal security concerns to justify political repression. The member states of the Association of South East Asian Nations (ASEAN)—Thailand, Malaysia, Singapore, Indonesia, and the Philippines—for all the differences among them, are developing an increasing sense of regional consciousness and demonstrating a collective capacity for coordinating their economic systems and asserting their joint political and security concerns. Under the guidance of conservative, anti-Communist leaders, they represent a new regional power in Asia that is likely to grow in importance. The emergence since 1975 of a unified Vietnam, allied to the USSR and determined to consolidate its control over Laos and Cambodia, is, of course, the most significant occurrence in communist Asia in recent years. North Korea, much like Korea of old, is going its own way and beholden to neither the Soviet Union nor the PRC. During the last decade, the countries of South Asia too have shown signs of overcoming internal fragmentation and achieving in varying degree political equilibrium and institutionalization. Only in Southwest Asia, adjacent to the turbulent Middle East, have revolution, foreign intervention, and resistance torn apart such societies as Iran and Afghanistan.

In all its diversity, the contemporary Asian experience encompasses three overarching trends that challenge Chinese understanding and confound Chinese policy. The first is the remarkable growth of the non-Communist Asian economies, and their increasing integration into the international economy. The economic success of non-Communist Asia challenges the relative economic autarky of the Maoist period, reduces China's appeal as a model for the rest of the continent, and raises the question of what China can learn from its neighbors' experiences. Second is the process of internal political consolidation in Asia, notwithstanding the persistence of ethnic, Communist, and religious insurgencies that test the unity of several Asian states, notably Burma, the Philippines, Iran, and Pakistan. On the whole, the prospects for further political fragmentation, the redrawing of existing state boundaries, or revolutionary political change seem much diminished compared to years past. This process of political integration suggests that Peking's policy of supporting guerrilla revolutionaries has reached a dead end, and that existing governments in Asia are stronger and more stable than China's leaders originally wished to admit.

Finally, the two superpowers remain active in Asia, and there is no reason to expect their involvement to diminish for many years to come. Because of continuing Soviet and American participation in Asian affairs, regional economic, political, and security issues will be placed in the context of global balance of power politics, making their resolution more difficult. But, whether viewed in economic, political, or military dimensions, Asia in the 1980s will have multiple centers of power, and there is little likelihood that any single state will be able to dominate the entire region. This multiple balance of power in Asia, in which the United States and the Soviet Union play important but not dominating roles, challenges the Chinese assumption that superpower hegemonism, particularly of the Soviet variety, is a clear and present danger in Asia.

In sum, China must overcome some significant conceptual handicaps in dealing with its Asian neighbors. It has been slow to understand the suspicion and fear that its size and resources have created in much of the rest of the region. While professing its membership in the Third World, it continues to regard other Asian nations with a degree of condescension. Its views of Asia have not always kept up with the pace of change in the continent. As a result, there has been a significant perceptual gap between China and the rest of Asia. In no small measure, China's problems in Asia derive from its tendency to view the region through the prism of a set of global foreign policy concerns that its neighbors, inclined to take a regional view of matters, consider inappropriate and in part threatening to their own interests.

Chinese Goals and Policies since 1949

Within Asia China has pursued three foreign policy goals. It has sought first of all to enhance its own security. This has meant forming a united front with one of the superpowers (the USSR in the 1950s, the United States in the 1970s) to contain what was perceived to be its more threatening expansionist rival (the United States in the 1950s, the USSR in the 1970s and 1980s). Its objective has been to deny its major adversaries bases in, access to, or control of Asian territories from which they could threaten China itself. This goal has also involved China in a search for secure boundaries and embroiled it in land and maritime territorial disputes with many of its neighbors. In some cases (Burma, Pakistan, Mongolia), negotiations have produced a peaceful resolution of boundary problems, but in others (India, the USSR, Vietnam) the Chinese have employed force in pursuit of their objectives.

Second, it is in Asia that China has asserted its own sovereignty and affirmed its identity as a powerful state. Since China's assertiveness has coincided with an age of postwar Asian nationalism, friction has inevitably developed between China and its neighbors. A central question for the future is whether China will be willing and able to work out long-term arrangements on an equal basis with such powerful Asian states as Japan, Vietnam, India, and the USSR to secure long-term peace and stability.

Third, China has looked to Asia in terms of both revolution and development. Particularly in the 1960s, Chinese Communist leaders proselytized their own model of guerrilla-style, peasant-based revolution and extolled the utility of Maoist agriculture-led economic development. More recently, they have examined with interest the economic development models and borrowed some of the techniques successfully employed in newly industrialized areas like Taiwan, Korea, Singapore, and Hong Kong. From Japan they have received development assistance in the form of financial credits, technology, and technical expertise. The PRC has also turned to ethnic Chinese scattered throughout Southeast Asia for contributions of capital and expertise in the task of modernization. The developing economies of Asia represent important trading partners for the PRC as well as competitors and are potential sources of ideas and capital.

A brief overview of the evolution of China's role in Asia since 1949 may further clarify these policy objectives, as well as China's conceptual approach to the region. In the early 1950s, Chinese leaders accepted a Stalinist two-camp view of international relations and, out of deference to their Soviet ally, temporarily soft-pedaled their conviction that their own revolutionary experience had greater relevance to Asia than did the Russian revolution. Communism seemed to be the wave of the future and China was part of that wave. China supported Communist insurgencies in Asia and seemed reluctant to accept the legitimacy of many of the continent's newly independent but Western-oriented states.

With the end of the Korean War, however, as the Chinese chafed under the Sino-Soviet alliance and began to show greater conceptual and diplomatic flexibility, they sought to draw upon the fund of anti-Western feeling that was a legacy of the imperialist age in Asia in order to promote a broad united front of non-Communist countries directed against the United States and its allies. The Panch Shil or Five Principles of Peaceful Coexistence (mutual respect for territorial integrity and sovereignty, nonaggression, noninterference in internal affairs, equality and mutual benefit, and peaceful coexistence), subscribed to by China and India during their era of good feeling, served as a kind of safe-conduct pass facilitating China's entry into polite diplomatic society. They opened the era of China's Afro-Asian diplomacy, symbolized by its participation in the Bandung Conference of April 1955.

Although this diplomacy soon fell afoul of the radicalization of Chinese doctrine and the Sino-Indian border conflict in the late 1950s, the Chinese notion that Asia belonged neither to the imperialist world nor to the socialist world survived intact. In the 1960s, as the Sino-Soviet split convulsed the world Communist system, China's declaratory policy was dominated by the exhortation to revolution in order to make a decisive break with the colonialist past, eliminate regimes which were collaborating with China's primary enemies, and bring into being a Third World revolutionary united front that China would presumably lead. In his concept of intermediate zones lying between the camps of socialism and imperialism, Mao Zedong expressed his belief in the potential for autonomous political action outside the field of force of the two superpowers. In this theory, Asia was linked to Africa and Latin America as standing in the forefront of the anti-imperialist struggle.

In the 1970s, PRC foreign policy focused on both the North-South and the East-West axes. China asserted its solidarity with the underdeveloped world and its struggle for a New International Economic Order (NIEO), and Deng Xiaoping, speaking at the United Nations, outlined Mao's theory of the Three Worlds in which Asia once again formed a troika with Africa and Latin America. By this time, of course, the PRC was deeply worried about the growing might of the USSR, now perceived as an expansionist, interventionary, social-imperialist superpower. Thus Mao, the "Great Helmsman," sharply swung the wheel of Chinese foreign policy onto a course of reconciliation with the West as well as with the established, mostly conservative governments of Asia as part of an effort to forge a united front against perceived Soviet hegemonism.

In the 1980s, even as the PRC moves toward a less confrontational relationship with the USSR, Chinese leaders continue to identify the Soviet Union as the primary threat to world peace. Directly in Southwest Asia, and indirectly in Southeast Asia through its Vietnamese ally, they see the Soviet Union thrusting outward into Asia. China has defined its own role in checking this trend in very modest terms. In addition to slowly modernizing its own military capabilities, China provided military assistance and political support to the so-called front-line states of Pakistan and Thailand and incessantly warned all those who would listen of the dangers of complacency in responding to Soviet expansionism. But Peking showed only intermittent interest in an operational security alignment with the United States, and, by the early 1980s, Chinese leaders were returning to a position of greater although still unequal balance in their relations with the two superpowers.

Of course, no state can operate in the international arena only on the plane of political abstractions. Despite their rhetorical emphasis on building united fronts against hegemonic superpowers, at the level of actual diplomacy the Chinese have been chary of entering into multilateral arrangements on a basis of equality that would entail reciprocal and mutually binding obligations. Rather, the PRC has preferred to develop its relations with its Asian neighbors largely on a bilateral basis, a curious echo of the imperial Chinese tribute system. This preference for bilateral diplomacy may in part also reflect China's past unhappiness with participation in the Soviet bloc; it certainly has the effect of magnifying China's power. In all its bilateral dealings in Asia with the exception of the USSR and, in economic terms, Japan, China is the stronger partner in one respect or another. The practice of bilateralism strengthens China's hand and over the long run could help China position itself for a dominant role in Asia.

Thus, China has not sought to create any formal alliance of Asian states in which it might play the major leadership role. (In the early 1960s, to be sure, the Chinese appeared to be assuming the role of catalyst in a loose grouping of Communist and radical states—the PRC, North Korea, North Vietnam, Cambodia, and Indonesia.) China's primary approach has been a negative one: to weaken, break up, or prevent the emergence of Asian states with an actual or presumptive anti-China bias. In this vein, the PRC condemned the South East Asian Treaty Organization (SEATO), Asian and Pacific Council (ASPAC), Association of Southeast Asia (ASA), and, during its early years, ASEAN as presumed creatures of American imperialism. It also opposed the proposal for an Asian collective security system that Moscow has floated since 1969. China's objective has been to contain the involvement of the superpowers in Asia, to prevent them from playing a hegemonic role, and thus to preserve China's own freedom of action in the region. However, recognizing that as Asian-Pacific powers neither the United States nor the USSR can be excluded from Asia, China aligned itself first with Moscow against Washington in the 1950s and then with Washington against Moscow since 1972 in an attempt to counterbalance the stronger threat to Chinese interests. And this shifting pattern of alignment has been accompanied by Chinese attempts to encourage the formation of a broad united front of diverse partners whose only common interest is to contain the more dangerous of the superpowers.

China has also been very critical of close bilateral relations, especially those involving security cooperation, between Asian countries and the superpowers when it has judged these to be animated by anti-Chinese intentions. Peking has feared that Asian countries large and small—Japan, South Korea, Thailand, the Philippines, India, Vietnam, Afghanistan, and Mongolia—were being used as pawns or proxies by the United States or the USSR. However, where China has judged such relations useful to its overall objective of containing the stronger superpower, as in the case of the U.S.-Japan relationship since 1972, it has extended its approval. China has also learned to appreciate the virtues of such regional groupings as ASEAN once Peking became convinced that its members were not banded together to confront the PRC.

When looked at in subregional terms, China has had a highly differentiated view of Asia over the years since 1949. Northeast Asia has probably been the area of greatest interest and concern to the PRC. The Korean War, in which China reluctantly intervened, and the U.S.-Japan security treaty convinced Chinese leaders that a serious threat to their security emanated from this direction. Presently, the Chinese perceive Northeast Asia as a locus of increased Soviet military activity and the area where a Soviet-Chinese military confrontation would most likely occur. The unresolved situation on the Korean peninsula is another source of anxiety because renewed conflict there could force the Chinese to activate their alliance with Pyongyang and destroy the entente with the United States and Japan. The PRC's strong interest in Northeast Asian stability is reinforced by its desire to expand economic cooperation with Japan to promote modernization.

Southeast Asia is the next most important subregion in Asia from China's perspective. Again, security concerns have dominated China's agenda in this area. In the 1950s and 1960s the PRC actively supported revolutionary movements in Southeast Asia and courted Indonesia's Sukarno in an effort to undermine the pro-Western governments that the United States had mobilized to contain China. Sino-American confrontation was narrowly averted during the Vietnam War, but Hanoi's victory brought little joy to the Chinese, who soon found themselves facing a powerful Vietnam determined to exercise its sway over all of Indochina and increasingly linked to the

Soviet Union. In response to these developments, China accelerated the normalization of its relations with the ASEAN states and exerted both military and diplomatic pressure against Vietnam in an attempt to dislodge it from Cambodia. Toward Burma, China has acted the role of the *padrone,* expecting deference as a matter of course and acting indulgent or severe as the mood strikes.

Chinese interest in South Asia has been of a lesser order of magnitude. The early promise of close Sino-Indian relations based on anticolonialism and a species of Asian nationalism foundered on the rock of conflicting national interests in the Himalayan wastelands. India's sympathy for Tibetan freedom fighters, the sanctuary provided to the Dalai Lama and his entourage, and India's close ties with the Soviet Union further irritated the Chinese leadership. Fifteen years of a Sino-Indian cold war following the border war of 1962 was ended with the exchange of ambassadors in 1976, but the normalization of Sino-Indian relations proceeded at a very deliberate pace. Indeed, negotiations aimed at resolving the territorial and other issues between the two countries were not undertaken until five years later. By contrast, Sino-Pakistani relations have been remarkably amicable throughout the twists and turns of Chinese foreign policy, and Peking has provided substantial military and economic assistance to Islamabad's conservative Muslim rulers.

The PRC has had relatively little interest in Southwest Asia, a region remote from China's economic and population centers. More recently, however, strategic concerns relating to the Soviet Union have drawn Chinese attention to the area. Just a few months after then-premier Hua Guofeng's state visit to Teheran in 1978, the Chinese saw Iran dissolve into revolutionary chaos. The Soviet invasion of Afghanistan appeared to jeopardize the security and internal stability of China's long-term friend Pakistan, as well as the West's lifeline to Persian Gulf oil. China reacted by reiterating its commitment to Pakistan and by channeling small arms and supplies to anti-Soviet Afghan guerrillas. But Peking had little leverage in either situation, and Southwest Asia has remained at the bottom of China's list of regional concerns despite a brief rhetorical flurry that suggested otherwise.

If we consider Asia along another axis—Communist versus non-

Communist—it is noteworthy that at present China's relations with the former are generally quite bad, whereas with the latter they are good with a few exceptions. China enjoys amicable relations only with North Korea (DPRK) among its seven Communist neighbors in Asia (the USSR, Afghanistan, North Korea, Mongolia, Vietnam, Laos, and Cambodia). Linked to the DPRK by a 1961 treaty of friendship, cooperation, and mutual assistance, Peking echoes Pyongyang's line on Korean issues but clearly would be distressed by a renewal of conflict on the peninsula. Chinese interest in North Korea is sustained by fears of Soviet competition for influence in Pyongyang, but Peking's disdain for Kim Il-sung's brand of socialism limits PRC-DPRK relations. A modest level of trade and a program of cultural exchange round out relations between two countries that may be allies but are hardly close friends.

The Sino-Soviet conflict has infected China's relations with all its other Asian Communist neighbors. Closely tied to the Soviet Union since the 1920s, Outer Mongolia (MPR) has become a forward base for Soviet military deployments directed against China. The continued sinicization of Inner Mongolia by Han Chinese settlers has undoubtedly encouraged MPR leaders to cling more tightly to the USSR. Lacking direct access to Afghanistan since 1980, when Moscow occupied the Wakhan corridor forming the short border between Afghanistan and China, Peking has worked through its close ally Pakistan in support of the resistance war against the Soviet-imposed Kabul government of Babrak Karmal.

Sino-Vietnamese relations are a fascinating case study of the foreign policy difficulties of the PRC in contemporary Asia. The roots of Sino-Vietnamese hostility extend to the era of imperial Chinese rule over Vietnam. In more recent times, Hanoi's and Peking's goals diverged at the 1954 Geneva Conference, when China joined the USSR in pressuring Ho Chi Minh to accept a temporarily divided Vietnam as the price for improving relations between the socialist camp and the West. This divergence increased markedly during the Vietnam War, when Mao first rejected Communist bloc efforts to provide joint assistance to Vietnam, then criticized Hanoi for negotiating with Washington, and finally veered off to strike his own strategic bargain with the United States while B-52s were still pulverizing Vietnam. Despite these injuries, Chinese and Vietnamese leaders managed to maintain a good outward face on their relationship as long as the war continued.

Victory engendered greater strains in the relationship than war ever had. To make matters worse, China soon lost its master diplomat Zhou Enlai, who might have been able to control the escalating spiral of hostility. Dizzy with success, Hanoi moved rapidly to integrate the two halves of war-ravaged Vietnam and extend its influence into Laos. Meanwhile, China cultivated relations with the new Pol Pot government in Phnom Penh which, suffering from its own delusions of grandeur, provoked fights along its border with its vastly more powerful Vietnamese neighbor. Wishing to curb Hanoi's power, Peking showed no interest in holding its fractious Cambodian partner in check.

In 1978 things fell apart. Reacting strongly to Vietnam's expropriation and persecution of ethnic Chinese, particularly in south Vietnam, where many were small merchants, Peking roundly denounced Hanoi and provided refuge to some two hundred fifty thousand panic-stricken ethnic Chinese from Vietnam. Then, in July 1978, China unilaterally terminated its economic assistance to Hanoi and recalled its technicians—all in a repetition of the crude pressure tactics that Nikita Khrushchev had applied against China itself just eighteen years earlier.

Determined to eliminate the abominable and intractable Pol Pot regime, Hanoi moved to secure its northern flank by signing a friendship treaty with the USSR in November 1978 and then sent troops into Cambodia to sweep Pol Pot from power. Just six weeks later, China launched its punitive war against Vietnam, supposedly designed to teach Vietnam a lesson. This "pedagogical war," to borrow Lucian Pye's tongue-in-cheek appellation, resulted in the further militarization of yet another of China's frontier zones and a dangerous rise in the level of regional tension.[1]

Since then, bolstered by the complaisance of the United States and ASEAN, the PRC has continued to pursue a confrontational policy

1. Lucian Pye, "China and Southeast Asia," in Richard H. Solomon, ed., *The China Factor* (Englewood Cliffs, NJ: Prentice-Hall, 1981), p. 241.

of feeding the guerrilla resistance to the Heng Samrin government in Phnom Penh, and harassing Hanoi by supporting tribal insurgents in northern Laos. The formation in the summer of 1982 of a Cambodian government-in-exile nominally headed by Prince Sihanouk and incorporating both the Khmer Rouge and their erstwhile rivals, Son Sann's guerrillas, demonstrated a new tactical flexibility on the part of all the anti-Hanoi forces but only marginally improved the prospects for altering the military balance of forces within Cambodia. Meanwhile, along the Sino-Vietnamese border a smaller but tougher Vietnamese force, armed with modern equipment including advanced Soviet anti-aircraft missiles, faces a larger but flabbier Chinese force in a tense atmosphere marked by sporadic skirmishing. The People's Liberation Army (PLA) cannot be confident of its ability to crush Vietnamese resistance in the event of war.

With the exception of North Korea, then, the Communist states of Asia have lined up in a bipolar, Cold War configuration pitting the USSR, Mongolia, Vietnam, Laos, Cambodia, and Afghanistan against the PRC and the remnants of so-called Democratic Kampuchea. It seems doubtful that the emergence of such a configuration was inevitable in the post–Indochina War period. Rather, China has contributed much to the establishment of this pattern by badly overreacting to Vietnam. Chinese leaders have insisted on viewing Hanoi as a mere client of Moscow (the Cubans of the Orient) rather than as an independent regional power center. The truth of the matter may be that China opposes Vietnam less because it is a Soviet ally than because it dislikes the idea of having on its southern periphery a state which is disinclined to bend before China's will. It may be some time before the Chinese are prepared to reconsider their present stance, seek to detach Vietnam from its somewhat uncomfortable perch within the Soviet bloc, and work out a *modus vivendi* with Hanoi.

In recent years, in sum, China has viewed relations with its Asian neighbors primarily through an anti-Soviet prism. It has extended its approbation to those states—Pakistan, the members of ASEAN, and Japan—which have reason to be wary of the USSR. In contrast, Peking's diplomacy toward states that are either allied with or else too friendly toward Moscow—Vietnam, Mongolia, and India—has been marked by the excessive rigidity and sterility that the Chinese sometimes confuse with adherence to principle.

But the notion of building an anti-Soviet united front has been much more than a policy designed to protect the PRC from an alleged Soviet threat. It has provided the rationale, the integrating mechanism, and a measure of consistency for the disparate pieces of China's policy toward Asia. It has defined the political and strategic role that China has sought to play in the region. And it has provided the instrumentality by which China has sought to transcend its relative weakness and play a key role on the stage of world affairs. Anti-Sovietism, in short, has offered a sense of direction and identity to a Chinese leadership that still seems to need an overarching purpose in facing the external world.

By constructing its Asian policy around the concept of anti-Sovietism, China has demonstrated once again its tendency to place its regional relations in a global context. For Mao's successors, just as for the late Chairman himself, Asia has been less a geographic reality than a political abstraction, embodying their hopes for a fundamental change in the global distribution of power. Thus, just as "Asia" was harnessed to the chariot of anti-Americanism during the Bandung era, China envisioned a similar role for "Asia" vis-à-vis Soviet hegemonism in the 1970s.

In all these ways, the anti-Sovietism of the recent past is reminiscent of the anti-imperialism of the 1950s and 1960s. But in the process of containing the Soviet Union, the PRC has adopted a very different vocabulary from that employed in its confrontation with the United States in earlier decades. The revolutionary rhetoric of the earlier period was less suited to the task of dealing with the USSR, which was, after all, a Communist state that trumpeted its commitment to supporting revolutions. Instead, China has had to appear as a responsible member of the international system promoting stability and order. The realignment of the 1970s produced a sea change in China's orientation in Asia. China became more responsive to geopolitical realities than to revolutionary aspirations, to the viewpoints of governments in power than to rebels in opposition, to those who control strategic territories and lines of communication than to those who enjoy popular support or legitimacy. Thus, Peking's rhetoric of revolutionary diplomacy yielded to the language and logic of real-politik.

Issues in China's Asian Policy

What are the key issues in China's current policies in Asia, and what assets and liabilities does China bring to bear in its interactions with its Asian neighbors? We shall explore these questions by looking in turn at historical, economic, military, ethnic, and ideological factors. Before doing so, however, it is important to note that in a geographical sense China and Asia are growing closer together. To be sure, along a considerable part of China's borders, adversary political relationships superimposed upon difficult terrain have combined to restrict the utilization of existing links. But the main trend since 1949 has been the establishment of new land, sea, air, and electronic links connecting China with other parts of Asia and facilitating the flow of people, goods, weapons, ideas, and information. Many of these links connect China not only with Asia but with the world beyond and thus represent a concrete expression of China's dual status as a regional and a would-be global power.

History

Chinese leaders have tried to use history to cement their relations with selected Asian states, but memories of the past have as often been a liability as an asset in Sino-Asian relations. In Peking's view, Western imperialism and colonialism provided the origins of a natural bond among Asian peoples who suffered the traumatic loss of their independence, national selfhood, and cultural autonomy. The possibility that opposition to Western imperialism could serve as the common denominator of independent but convergent Asian nationalisms animated PRC policy in the Bandung period and sustained Prime Minister Nehru's hope for an era of Sino-Indian amity. As memories of Western imperialism fade among the Western elites, Peking has sought a new basis for unity in the Third World's demands for the creation of a New International Economic Order and in the struggle against superpower global hegemony. The Chinese have also invoked the memory of their past cultural intercourse with Japan,

India, Vietnam, and the states of Southeast Asia at various times to demonstrate that China has been a good neighbor.

Many Asian countries, however, find in history reasons for their own wariness of the PRC. Throughout Southeast Asia, albeit in varying degrees, the image of imperial China with its sense of cultural superiority sustains contemporary suspicions that the People's Republic aspires to an updated and less passive version of the old tribute system. The Soviet Union, ever eager to stoke the flames of suspicion, harps on the theme of Chinese expansionism as it pursues its own Asian policy objectives.

The series of unresolved territorial disputes between the PRC and many of its immediate neighbors is an obvious historical legacy that contributes to instability in Asia. In the late 1950s and early 1960s China signed boundary agreements with Pakistan, Burma, and Mongolia, yielding portions of contested territory in a spirit of compromise. At about the same time, however, more serious boundary disputes with India and the USSR emerged, resulting in armed conflict in 1962 and 1969 respectively. Later a boundary dispute with the SRV developed too. The PRC seized the Paracel islands from South Vietnam in 1974 and, citing historical evidence, laid sweeping claims to the archipelagos, reefs, and islands of the South China Sea, some of which were garrisoned by Taiwan, the Philippines, and Vietnam. China also clashed with Japan over ownership of the Senkaku (Diaoyutai) islands and with both Tokyo and Seoul over maritime rights in the waters of the continental shelf.

The issue of Taiwan, although dissimilar in many respects, also represents a case of China asserting its desire to incorporate a territory which has functioned de facto as an independent entity since 1949 and whose population has evinced no interest in becoming a province of the PRC. Finally, although Peking has long tolerated the anomalies of a British as well as a Portuguese colony on Chinese soil, PRC assertions of its determination to reestablish sovereignty over Hong Kong may disrupt the economy of this vital enclave from which the PRC earns substantial sums of foreign exchange.

Thus, the PRC showed itself to be a non–status quo power with respect to existing state boundaries. What is more, Peking was not shy about applying military force in attempts to validate its claims.

The seizure of the Paracel islands in 1974 and the Chinese military engagements against India in 1962 and Vietnam in 1979 are the best-known examples in this regard.

Although most of these territorial and boundary disputes are presently quiescent, one cannot assume that they will remain so indefinitely. Of course, China alone does not bear the onus for the failure to resolve these disputes. From the viewpoint of her neighbors, particularly the smaller states of Southeast Asia, however, Peking's territorial pretensions and its occasionally pugnacious disposition are far from reassuring.

Economics

Until recently, China by choice played a very small role in the international economic system. As a large continental power with abundant natural resources and a very high rate of domestic savings, during much of the Maoist period China proclaimed its economic autonomy and touted its own self-reliant system of development. The Maoist model of development was hailed by Asian leftists critical of their own countries' dependence upon the international capitalist economy. But now the Maoist developmental model is in eclipse, its failings exposed by Mao's successors, who have steered China outward into the broad but often turbulent waters of the international economy.

In this new stage, Japan is China's natural partner in development. China's vast store of natural resources (including primary energy and other raw materials) can be exchanged for the advanced technology and high-grade capital goods that Japan produces in abundance. Reflecting this reality, Sino-Japanese trade increased tenfold in the decade following diplomatic normalization in 1972, and Japan became China's most important trading partner. A similar though lesser potential exists for Chinese trade with Taiwan and the Republic of Korea, but political barriers keep the existing indirect trade at relatively low levels. With the exception of Japan, the Asian states are not major trading partners of the PRC. Sino-Asian trade (excluding that with Japan and Hong Kong) was only 7.8 percent of China's total trade in 1981.

With respect to other developing Asian states, China could become a significant competitor as well as a partner if its modernization program succeeds. As a major exporter of labor-intensive products such as textiles, light manufactures, and simple consumer goods, China already competes to some degree in the same markets with such states as India, Malaysia, and Sri Lanka. However, South Korea, Taiwan, and most of the ASEAN states will probably be able to stay at least a step or two ahead of China technologically, thus minimizing the PRC's ability to compete with them directly. In such cases, the PRC may prove to be a partner in development exchanging raw materials, primary energy, and simple manufactures for more sophisticated goods as well as services.

China is making the transition from being a donor to a recipient of foreign aid. Between 1953 and 1977, the PRC extended approximately $3.8 billion in aid to Asian states. Vietnam, North Korea, Pakistan, and Cambodia were the major recipients of China's largesse, receiving a total of $2.8 billion in aid.[2] China's aid disbursements have been drastically reduced if not eliminated, and China itself is now competing for concessionary aid with other Asian LDCs from such sources as the World Bank, the United Nations Development Program, and foreign governments such as Japan's. Given China's enormous needs and the limits of available credits, Peking's entry into the aid market has caused apprehension among Asian and other LDCs that their own share of a fixed or even shrinking pie will be reduced. Aid donors like Japan have had to balance the competing aid requests of China and other LDCs, and are unable to comply with all of Peking's requests for assistance.

China's verbal and political support for the concept of the New International Economic Order has not thus far been translated into active Chinese participation in Third World collective economic arrangements to improve the terms of trade with the developed world. However, in one arena—shipping—the PRC has contributed to weakening the developed countries' monopoly in Asia and thereby aided developing Asian countries. The PRC has doubled its merchant marine tonnage over the past several years and, facilitated by extremely low labor rates, the China Ocean Shipping Company has

2. *The Aid Programme of China* (Paris: OECD, 1979), pp. 6–7.

offered Asian business shipping rates 10 to 15 percent below those of the European-dominated Far Eastern Freight Conference.

Summing up, the PRC is a natural economic partner for Japan at this stage of Chinese development and may become so for the newly industrialized countries too, though the potential for competition with them cannot be denied. The PRC is likely to continue its increasing integration into the international economy as long as such a policy contributes to the success of its economic modernization. A sharp setback to this process or a major shift in the domestic political balance leading to a kind of neo-Maoist rule might produce a new period of Chinese autarky and sharply reduced economic ties between China and the rest of the world.

Strategic Threats and Military Issues

Since the middle of the nineteenth century, Asia has been a circumference of threat from which hostile military powers have menaced Chinese security, but since 1949 it has also been a setting in which the PRC has employed its own armed forces against its enemies. China has tried to shift the military balance along its border in its favor, but it has met with only limited success, in part because of American and, more recently, Soviet policies of containing a presumed Chinese threat. In addition, increases in the military capabilities of India, Vietnam, Taiwan, the two Koreas, and Japan have at least kept pace with if not outstripped the growth of PRC military power, with the important exception of China's nuclear arms capability. Nevertheless, taking into account political as well as military factors, on balance China enjoys somewhat greater security in the 1980s than it did in 1949.

Contemporary Chinese leaders have inherited from Mao Zedong a vision of international politics that attunes them to the problem of strategic threat. In dealing with the concrete political and security issues of Asia, however, this legacy has not always served them well. That China must share the crowded stage of Asia with countries whose policies displease it is a fact its leaders have been reluctant to acknowledge.

China's current security concerns focus on the Soviet Union and its ally Vietnam. Although the Chinese for propaganda purposes have systematically exaggerated the size of the Soviet forces along their border, there can be no doubt that Chinese leaders are concerned with the vast superiority of both Soviet nuclear and conventional forces in the East Asian region. However, Peking has usually emphasized that the primary threat posed by these forces is to the United States and Japan, and only secondarily to China itself. This formula is a tacit recognition that the PRC can do little to alter the Sino-Soviet balance of power, and it also may facilitate the easing of tensions with Moscow.

The Vietnamese threat, of course, is of a different order of magnitude. With its successful occupation of Cambodia, Hanoi showed up Peking's inability to protect its rambunctious client regime in Phnom Penh and frustrated PRC desires to maintain a significant degree of influence in Indochina. Yet the Vietnamese threat, as perceived by the ASEAN states, has actually helped China to improve its position in the subregion. Of course, the real worry for Peking's strategic planners is that Vietnam's alliance with Moscow facilitates the Kremlin's containment of China by providing basing rights for the Soviet navy and air force and enlisting Vietnamese military pressure on China's weak southern flank.

China's own threat to the security of its Asian neighbors is limited by the constraints on Chinese military power and the weakening of China's revolutionary credentials. China's conventional military power in Asia is sufficient to overawe only those states with whom it is least likely to come into conflict at the present time. The Chinese possess a limited capacity to conduct cross-border operations, as the Sino-Indian war of 1962 and the Chinese incursion into Vietnam in 1979 demonstrated, but the PLA has lost the decisive advantage it had over India a generation ago, and the Vietnam venture revealed critical weaknesses in China's military machine. By all accounts, the Chinese are badly outclassed by the technologically superior Soviet forces along their lengthy common border. The PLA is particularly weak in air- and sea-lift capabilities, and this deficiency presently limits its potential to operate outside of its own borders against such hypothetical adversaries as Taiwan, Japan, and insular Southeast Asian states.

Yet despite the low priority given to defense modernization, progress is being made in certain key areas. China's navy is outgrowing its heretofore exclusive role as a coastal defense force and may before long be in a position to back up sweeping PRC claims in the South China Sea and show the flag in Southeast Asian ports. Technology transfer from the West may rapidly upgrade the avionics of the Chinese air force and place a 1980s-generation fighter aircraft in Chinese hands. With respect to nuclear weapons, the PLA now possesses both intermediate- and long-range ballistic missiles capable of reaching targets anywhere in Asia. This gives China a unique status among Asian states, but further nuclear proliferation is likely to alter this situation over the next decade.

These developments might severely destabilize the Taiwan-PRC balance of military power and intensify latent anxieties in Southeast Asia. Of course, Moscow can be expected to compensate or, more likely, overcompensate, for any PRC force modernization in order to maintain its military advantage over Peking, while Tokyo may also increase its defense spending.

China has also had an impact on the Asian military balance through provision of conventional arms to its friends. Pakistan has received by far the largest amount of Chinese military assistance including jet aircraft, tanks, and other equipment. The PRC has also provided substantial amounts of equipment to Pol Pot's government in Cambodia and has continued to arm and supply their guerrilla warfare since 1979. China also supplies lesser quantities of arms to the Afghan insurgents, and has transferred military aircraft to North Korea. The supply of Chinese military goods to Communist insurgents in several Southeast Asian nations has apparently diminished in recent years.

As already indicated, China has demonstrated on several occasions its willingness to employ force in pursuit of its foreign policy objectives notwithstanding the risks involved. As one British observer has privately remarked, "The Chinese are prepared to thump their neighbors, call others hegemonists, and behave a bit like hegemonists themselves." Peking's punitive expedition against Vietnam in 1979 nourished Southeast Asian suspicions concerning China's supposed commitment to the goals of achieving peace and stability in Asia. Might not China's readiness to resort to force portend a still greater bellicosity once the PLA becomes modernized? Would the future see China pursuing its great power objectives in Asia through the threat or use of force against weaker neighbors? Such Asian anxieties require continued careful scrutiny of Chinese foreign policy behavior.

In sum, in military terms the PRC is able to defend itself against any threat to its security emanating from Asia with the exception of that from the Soviet superpower. And even in the Soviet case, the PRC has achieved a position of minimum nuclear deterrence. In the event of a conventional war, China could be crippled but not destroyed or occupied by the USSR. Conversely, China presently poses only a modest threat to the security of its Asian neighbors with the exception of Vietnam, which, however, enjoys Soviet protection. As long as China devotes itself primarily to the enormous task of modernization, this situation is unlikely to change very much, but as China grows increasingly powerful, its neighbors cannot assume that Peking will always exercise restraint in the pursuit of its objectives.

National Minorities and Ethnic Chinese

An ethnological map of Asia is a crazy quilt of peoples. Most of the approximately 60 million non-Han Chinese minorities live in the peripheral territories of the PRC and many of them—the Kazakhs, Uighurs, and Kirghiz of Xinjiang, the Mongols of Inner Mongolia, the Zhuang, Nong, Meo, Lao, and Tai of China's southwest—spill across the borders into neighboring countries. Because of what it has admitted were often harsh and intolerant policies, Peking has not found it easy to gain the loyalties of many of these national minorities, and one result has been continuing Chinese concern over the security of its border territories.

Both China and its neighbors from time to time have exploited these transnational ethnic groups for purposes of harassment, destabilization, intelligence gathering, and so forth. In 1962, for example, the Soviet Union fanned the flames of ethnic discontent in Xinjiang and induced some sixty thousand Kazakhs to flee into Soviet territory. For many years Tibetan rebels against Chinese authority found refuge in Nepal's high country and spilled over into India as well from whence they conducted guerrilla warfare against the Chinese army of occupation in their homeland. Indian sympathy for Tibetan self-determination hinders improvement of Sino-Indian relations. Reports in recent years indicate that the Chinese are supporting anti-Vietnamese Meo guerrillas in northern Laos and encouraging Montagnard rebellion in the highlands of Vietnam itself.

However, it is not China's transnational ethnic minorities but the Han Chinese themselves who, as ethnic minorities outside of China, represent the most important and contentious human connection between the PRC and its Asian neighbors. Whether because of their weight within the general population, their economic role as the key commercial class, their involvement in antigovernment insurgency, their allegedly questionable loyalties, or their clannishness, ethnic Chinese have been a significant factor in the politics of Malaysia, Singapore, Thailand, Vietnam, and Indonesia, and an important consideration in the relations between these states and the PRC.

From Peking's point of view, the existence of ethnic Chinese communities in Southeast Asia has been a mixed blessing. Official policy toward them has gone through cycles of estrangement and embrace, reflecting an unresolved ambivalence in thinking. Two major questions have been whether, and if so how, China should protect the interests of these ethnic Chinese; and what contribution, if any, ethnic Chinese in Southeast Asia can make to the attainment of China's national objectives.

As part of its Bandung-era good neighbor policies, beginning in the mid-1950s Peking abjured any special relationship with or responsibility toward the ethnic Chinese of Southeast Asia and encouraged them to adopt local citizenship and discard their sojourners' attitude. China's adherence to this stance has been sorely tested, however, whenever violent xenophobic outbreaks endangered the safety of ethnic Chinese minorities. Anti-Chinese pogroms in Indonesia in the early and middle 1960s inspired protests and attempts by the PRC to rescue some of the victims of mob violence. Peking condemned mistreatment of the Chinese minority in Vietnam during 1977 and 1978 and accepted some two-hundred fifty thousand refugees into its southern provinces for resettlement. China's punitive war against Vietnam in 1979 was occasioned in part by a sense of aggrieved ethnic pride.

Peking by no means has the whip hand on issues affecting ethnic Chinese in Southeast Asia. The internal consolidation of the states of the region has increased their ability to manage their local Chinese minorities, but communal and ethnic tensions persist and the process of national integration is incomplete. Although it is risky to generalize about the ethnic Chinese of Southeast Asia since their position varies considerably from country to country, it is clear that in parts of the region (Indonesia and Malaysia, for example), they are still held in considerable suspicion. The governments of several Southeast Asian states have taken measures to reduce the economic and political power of their ethnic Chinese minorities and to accelerate their cultural assimilation. Such policies present Peking with the choice of whether or not to attempt to protect their ethnic compatriots from excessive pressures.

The response to this dilemma is connected with the question of what role, if any, overseas Chinese communities can be expected to play in China's own modernization. In the post-Mao period, ethnic Chinese living abroad once again have been cast in the role of potential major contributors to China's developmental process. Amidst a flurry of apologies for the outrages of the Cultural Revolution, PRC leaders court ethnic Chinese in Asia and elsewhere as sources of capital, technology, entrepreneurial skills, and so forth. A place of honor has been reserved for them in the renascent nationalist united front whose spiritual father is Sun Yat-sen. Overseas Chinese capital may play a particularly important role in the development of Guangdong and Fujian, the provinces having the most links with Chinese living abroad.

Yet the wooing of these ethnic Chinese creates a triple bind for Peking. First, it implies a reciprocal obligation to aid the overseas Chinese in case they again become objects of persecution in one or another country. Second, China's appeal for support on the basis of consanguinity threatens the fragile national integration of several Southeast Asian states and, in fact, counterposes the old imperial concept of *jus sanguinis* to the modern concept of *jus soli*. Third, the ethnic Chinese who return to the PRC as tourists, visiting experts, and so forth bear the cultural baggage of the capitalist societies from whence they come and are thus perceived as a species of ideological and cultural Typhoid Mary.

In sum, the concept of ethnicity occupies an important place in China's relations with several of its Asian neighbors. The ethnic Chinese by their very existence are a potential irritant whose political role may be defined very differently depending upon one's angle of vision. To the degree that they remain less than fully integrated into the countries where they live, they are unfortunately vulnerable both to often-unfounded suspicions of doubtful loyalty and to spasmodic waves of persecution. Yet this very vulnerability conceivably could be used by the PRC as a pretext for intervention in the internal affairs of other states in order to protect beleaguered Chinese brethren. The analogy of Germany's intervention on behalf of *Auslands-deutschen* during the interwar period comes to mind.

The expulsion of ethnic Chinese from Vietnam in 1978 and the sporadic outbreaks of anti-Chinese violence in Indonesia and elsewhere suggests that it will be some time before the ethnic Chinese issue fades in importance. One should not exaggerate the extent to which PRC policy can actually affect the attitudes which make ethnic Chinese vulnerable. At most, by a stance of consistent disengagement and a clear message to ethnic Chinese not to expect any major exertion on their behalf, Peking can contribute marginally to reducing Southeast Asian suspicions, but as long as PRC leaders see some advantage in cultivating the goodwill of the ethnic Chinese living abroad, the possibility that China will act to protect its ethnic compatriots will continue to exist.

Ideology and Revolution

During the Maoist period, China's image as a revolutionary city upon a hill attracted radicals in many places who were critical of their own governments and societies. Among a much wider circle that included certain development economists, the Maoist economic model of decentralized, agriculture-based growth appeared to present an attractive alternative to the urbanized, foreign trade–dependent growth models of Japan, Taiwan, and South Korea. However, the policy reversals of the Deng era, coupled with Chinese admissions of failures and rank deceptions during the Maoist years, have tarnished the reputation of this Maoist model probably beyond restoration. Chinese disavowals of their 1960s ideological polemics against Soviet revisionism have shattered yet another arrow in the Maoist quiver. Whether in the realms of ideology, culture, or development, China is no longer an attractive model to more than a relative handful of Asians. In fact, for some of China's young people, particularly those in the cities who are disenchanted with the repressive and puritanical official orthodoxies, the Americanized Asian culture of places like Hong Kong, Tokyo, and Taipei is a siren song luring them to a more attractive and liberating life-style.

Chinese support for Communist revolutionary movements in Asia has declined steadily over the past several years. China has long since ceased to be, if it ever actually was, the center of revolutionary change in Asia. On the whole, this retreat from support of Asian revolutionary movements has strengthened China's diplomatic position in the region although even Peking's attenuated ties with Communist insurgencies evoke great suspicion, particularly in Southeast Asian capitals.

In a more heroic age, Mao and his followers enunciated the doctrine of people's war and proclaimed the necessity for armed revolutionary struggles throughout Asia to purge the region of imperialism and colonialism. Even then, actual PRC support for revolution was carefully circumscribed, and the leitmotif of Chinese statements on revolution was that Asian and other revolutionaries should practice self-reliance. What is more, before deciding which particular revolutionary movements deserved their verbal support, Chinese leaders picked over the merchandise as carefully as customers in a thrift shop. PRC support of Asian revolutionary movements in the 1960s served China's overall strategic objective of enhancing its security through a species of revolutionary countercontainment aimed at those governments in the region closely linked to what was perceived as the primary enemy, the United States.

Despite these limitations, at one time or another in the 1950s and 1960s Peking had endorsed revolutionary movements in Burma, Thailand, Malaysia, India, the Philippines, Vietnam, Laos, and Indonesia, providing small arms, materiel, and supplies as well as advice. Other than in Vietnam, nowhere in Asia did Chinese-supported revolutionary movements actually succeed in toppling any postcolonial regime, and in most places (India, Thailand, the Philippines, Malaysia) revolutionaries of a Maoist persuasion were more often a bloody nuisance than an integral challenge to the state.

By the 1970s a combination of factors had sapped Chinese interest in Asian revolutionary movements. In the first place, as just noted, these movements appeared to be stuck on a treadmill. Second, as the furor of the Sino-Soviet ideological dispute subsided, CCP leaders felt less need to invest resources in support of Asian Maoists. Third, significant changes in the Asian politico-strategic environment—the American defeat in Indochina, the emergence of a powerful united Vietnam, and the intensification of Sino-Soviet rivalry in Southeast Asia—pointed Peking in the direction of establishing official ties with Asian states, which in turn were more receptive to the PRC than heretofore. The domestic ascendancy in China of postrevolutionary stabilizers—leaders such as Deng Xiaoping, Hu Yaobang, and Zhao Ziyang—has accelerated the process whereby China formally distanced itself from Communist revolutionaries in Asia.

Chinese leaders have been unwilling to sever all ties with their guerrilla Communist brethren. Nevertheless, under continuing pressure from Southeast Asian leaders, the PRC has downplayed its party-to-party ties to a great extent while strengthening its state-to-state relations. This attempt to assert a distinction in principle between party-to-party and state-to-state relations—so-called dual-track diplomacy—has been correctly viewed in Southeast Asia as a transparent attempt to work both sides of the street. Premier Zhao Ziyang, on visits to Southeast Asian capitals in the early 1980s, sought to reassure his hosts that residual CCP relations with insurgent Communist parties would not detract from China's paramount interest in improving relations with the ASEAN states, but his statements fell short of quieting all Southeast Asian doubts. The CCP's continuing links with the Burmese, Malayan, and Thai Communist parties fuel ASEAN suspicions that China may one day revitalize these ties as an instrument of an expansionist diplomacy. In July 1979 and June 1981 respectively, the PRC-based Voice of People's Thailand and Voice of the Malayan Revolution radio stations, long-time irritants to Bangkok and Kuala Lumpur, were closed down only to be succeeded by new, albeit less powerful, transmitters no longer on Chinese soil. This symbolizes China's willingness to go part but not all of the way toward meeting ASEAN demands that it sever links with local Communist parties.

Chinese leaders, perhaps reluctant for domestic political reasons to repudiate insurgent Asian Communists explicitly, may also fear that Hanoi could inherit the loyalties of jungle Communists who already feel orphaned by the shifts in Chinese policy. Furthermore, in the unlikely event that Vietnam invades Thailand, Chinese-supported guerrilla Communists could become a thorn in the side of SRV forces. Finally, as some Southeast Asians already believe, it may be that China preserves minimal links with Southeast Asian Communist parties against a future time when it may wish to expand its influence and power in Asia by means of revolution.

Asian Views of China

China dominates the map of Asia. It shares land or sea frontiers with no fewer than thirteen Asian countries: Afghanistan, Bhutan, Burma, India, Japan, Laos, Mongolia, Nepal, North Korea, Pakistan, the Philippines, Vietnam, and the USSR. Its territory constitutes nearly half of non-Soviet Asia, and its population of over one billion people is nearly equal to that of all the other Asian states combined.

To be sure, the enormous economic and military potential of China has not yet been realized. At no point in its long history, not even at the apogee of its strongest dynasties, has China actually dominated more than a portion of Asia, although its political and cultural influence has extended well beyond its borders and its presence has been widely felt. Nonetheless, the brief life span of the People's Republic has already witnessed the extension of China's political, economic, military, and cultural influence to a degree unknown in the recent history of the region. China's neighbors, uncertain as they are of China's long-term intentions, view this development with an interest tinctured by apprehension.

Whether China will attain or even aspire to a dominating position in Asia over the coming decades is a question that elicits a wide array of responses within the region. Asian views of contemporary China run the gamut from fear of China as an expansionist power to the belief that the PRC, unable to resolve its internal political and economic problems within the foreseeable future, will never achieve par with the superpowers as a factor in Asian let alone in global politics. Although Asian views of China thus defy easy generalization, it may still be useful to make a few observations on this topic with particular reference to views commonly held in Japan, Southeast Asia, and India.

Since China and Japan normalized their diplomatic relations in 1972, the intensification of Sino-Japanese contact has had the paradoxical effect of stripping away much of Japan's earlier sentimental fascination with the Chinese. For Japanese leftists, the decline of ideology in the PRC and the post-Mao rightist policies have punctured the revolutionary China bubble. Among the business community and Japanese officialdom, erratic Chinese economic policies and Peking's inability to meet its commitments for deliveries of primary resources have similarly engendered a more skeptical mood regarding China's present and future roles in Asia. Japanese leaders, their vision unclouded by the hoary American obsession with China as an emerging superpower, appear more concerned that China's present modernization efforts may fall short, as so many Chinese efforts have done in the past. In this case, the PRC might turn inward on itself, producing an immense gap in Asia that the USSR might seek to exploit. Viewing China in regional rather than global terms, the Japanese shy away from tilting too far toward Peking, since they realize that Japan's security depends upon maintaining nonhostile if not necessarily cordial relations with Moscow. Yet despite a certain disillusionment with the China market, Japan is basically confident that the logic of Chinese modernization will further strengthen the Sino-Japanese economic relationship. Economic imperatives will triumph over political vicissitudes.

Very different images of China prevail in Southeast Asia. Uncertainty about China's future course in Asia is compounded of memories of China's historical empire, doubts about the role of ethnic Chinese in local politics, and suspicions concerning the residual ties between Peking and local Communist parties. In sharp contrast to the United States, which in recent years has hailed the emergence of China as a factor for peace and stability in Asia, Southeast Asian nations to varying degrees are skeptical about the notion that an increasingly powerful China can be relied upon to act benignly. Skilled practitioners of balance-of-power politics, the non-Communist leaders of the ASEAN states believe that the continued involvement of the United States in regional affairs is an essential counterweight to the short-term threat of Vietnam and the USSR and the longer-term threat of the PRC. They fear that Washington may concede primacy in regional affairs to Peking as a side-payment for friendly Sino-American relations.

Southeast Asian elites are relatively unconcerned that the dominant ethnic groups in their countries will be attracted to China as a model or to Chinese-style Communist revolution as a vehicle for socio-political change. However, in countries with significant ethnic Chinese minorities, the feeling persists that Peking seeks to manipulate ethnic solidarity for its own purposes. Similarly, as earlier noted, Southeast Asian elites perceive the CCP's only grudging disengagement from the guerrilla Communist parties of the region as evidence that China may revitalize its remaining ties at some future time and use both ethnic Chinese minorities and local Communist parties as instruments of an expansionist foreign policy. Although there is more than a little political paranoia in such perceptions, Southeast Asians are undoubtedly correct in refusing to accept at face value Peking's assurances that China will never be a superpower.

Apart from this apprehension rooted in geopolitical realities, non-Communist Southeast Asians, particularly those of insular Southeast Asia, have relatively little interest in Chinese domestic or foreign politics. As long as the potential Chinese threat can be contained through a combination of balance-of-power diplomacy, careful management of local ethnic Chinese, and suppression of insurgent Communists, anxiety about China will remain at relatively low levels. Communist Vietnam, of course, has already had a taste of China's military power. Peking's hostility reinforces Hanoi's own rigid diplomacy and tightens the bonds between Vietnam and the Soviet Union. Traditional Vietnamese enmity toward China flourishes once more, and Hanoi sees Peking as a direct threat to its security as well as to the pursuit of its interests in Cambodia and

Laos. Of all the Southeast Asian nations, then, the Socialist Republic of Vietnam has the most negative view of the PRC.

Underlying most Indian views of China is a vein of resentment that the PRC is perceived as a greater factor than India in world affairs. In the 1950s Nehru based his China policy on the notion that the shared experience of humiliation at the hands of imperialist powers gave India and China a common outlook on international affairs. But Nehru's determination to defend Indian territorial claims against perceived Chinese expansionism precipitated the border war of 1962 and led to the humiliation of the Indian army by the PLA. This event produced lasting effects, including New Delhi's tilt toward the Soviet Union and the adoption of positions that anger the PRC on contemporary Asian issues, such as recognition of the Heng Samrin government in Phnom Penh.

Perhaps the dominant Indian view is that China is an expansionist nation quick to use military power to pursue its objectives and determined to achieve a position of dominance in Asia at the expense of major countries like India herself. Indians view China's alignment with Pakistan, its meddling in the Indian ethnic and ideological rebellions of the 1960s, its criticism of India's incorporation of Sikkim and of New Delhi's policy toward Bhutan as evidence of Peking's desire to deny India its rightful position of leadership on the subcontinent. Indians believe that an increasingly powerful China cannot be trusted to play a responsible and pacific role in Asia, but instead will make new demands backed by power. Like the Southeast Asians, they think that the United States, rarely mindful of Indian interests or concerns, encourages Chinese pretensions by treating the PRC as a major fulcrum of global politics.

The upsurge of nationalist feelings in India that accompanied the border war with China in 1962 supplanted the sentiments of Sino-Indian friendship that Nehru had earlier fostered. Consequently, even among Indian intellectuals, relatively few were attracted to the radical political and social experiments of the Cultural Revolution era. Most Indian leftists preferred either the salon Marxism of the British universities at which they had trained, or else the bureaucratic Muscovite variety. Post-Mao Chinese admissions of economic failures and persistent poverty in the PRC confirmed Indian beliefs that the once-touted Chinese developmental model was less effective than India's mixed economy in relieving misery. Another dimension of Indian interest in Chinese development arises from the parochial but legitimate fear that the PRC is well on its way to becoming a major competitor for soft loans from the International Development Association and other foreign lenders.

With China on their doorstep, the countries of Asia cannot afford to take a detached, long-term view of China's future role in Asian and world politics. They must concentrate on the here and now. However, when they do assume a more contemplative pose, their views of China differ considerably. The Japanese hope for and predict the further expansion of Sino-Japanese ties, particularly in the economic arena, under conditions in which the PRC strengthens its connections with the international system as presently constituted. A China developing within the parameters of the international status quo is a desirable long-term partner from Tokyo's perspective. Japanese fears focus on the possibility that Deng Xiaoping's pragmatic model may misfire and internal disarray may deflect China's attention from the international arena and produce a neo-isolationist foreign policy or an internal collapse.

Indians and Southeast Asians are uncomfortable with the prospect of growing Chinese strength rather than the possibility of renewed weakness. Sometimes slighted in the global calculations of the same superpowers who tend to exaggerate China's importance, India and Southeast Asia look at China with a skeptical eye. Rejecting the idea that China or any other major power has a right to exercise a predominant role in the affairs of all of Asia, the Indians and Southeast Asians wish to be masters in their own subregions of the continent, the former through the assertion of their own strength and the latter by increasing cohesion through multilateral ties (ASEAN) and balancing among the external powers.

The Prospects for China in Asia

What role is China likely to play in Asia during the remainder of the 1980s? Let us conclude this chapter with a brief consideration of this question.

Generally speaking, China's present policies in Asia are consistent with the post-Mao domestic policies of establishing a stable political environment and promoting economic development along pragmatic lines. Chinese leaders have demonstrated their interest in furthering good relations with such Asian neighbors as Japan, Pakistan, and the ASEAN nations and in exploring the possibility of normalizing China's long-strained relations with India and the USSR. (PRC policy towards Vietnam is a notable exception in this respect.) Such policies facilitate China's exanded participation in the international economy and convey the image of a responsible power willing to contribute to stability and cooperation in Asia. There is no reason to doubt Peking's assertions that China's modernization requires a stable international environment in Asia as elsewhere. Yet China's willingness to develop its political and economic links with its Asian neighbors into new forms of cooperation and interdependence will depend on how successful Peking's current leaders are in holding together their domestic political coalition. If they can manage this task, the most likely path for China to pursue in Asia will be to seek recognition as a major power via cooperation rather than conflict. The collapse or significant weakening of the domestic coalition, however, might well produce changes in China's Asian policies.

In the unlikely event of a neo-Maoist regime emerging in Peking, China would likely reduce economic intercourse with Japan and the ASEAN states, reaffirm a stricter construction of the doctrine of self-reliance, and possibly revitalize CCP links with the guerrilla Communists in Asia. Yet unless the international environments of the Asian states change significantly, there is little prospect that a revolutionary redirection of Chinese policy would produce measurable results. Asian states would be able to counter any Chinese attempts to destabilize existing governments via suport of revolutionary insurgency.

Alternatively, a neo-Maoist regime might mouth the rhetoric of Third World revolution as a cloak for an isolationist foreign policy. A Chinese retreat from Asia would severely destabilize the existing balance of power, which depends on Chinese participation. Reverberations would be felt from Japan and Korea in the northeast all the way to Pakistan and Afghanistan in the southwest, as the Soviet

Union, the United States, Japan, India, Vietnam, and the ASEAN states tried to readjust their relations to meet the new situation. Asia without a strong Chinese presence would be a more volatile region.

There is little likelihood that China will assume the role of a traditional expansionist power in Asia within the next decade or so. However, it is conceivable that a praetorian regime dominated by conservative bureaucrats and the PLA might strike a militant nationalist posture as a substitute for a largely discredited Marxist-Leninist ideology. Such a regime might heat up dormant territorial disputes with Japan, the USSR, India, Vietnam, and other bordering states. If no progress is made on the Taiwan issue, Peking might mobilize national opinion in support of military pressure against Taipei. The resumption of dual-track diplomacy in Southeast Asia through support to local Communist parties could also be part of a praetorian regime's policy in Asia.

But the military, economic, and political strength of its neighbors —particularly the USSR, Vietnam, Japan, India, and the ASEAN states—will define the boundaries within which China's own power may be asserted. China will still lack the military power to overawe its neighbors, particularly if the superpowers retain their current levels of involvement in the region. Conflicts instigated by the PRC would not only remain limited, but would stimulate further military preparedness on the part of China's neighbors, and give Moscow the opportunity to lobby more effectively for an Asian collective security system aimed at Peking. Thus, unless unforeseeable vacuums of power develop in Asia, it is difficult to conceive of China acquiring the hegemonic role that the United States long had in the Western hemisphere or that the USSR plays in Eastern Europe and the Communist bloc.

Whatever the direction of China's future policy in Asia, it is almost certain that Peking will want to play an independent role, unconstrained by formal alliances or binding relationships with countries of the region. The Chinese are also likely to remain a proud people with a deep sense of their own greatness and a reluctance to acknowledge rival interests in what they perceive as their primary arena. Never inspired by a pan-Asianist ideology such as the Japanese espoused during their imperial expansion in the first half of the twentieth century, the leaders of the PRC will continue to view Asia and their own role in Asia within a global rather than a purely regional context. But Asia will continue to be the focal point of China's foreign policy. Whether China will contribute more to the attainment of peace and the promotion of justice or to the generation of conflicts over territory, resources, and spheres of influence will depend in good measure on what role China's leaders choose for their country in Asia and how skillfully they play the role they have chosen.

5 China and the Global Strategic Balance JONATHAN D. POLLACK

Among the factors influencing Chinese foreign relations, China's relationship to the global strategic balance has always been pivotal. For better or for worse, the postwar world continues to be dominated by the power rivalry between the United States and the Soviet Union. By any reasonable measure—economic capabilities, conventional military strength and reach, or their enormous nuclear arsenals—the United States and the Soviet Union remain great powers distinct from all others, with a unique capability to affect war and peace in the international system.

China's leaders profess considerable distaste for this state of affairs. They assert that the politics of "superpower hegemonism" offer neither understanding of nor solutions for the long-term problems and crises of international politics. Indeed, the Chinese view the Soviet-American rivalry as a relic of history, to be supplanted ultimately by a more egalitarian, far less coercive international order. Despite China's self-characterization as a Third World state and its long-standing critique of the domination of international politics by a few great powers, the Chinese have few illusions about the workings of the contemporary international system. They recognize that they must function within the existing international system, even if they insist that their actions and objectives are intended to transform global politics. For China, there is no escape from either the Soviet-American rivalry or the attendant conflicts that have made Asia the major battleground of the postwar era.

The opinions expressed in this essay are my own and do not represent the views of The Rand Corporation or any of its research sponsors.

Where does China fit within the global strategic balance, both historically and at present? How important is China in the global power equation? Is China likely to possess sufficient power and standing to affect significantly the future of the strategic balance and, if so, in what ways? Do the other major powers view China's role in the same way that leaders in Peking do? And how will China's growing involvement in the international strategic system alter the beliefs and practices espoused by leaders in Peking?

To assess these questions, I will explore in this chapter three interrelated themes: first, China's shifting relationship to the Soviet-American power balance since 1949; second, the basic patterns in contemporary Sino-American relations and Sino-Soviet relations, as they contribute to defining China's global role; and third, China's importance in the contemporary international system, as perceived by China and by other major powers. I will then draw some general conclusions about the likely evolution of the global strategic balance through the remainder of the 1980s.

China in the Postwar World

With the establishment of the People's Republic in 1949, the leadership of the Chinese Communist Party (CCP) had to take on the task of defining an international position and direction for their country. The CCP was no longer a revolutionary movement whose political and military horizons were bounded by China's geographical limits. It not only had to consolidate its political, economic, and administrative power within China, but it had to identify and work toward an international role congruent with both China's power and security objectives and the constraints imposed by the actions of others.

As the principal architect of Chinese security strategy, Mao Zedong clearly understood that his preeminent foreign policy objective was to diminish China's vulnerability to external power and military pressure. Since the United States and Soviet Union were the predominant military powers in the postwar world, China's relationship to the two superpowers constituted the central question for the security of China. In the broadest of terms, therefore, Mao offered three general maxims for Chinese security: (1) identify the principal political and military threat to China, and do not allow China to be embroiled in conflicts of less than vital interest; (2) whenever possible, avoid international isolation or outright confrontation with one or both superpowers; and (3) lean toward the less threatening and more helpful of the two superpowers, but never in irrevocable fashion. All three maxims offered sound general principles, but there has frequently been a divergence between theory and practice. In several key instances, Mao did not heed his own advice, especially in periods when the debate about security became deeply enmeshed in domestic political conflict. On other occasions, Soviet and American leaders did not always act as China's leaders anticipated or hoped. Reviewing the successes and failures of Chinese foreign policy over the past three-and-one-half decades enables us to see more clearly both the strengths and the limits of China's power position and approach to global strategy.

As noted earlier, China's search for security was qualitatively different from the CCP's revolutionary experiences. As one nation in a world of sovereign states, China experienced a significant reduction in its freedom of action and room for maneuver. Even more important, the PRC was severely disadvantaged in relation to the structure of world power the Chinese leadership confronted in 1949. By the time of the Party's victory over the Guomindang, the international system had undergone a major ideological, political, and military polarization. The Soviet-American wartime alliance had been supplanted by a stark political, ideological, and military confrontation in Europe, with the European nations now playing a subsidiary role in the broader Soviet-American competition. An event as dramatic as the CCP triumph thus assumed global significance, all the more in view of China's adherence to Marxism-Leninism.

Even if the PRC leadership had wished to insulate itself from the Soviet-American rivalry, circumstances did not permit such detachment. The consolidation of Communist rule on the Chinese mainland virtually guaranteed that the Cold War would extend to Asia as well as Europe. The United States, having long sought to infuse the Nationalist government with at least symbolic standing as a major world power, now sought to deny the legitimacy of the new Chinese government through political, economic, and military means, and to impede the PRC's territorial consolidation and economic rehabilitation. At the same time, the United States was increasingly committed to a renascent Japan closely aligned with U.S. political and strategic goals in the Pacific. A confrontation with American power in East Asia ill served China's long-term interests, but the ingredients for such a confrontation were all too evident in the fall of 1949.

Thus, China was severely disadvantaged in relation to American power. The Soviet Union had rapidly consolidated its control of Eastern Europe, enabling Moscow to compete against the United States with a series of buffer states to the west. China had no such geographic advantage. In dire economic circumstances and highly vulnerable to American power, China therefore recognized the imperative need to seek at least a partial accommodation with the Soviet Union.

In critical respects, the Sino-Soviet alliance of early 1950 represented a marriage of convenience. Yet it is doubtful whether any Chinese leaders—including Mao—saw any reasonable alternative. China and the USSR shared both a long border and (at least nominally) a common ideology. The achievement of correct if not wholly intimate interstate relations with the Soviet Union was a vital need for the Chinese, if only to avoid the nightmarish vision of hostile relations with both Moscow and Washington. Although excessive dependence on the Soviet Union was hardly desirable, the potential gains for Chinese security and economic needs far outweighed the risks.

The consummation of the Moscow-Peking alliance further abetted the stark polarization of the international system. Some of the dangers inherent in such a situation rapidly became evident, as the onset of the Korean conflict in June 1950 brought American military power to China's northeastern doorstep, compelling the PRC to intervene on behalf of North Korea. The PRC thus found itself on the front lines of a major military conflict. China's vulnerability to external power had now been accentuated rather than diminished.

Thus, the role of junior partner in the Sino-Soviet alliance entailed costs as well as gains. In the Korean War, the PRC bore the brunt of the responsibility for assisting North Korea. It suffered major losses in combat and had to defer key parts of its internal economic rehabilitation program. The conflict further heightened China's dependence upon the Soviet Union for both military and economic aid. The Soviets, although forthcoming in their assistance, exacted a high price: China was fully incorporated into the socialist camp, with virtually no opportunity for serious economic or political dealings with the major non-Communist powers. U.S. policy further abetted these circumstances. The United States, regarding the PRC as a major adversary, imposed a full economic blockade against Peking, ringed China with a series of military bases, and provided the rival Nationalist government on Taiwan with vital economic and military aid. Thus, the Chinese experienced the worst of both worlds: political domination by their far more powerful and developed ally and isolation and encirclement imposed by the world's leading military power.

As early as the mid-1950s, China tried to break out of these unappealing circumstances. As the immediate American military threat eased in the wake of the truces in Korea and Indochina, the PRC initiated a direct dialogue with the United States through ambassadorial discussions in Geneva and subsequently in Warsaw. At the same time, the post-Stalin power struggle in the Soviet leadership afforded the Chinese new leverage in their dealings with the USSR. China was therefore able to embark on a more independent foreign policy, seeking to build friendly relations with some of its non-Communist neighbors in Asia.

By the late 1950s, the Chinese (and Mao in particular) went a step further, actively seeking to redefine their alliance relationship with the Soviets as part of a larger effort to diminish Moscow's influence in Chinese affairs. In Mao's view, the Soviet leaders (especially Khrushchev) were not only seeking to control China. Khrushchev's interest in peaceful coexistence with the West also offered clearcut evidence of Soviet and American collusion at the expense of Chinese interests. Under these circumstances, China began to take public issue with Soviet policy, which in Mao's view consigned China to subordinate status in both global and Asian politics. Equally important, China initiated a major effort to develop its own nuclear weapons, since an independent nuclear deterrent was essential for China to guarantee its own security.

China's effort to forge an independent foreign policy was still frustrated by U.S. policy toward the PRC. Peking could not define a more symmetrical position in relation to Washington and Moscow as long as the United States continued to view China as a threat to global peace and stability equal to or greater than the USSR. Throughout the late 1950s and early 1960s, the United States judged China to be the principal source of "revolutionary Communist expansionism"—a view made more understandable by Peking's strident attacks on "Soviet revisionism" and Moscow's alleged "capitulation to U.S. imperialism's global counterrevolutionary strategy."[1] Despite the mounting evidence of Sino-Soviet estrangement over ideology and foreign policy, the United States failed to exploit the political and diplomatic opportunities inherent in such circumstances. Indeed, the perception of a common American and Soviet interest in forestalling the further spread of nuclear weaponry—with China as the obvious candidate—led Washington to pursue common ground with Moscow in the field of arms control, to the detriment of Chinese interests. Peking, therefore, acted in defiance of both superpowers, even if this posture entailed additional risks to China's security and economic well-being.

Peking's defiance was fueled by internal politics. Mao was not only defying Moscow in international affairs; he was also trying to purge the CCP of those opposed to an increasing radicalization that would subsequently lead to the xenophobia and convulsion of the Cultural Revolution. In a marked departure from a decade-long effort to forge expanded relations abroad, China increasingly withdrew from both diplomatic and foreign policy involvement, leaving itself isolated and vulnerable in the midst of domestic turmoil and violence.

At this time U.S. military involvement in the Vietnam conflict began to grow appreciably. Many predicted that the growing military tensions in Southeast Asia would mute the Sino-Soviet conflict, and draw Peking and Moscow closer together. But Mao publicly rejected the calls of Khrushchev's successors for joint Sino-Soviet action to oppose the United States in Vietnam; in spirit if not in letter, the

1. See, in particular, *Two Different Lines on the Question of War and Peace: Comment on the Open Letter of the Central Committee of the CPSU (V),* 19 November 1963 (Beijing: Foreign Languages Press, 1963).

Sino-Soviet alliance was now dead. China assisted Vietnam on its own—even as it warily allowed the shipment of Soviet military aid through China—but conveyed to the United States that it wished to avoid a wider Sino-U.S. conflict. In the eyes of the Chinese strategists, America's Vietnam involvement was from the outset doomed to failure. In a region of marginal strategic value to U.S. interests, the United States could only grow more enmeshed in a quagmire in which there were no reasonable limits, nor was there any easy means of extrication.

Such an evaluation was vindicated in the remainder of the 1960s and in the early 1970s. As a result, however, the Soviet Union steadily augmented its military power, without provoking serious American reactions. Even worse for Chinese interests, much of this growth in Soviet power occurred on China's northern doorstep. Soviet alarm over Cultural Revolutionary xenophobia—exacerbated by Mao's references to Chinese territory that had been seized by the czars and was still held by the Soviets—led Moscow to upgrade its defenses along heretofore thinly manned borders opposite China. Peking's worst strategic nightmare was coming to pass: China, convulsed in internal disarray without credible allies or even powerful friends, faced acute political and military pressure on separate geographic fronts from both superpowers.

But the Chinese themselves were largely responsible for these inauspicious developments. The "plague on both your houses" mentality then evident in Chinese foreign policy had led to severe isolation, internal dislocation, and a societal vulnerability all too tempting to external adversaries. China was far weaker than either the United States or the USSR, yet Peking's internal and external course alienated and affronted both superpowers, and precluded effective collaboration with either. All three of Mao's cardinal rules of international strategy were being neglected; the internal disarray evident in the Cultural Revolution had spread throughout the Chinese political process, including foreign policy.

The full implications of China's isolation and vulnerability began to be felt in the late 1960s. The Soviet invasion of Czechoslovakia in 1968 and a series of bloody clashes along the Sino-Soviet border in 1969 made it abundantly clear that Peking faced a major Soviet military challenge to its north. Sino-Soviet differences had now been fully transformed from a war of words and ideas into a potential war with guns. China therefore had to put its domestic house in order as well as make a series of difficult but critical choices in its foreign policy strategy. Overtures from Peking to the newly elected Nixon administration were answered: both states were prepared to enter into political dealings for mutual advantage, culminating in the Nixon visit to China in February 1972.

Thus, China's long-sought independence and leverage had finally been achieved, but only after a period of acute internal and external crisis. This included the death and political disgrace of Defense Minister Lin Biao, Mao's constitutionally designated successor. Lin was the apparent architect of China's "dual adversary" strategy toward both superpowers and, not accidentally, the major political beneficiary of China's convulsive course at home and abroad. Both Mao and Zhou Enlai had increasingly realized the acute danger inherent in China's continuing to function as the odd nation out in the U.S.-Soviet-Chinese relationship.

Mao and Zhou's overtures to the United States reflected classic unsentimental balance-of-power calculations and bore little relation to the ideological pronouncements that Peking had held dear for much of the 1960s. A posture of informal alignment with the United States would permit China to have vital breathing space at a time of acute vulnerability. It could thus seek to deter any further escalation of Sino-Soviet hostilities to the north, as it progressively eased tensions with the United States to the east and the south. In fact if not in name, Peking was willing to form a security alignment with Washington, even as the United States was still trying to salvage a political victory in Vietnam against China's erstwhile socialist ally.

In grasping such opportunities, the Nixon administration not only capitalized on the possibilities inherent in the Sino-Soviet conflict since the late 1950s; it also accorded China an independent strategic value within the global balance of power. Although the Chinese from the first realized that the U.S. agenda in forging ties with Peking differed from their own, this did not diminish the fact that the new Sino-American relationship also marked the realization of China's long-sought strategic objective. Not only could China seek to parlay its relationship with the United States into more effective opposition to the growth of Soviet power in Asia. What is more, the American connection also accorded Peking unparalleled international stature and legitimacy in both the socialist and capitalist world. It is little wonder, therefore, that Mao's role in creating this "revolutionary line in foreign affairs" remains among the few areas where the late chairman's role in Chinese politics remains largely sacrosanct.[2]

Thus, the full logic of a triangular world had finally emerged. Before the late 1960s, China had yet to gain full acceptance as an accredited major power acknowledged by both Washington and Moscow. Until the United States as well as the Soviet Union were prepared to confer such stature, China could not and did not play an international role commensurate with its size, power potential, and centrality in postwar East Asia. Neither state, to be sure, had been able to ignore Chinese power. The United States had fought a war with the Chinese in Korea, and for two decades had deployed substantial military forces both to contain and to deter China from undertaking any provocative international actions. The Soviet Union, for its part, now found itself committing substantial military forces to a potential conflict with the PRC. With the growing accommodation between the United States and China, however, a new stage had been reached: Both global powers now had to weigh the implications of their actions toward China against the effect of these actions on their relations with each other.

For the Chinese, their long-sought international legitimacy was a major political breakthrough, especially in view of China's vulnerabilities at the close of the 1960s. However, full triangularity created problems as well as opportunities. China had long condemned the "hegemonism of big power politics," yet it benefited by the inclusion of a China factor in the Soviet-American global rivalry. Even as the Chinese continued to criticize the Soviet Union and the United States for their global ambitions, Peking clearly stood to gain from antagonism between the two superpowers. A sounder relationship with the

2. For the fullest official exposition of Mao's foreign policy doctrines, see Editorial Department of *Renmin Ribao*, "Chairman Mao's Theory of the Differentiation of the Three Worlds Is a Major Contribution to Marxism-Leninism," *Peking Review*, 4 November 1977, pp. 10–41.

United States permitted China to deflect Soviet political and military pressure directed against it—provided that Peking's ties with Washington tempered rather than provoked Moscow. At the same time, China did not want to risk embroilment in any Soviet-American confrontation. China, in effect, could gain from superpower rivalry, even from a degree of tension, but not from an overly antagonistic Soviet-American relationship that verged on major crisis.

As a consequence, the Chinese leadership needed to weigh carefully not only its own interests in Sino-American relations but also how it perceived American interests and strategies toward both China and the Soviet Union. In this regard, Peking was persuaded that the United States at long last intended to disengage from Vietnam, and in other respects would curtail U.S. military activity in the Western Pacific. In addition, to the extent that the United States pursued better relations with both Peking and Moscow, new pressures would be placed on Hanoi to negotiate with Washington. Yet the Chinese also understood that the Nixon administration gained additional leverage in its dealings with the Soviet Union by enjoying high-level access to leaders in Peking. The United States, in effect, could trade on its improving relations with Peking to elicit greater responsiveness from Moscow on matters of vital interest to superpower relations, most notably agreements on strategic arms control as well as a negotiated peace in Vietnam.

Thus, triangularity posed an additional risk for the Chinese: that the United States would simply seek to parlay its ties with Peking into improved ties with the Soviet Union. China's experience in the Sino-Soviet alliance had been a sobering one. Peking would never again permit excessive dependence on an outside power, let alone cede any of its sovereign political prerogatives. China's acute vulnerability to Soviet power made partial accommodation with Washington a compelling political and security need, but the Chinese did not want to become a vehicle for larger American strategic designs. The improvement in Sino-American ties did persuade the Chinese that they would not fall prey to Soviet-American collusion at their expense, yet Peking also recognized that Soviet-American relations (with the exception of the Vietnam issue) had a distinct and different agenda from U.S.-Chinese ties. Above all, China did not wish either the Soviet Union or the United States to perceive Peking as an appendage of American power, since that created the worrisome probability that China (and Chinese interests) could be taken for granted—a direct contradiction of the principles of triangularity.

Many of these dilemmas and difficulties became more apparent over the remainder of the 1970s. Despite the clear gains for Chinese security early in the decade, the Chinese continued to witness the steady augmentation of Soviet capabilities and the further retrenchment of U.S. power, especially in Asia. By mid-decade, Peking increasingly feared that Washington was dealing with China only to gain leverage in arms control negotiations with the Soviet Union, the results of which were judged detrimental to Chinese interests. Not only was China being taken for granted; a string of Soviet successes in the Third World had gone unanswered by the West. The U.S. defeat in Vietnam further fueled China's anxieties. Some Chinese saw an ominous geopolitical momentum to these developments, with Moscow supplanting the United States as the world's leading power. The United States, in the view of many Chinese observers, was now a defensive and even passive power, and some in Peking questioned whether the United States was still enough of a superpower to be a credible partner for China.

Peking's concerns went beyond patterns of political and military alignment. In the wake of Mao's death and the ouster of China's radical leadership, China's leadership began to recognize the depths of the PRC's internal problems. China was in urgent need of technological assistance from abroad to tackle long-deferred tasks in economic development. Two decades of internal conflict found China lagging even further behind in education, science and technology, basic economic development, and military power. The pervasiveness of the Soviet political and military challenge in Asia—driven home by growing Soviet-Vietnamese collaboration to oppose China—made imperative the search for new sources of technological, economic, and even security assistance.

The only possible source for such aid was the West and Japan. As a result, China increasingly argued that the Soviet strategic challenge was so pervasive and threatening that the PRC could no longer equivocate about ties with the United States and the other major

Western powers. Joint collaborative efforts were thus required "to frustrate the war schemes of the Soviet hegemonists."[3] Peking seemed closer to an explicit security relationship with one of the superpowers than at any time since the high point of the Sino-Soviet alliance in the 1950s. The normalization of Sino-American relations at the end of 1978, followed immediately by China's border war against Vietnam and some months later by the Soviet invasion of Afghanistan, portended a stark repolarization of Asian international politics.

Thus, the dramatic improvement in Sino-American relations at the end of the 1970s was based on a conjunction of internal and external needs. It reflected not only heightened Chinese anxieties about Soviet political and military encirclement, but also the ascendance of leaders in Peking (in particular Deng Xiaoping) who were prepared to cement ties with the West. Deng judged a united front strategy against Moscow as the most credible, effective way to prevent further Soviet geopolitical gains in Asia. To the extent that Deng could persuade leaders abroad that China was almost reflexively opposed to any Soviet political or military actions, China could expect the United States and other Western powers to provide assistance vital to China's modernization effort.

At the same time, Deng understood a concomitant need not to provoke Moscow or exacerbate Sino-Soviet tensions. Notwithstanding the somewhat extravagant flavor of China's united front rhetoric, Peking did not seek a major confrontation with Soviet military power, least of all along the Sino-Soviet border. Nor did the Chinese want to see U.S.-Soviet tensions escalate to an acute level, especially if this threatened China. The goal of a security alignment with the West was to deter Moscow, not to provoke it. While the Chinese leadership refrained from forging any formal security relations with the United States, they did conclude that informal security ties could serve as a tacit signal to Moscow that China was considering the option of leaning further to the West in the event of undiminished Soviet pressure against China.

3. For an authoritative defense of China's united front strategy with the United States, see *Red Flag* Commentator, "The Plotter of a Siege Is Being Besieged," *Hongqi,* November 1978, in *Foreign Broadcast Information Service Daily Report: People's Republic of China,* 29 November 1978, pp. A9–13.

China's most compelling needs, however, were in the area of national economic development. China's modernization prospects hinged on several key considerations: (1) diminishing direct Soviet pressure against China, thereby making defense needs less imperative; (2) devising a credible, consistent basis for heightened economic and technological exchanges with the West; and (3) creating a stable and peaceful international environment that would be congruent with orderly economic development. All three factors reflected a dramatic departure in Chinese economic strategy from the previous emphasis on voluntarism and domestic mobilization and toward a more orderly pursuit of development goals. Thus, a united front strategy posed risks as well as potential gains. If China's preeminent interest was in a peaceful international environment, excessive polarization between China and the West, on the one hand, and the Soviet Union, on the other, could easily undermine such a goal. There was no firm guarantee that both China and the United States shared a common viewpoint on the best means of restraining Soviet power. It remained for the two countries to achieve a common set of assumptions about the character and objectives of their security dealings that would also be comprehensible to leaders in Moscow.

By the close of the 1970s, however, many of China's political and strategic objectives had been achieved. The contrast with Peking's political and military environment at the outset of the decade was palpable. Though still subject to severe military pressure and efforts at encirclement, China was no longer isolated internationally. With increasingly diversified economic ties, it could use the prospect of its untapped economic potential to induce broadened trade and technology purchases from the West. And, though lagging severely behind its major military rival, China did not face the likely prospect of serious military conflict, except along the Sino-Vietnamese border. The goal was to use these latent possibilities to China's overall advantage, hoping ultimately to redefine China's long-term relationship to both superpowers.

China and the Superpowers in the 1980s: A Delicate Balance?

As a result of its emergence into the international arena in the latter half of the 1970s and the early 1980s, the PRC is now more engaged in global politics than at any previous time in its history. Yet the character of China's international dealings, including its relations with the two superpowers, still remains unsettled. China's accustomed position in relation to the Soviet-U.S. power balance has been that of the vulnerable, encircled, perpetually threatened power. In terms of relative power capabilities, the disparities between the PRC and the superpowers will not change dramatically in the near future. But new strategic and political problems and opportunities have developed for Peking in the early 1980s. Depending on their resolution, China could enjoy leverage and flexibility significantly greater than in the past, or it could encounter new pressures and uncertainties. What would these changes imply for the future of the international strategic system? To consider this issue further, we need to turn to the present status and likely directions of Sino-U.S. and Sino-Soviet relations.

In the early 1980s, China's relations with the United States again assumed an unsteady course. The realization of full diplomatic ties in late 1978 and the burgeoning economic, governmental, and institutional dealings between the two countries created high expectations and even euphoria about the prospects for Sino-American relations. These remarkable breakthroughs also extended to informal security ties: The U.S. secretary of defense and his Chinese counterpart exchanged visits in the first half of 1980, helping lay the basis for the possible transfer of U.S. defense technology to the PRC and for the initiation of limited strategic cooperation on matters of common concern to the United States and China.

Leaders in Peking defined U.S.-China security relations in terms of a coalition, not an alliance. The United States and China could undertake parallel, mutually supportive actions, but without either country's being called on to engage in higher levels of security collaboration. Formal security ties were too binding: They restricted Chinese freedom of action and, even worse, threatened to embroil Peking in a Soviet-American confrontation, whether or not the Chinese judged their own security interests at risk.

But even though the Sino-U.S. relationship in no sense constituted an alliance, it nonetheless represented a major international breakthrough. An East Asian security coalition comprising the United States, China, and Japan loomed as a serious possibility, with the goal of restraining provocative Soviet actions in Asia.

Such expectations proved exaggerated or premature. China has instead assumed a far more assertive and independent political posture; moreover, it again describes the United States as a "hegemonic superpower" that threatens rather than guarantees international peace and stability. Although a Sino-U.S. security dialogue continues, it is now diminished, with uncertain prospects in the immediate future for significant strategic ties between Washington and Peking.

Numerous hypotheses have been offered to explain these major departures from Chinese policy of the late 1970s. The prevailing view is that China's unhappiness with Reagan administration policy toward Taiwan led Peking to reevaluate the possibilities (at least in the near term) for expanding ties with Washington, including the further institutionalization of a Sino-U.S. anti-Soviet united front. There is considerable support for this interpretation, yet it does not offer a fully persuasive explanation for Chinese behavior. A number of additional factors placed serious limits on the further development of Sino-American security ties. In retrospect, the late 1970s are better viewed as a transitional period in Chinese policy than as a fundamental and enduring realignment. Bold steps may have been needed to shake China loose from its previous complacency, but they did not offer a realistic basis for a long-term strategic course.

Several recurring concerns in PRC security strategy stand out as even more pivotal issues than Taiwan. China's abiding suspicions about alliances with states far more powerful than itself continued to argue against open-ended security arrangements with either superpower. A "never again" mentality thus pervades China's foreign policy. Its experience in the 1950s had left Peking perpetually suspicious of excessive dependence on a major external power. Although it may have had to provide initial assurances to the United States that its dealings with the West were of a long-term, strategic nature, Peking appears to have anticipated that inescapable differences in national power and security needs would drive the United States and China apart. In Peking's view, the United States, as the far more powerful partner, would inevitably seek to take advantage of China's weakness and vulnerability, and thus could not be expected to support a genuine commitment to "a strong and secure China."[4]

Such an inevitability seems to have taken place even sooner than might have been anticipated. The election of the Reagan administration, and its adoption of a staunchly anti-Soviet orientation, appeared to portend an accelerated pace of Sino-U.S. security dealings. Yet the new leadership in Washington expressed unease about overly close ties with a major Communist power, no matter how anti-Soviet its rhetoric. At the same time, the PRC judged the Reagan administration to be disrespectful or even contemptuous of past Sino-U.S. understandings over Taiwan. Possible transfers of various "dual use" technologies were also blocked or impeded, suggesting to China that the United States did not seriously intend to facilitate China's modernization, especially if to do so might strengthen the PRC militarily. In the view of leaders in Peking, these and related developments suggested that America's commitments were feigned rather than real and that the United States, in effect, had yet to decide whether China was friend or foe. China's perception of parallel strategic interests—and its willingness to call for accelerated Sino-American security cooperation—diminished just as rapidly as it had emerged.

In a manner reminiscent of the disintegration of the Sino-Soviet alliance, China again cast itself as the disadvantaged, aggrieved, and manipulated junior partner. But in a certain sense China was responsible for its own anxieties. In justifying its ties with the United States, China had insisted that (1) the Soviet threat was global in nature but increasingly oriented toward Asia and the Third World; (2) no single nation—and especially not China—had the capability to face Soviet power alone; and (3) China was acutely vulnerable and in urgent need of external assistance. From a U.S. perspective, China had presented itself as the needier, more expectant partner in the U.S.-China relationship. The PRC's characterization of its own contribution to countering Soviet power and assisting American needs was more negative than positive: Peking kept large numbers of Soviet and

4. The United States first expressed such a commitment to the Chinese during Zbigniew Brzezinski's visit to China in May 1978. See President Carter's instructions to Brzezinski, in Brzezinski, *Power and Principle—Memoirs of the National Security Advisor, 1977–1981* (New York: Farrar, Straus and Giroux, 1983), pp. 551–55.

Vietnamese forces committed against China that would otherwise be available for use elsewhere; it did not oppose and tacitly supported the U.S. political and military presence in East Asia; and it would not undertake a destabilizing regional role.

In China's view, however, all these contributions were vital to U.S. policy goals and global needs. From this perspective, the United States no longer had the capability to compete singlehandedly against the Soviet Union; thus it sought supplementary or surrogate forces to augment its own power. The United States would therefore be extremely forthcoming in its aid to China, including the long-deferred goal of military modernization. Peking was convinced that the United States could not take China for granted, because America needed China more than China needed America.

Although the Reagan administration clearly shared Peking's concern about Soviet political and military assertiveness, its prevailing beliefs differed significantly from those voiced to Peking. In the U.S. view, a Soviet military buildup had continued unabated and unanswered for a decade and a half. The most urgent need was to undertake a comparable effort to augment U.S. military capabilities in a manner that could challenge this perceived Soviet military advantage in peacetime and defeat the Soviet Union in wartime. China's role, therefore, while not marginal, was less than vital: China was far too technologically backward to do more than tie down Soviet forces that would otherwise be available for employment on other fronts. Moreover, the Chinese were perceived as far too vulnerable to Soviet encirclement and intimidation to take issue with U.S. policy, even if key U.S. policies (notably, those toward Taiwan) offended Chinese sensibilities and interests. Thus the Reagan administration took a position diametrically opposed to that of Peking: The United States *could* take China for granted, for China needed America more than America needed China.

Such differences contained all the ingredients for a test of wills between Washington and Peking. China's enduring suspicions about the motivations of a far more powerful benefactor were fueled by a perception of the United States as a resurgently hegemonic power that acted in disregard of the sensibilities and concerns of its new-found coalition partner. The singleminded U.S. preoccupation with challenging the Soviet Union in military terms downplayed what the Chinese saw as a far more pressing concern: forging a credible *peacetime* coalition that would restrain provocative Soviet actions in various areas of the Third World vulnerable to coercion, subversion, or penetration. In the absence of such efforts, security ties between the United States and China lacked credibility, purpose, and consistent direction.

Under such circumstances, the strategic underpinning of U.S.-Chinese relations had been placed in considerable jeopardy. By 1982, China's leaders had concluded that their security interests were better served by standing somewhat apart from the United States than by being closely aligned with it. Although both Washington and Peking subsequently sought to repair the strains in their relations and avoid what threatened to become a serious rupture in their dealings, substantial suspicions and uncertainties had been generated on both sides. From China's perspective, good relations with the United States remained very important, especially if China were to benefit more fully in the areas of economic collaboration and technology transfer. But China's relative importance in U.S. global strategy had unquestionably diminished. Since the United States intended to confront the Soviet Union on a worldwide scale irrespective of China's involvement or urging, Soviet anxieties would increasingly focus on combatting the U.S. military challenge, and China did not want to risk unnecessary embroilment in these superpower tensions. In addition, to the extent that the Soviet Union was preoccupied by its larger rivalry with the United States, it would be far less concerned about Chinese power, and might even be prepared to deal more reasonably with leaders in Peking. All these calculations had major implications for what arguably remained China's most compelling security concern—to counter the Soviet Union's long-term political and military challenge in Asia.

Leaders in Peking understand that the Sino-Soviet relationship represents a far more intractable problem than their disagreements and difficulties with the United States. Unlike the Soviet Union, the United States no longer poses a frontal military challenge to the PRC. The USSR maintains large, sophisticated, well-equipped military forces along a still partially contested Sino-Soviet border. A strengthening across the entire spectrum of Soviet military capabilities—ground forces, air forces, naval power, as well as strategic nuclear weaponry—has now been sustained for more than a decade. East Asia no longer represents a peripheral military front for the Soviet military leadership, a fact formalized by the establishment of an independent theater command in the region in late 1978. A long-term Soviet goal has been achieved at enormous expense: The Soviet Union has become a credible two-front power, with the capacity to pressure, coerce, and encircle China from the north, east, or south.

The pivotal strategic issue for Peking, therefore, is to define the most effective means of reducing or at least "managing" the long-term Soviet geopolitical threat to China. In addition to the predominantly military option, three other broad possibilities exist: aligning with another power or group of powers to offset Soviet military strength, diverting or preoccupying Moscow in areas of marginal strategic concern to China, or seeking a partial political accommodation with Moscow that specifies and restricts the areas of political conflict and crisis.

Such broad issues are not susceptible to easy or definitive judgments. It seems evident that Chinese assessment of Soviet power and the degree of threat it posed to China have repeatedly been affected by the PRC's broader foreign policy posture. For example, the heightened prospects late in the 1970s for an anti-Soviet united front argued for a more threatening depiction of Soviet political and military goals, although it also accorded with actual trends at that time. More recently, with China far less certain about both the propriety and the opportunity for collaboration with the United States, a decidedly more benign assessment of Soviet strategy has developed, but in the absence of any compelling evidence of change or redirection in the Soviet geopolitical challenge to China.

By its own actions and words, however, China has tried to preserve the possibility of some degree of accommodation with the USSR. China never asserted that it intended to use its informal alliance with the West to engage in a frontal military confrontation with Moscow. As noted earlier, a united front was intended principally to deter the Soviet Union, not to provoke it. By avoiding any major Sino-Soviet crisis or confrontation while at the same time expressing a continued willingness to improve Sino-Soviet bilateral ties when time and circumstances are more appropriate, China has thus left open the possibility of a less antagonistic Sino-Soviet future.

This prospect nevertheless depends critically on Soviet behavior. For all the foreboding talk of a relentlessly expansionist Soviet Union that regularly emanated from Peking in the 1970s and early 1980s, the Chinese also made it clear that they understood the limits of Soviet power. Some Chinese have long argued that Soviet capabilities could not match Moscow's presumed hegemonic ambitions, and that the USSR (like the United States before it) would inevitably face an agonizing reappraisal of its external commitments and goals. In this view, Soviet military power embodies weakness as well as strength. A major Soviet troop commitment along the Chinese border without commensurate political or military gains; growing restiveness in Eastern Europe necessitating an enormous military effort; major aid commitments to Cuba and Vietnam; a global strategic and naval competition with the United States likely to accelerate in coming years; and a bothersome (if not overly costly or risky) hot war in Afghanistan—none of these obligations and complications lend great confidence about the future security of the Soviet state.

When Soviet domestic vulnerabilities are added to this picture, Moscow's long-term prospects appear even less promising. An aged and ossified leadership structure; a continued decline in economic growth; military expenditures well in excess of 10 percent of gross national product; serious ethnic tensions, even within the armed forces; diminished access to Western economic and technological assistance—none of them offered grounds for much optimism. Nor do these considerations guarantee that the Soviet Union will act in a restrained or circumspect manner; rather, they make the costs and complications of additional Soviet expansion all too apparent. Numerous Chinese observers, therefore, see Moscow as an increasingly beleaguered if not enfeebled power, and certainly not an all-powerful military machine embarked on global conquest. Under such circumstances, there seems even less reason to worry about a direct Soviet military threat to China. Chinese strategic analysts have long argued that Soviet power is principally directed against regions, countries, and strategic locations far more vulnerable to penetration and subjugation than the PRC. Since the early 1970s, for example, spokesmen in Peking have consistently asserted that the Soviet Union is unwilling to incur the costs and risks of an attack on China, whether aimed at punishment or occupation of substantial amounts of Chinese territory.

Yet these expressions of long-term optimism leave unaddressed the broader Soviet geopolitical challenge to China. For more than a decade, a fundamental Soviet security objective was to encircle China from different geographic points, thereby compelling Peking to accommodate to Soviet pressure. The Soviet political and military presence to the north (in Mongolia and along the Sino-Soviet border), to the east (the Soviet Pacific Fleet), to the south (in Vietnam), and to the west (in Afghanistan) reflected a broad, underlying Soviet commitment to the containment of China not easily subject to change. There was, as well, a major commitment of Soviet strategic nuclear capabilities targeted against China, which has been steadily augmented in recent years. All these factors place Sino-Soviet relations in a much more worrisome light, all the more so in the context of uncertain Sino-U.S. relations.

Thus, the future of Sino-Soviet relations will depend critically on the resiliency of the positions and policies adopted by both Moscow and Peking. Both sides benefit by the avoidance of military hostilities along the Sino-Soviet border. The unresolved issue is whether such conditions will lead to a substantive change in relations. Changes in atmospherics were dramatically evident during 1982 and 1983: There were far lower levels of polemical exchanges, higher levels of trade, an increasing flow of official and unofficial visits between the two countries, and the initiation of consultations on interstate relations, held at the vice ministerial level. China's willingness to enter into such consultations—in the absence of any serious shifts in the Soviet political and military posture in Asia—suggested that Peking saw these discussions in a context different from previous negotiations. Whereas previous talks (including those initiated after the Sino-Vietnamese border war of 1979) seemed intended largely as tension management devices, the consultations begun in 1982 over the broader range of interstate relations were a visible demonstration of

China's long-term objective of foreign policy independence toward both Moscow and Washington. Yet China may have been making a virtue out of necessity: In the absence of stable Sino-U.S. relations, Peking may have had no reasonable alternative but to seek separate understandings with Moscow.

The principal Soviet goal in these discussions is to further decouple bilateral Sino-Soviet relations from the broader geopolitical rivalry between Peking and Moscow. In the months prior to his death, Soviet President Leonid Brezhnev conveyed such an interest, while still remaining unspecific on the more concrete measures that the USSR was prepared to undertake to diminish Sino-Soviet hostilities. These overtures gained new momentum with Yuri Andropov's accession to power in November 1982, when the presence of the Chinese foreign minister in Moscow fueled expectations of further movement. In the view of Soviet officials, China should not lock itself into a rigidly anti-Soviet stance that benefits neither Moscow nor Peking but only the United States—the principal beneficiary of unrelenting hostility between the two countries. If China were to convey a reasonable position in such talks and not inject what Moscow saw as extraneous "third-party issues," then the USSR would reciprocate these gestures.

In the Chinese view, however, these third-party issues—Vietnam, Mongolia, and Afghanistan—concern nothing less than Moscow's long-term objectives throughout Asia, and toward China. The PRC, therefore, argues that no significant improvement in Sino-Soviet relations can occur in the absence of serious attention to these issues. China's long-term security goal remains unchanged: to diminish (if not to eliminate) Soviet political and military pressure directed against China, thereby achieving correct if not necessarily amicable relations with both superpowers. Such an accomplishment would represent a major departure and breakthrough in China's international relations and further solidify a PRC position independent of both the Soviet Union and the United States.

Peking offers a substantial inducement for Soviet leaders to negotiate seriously: a commitment on China's part no longer to oppose reflexively every Soviet action and policy. At the same time, the Chinese have refrained from entering into extensive security collaboration with the West, even less any collaboration driven largely by an anti-Soviet design. The Chinese view these actions as serious concessions to the Soviet Union that demonstrate Peking's interest in more than tactical adjustments in its relations with Moscow. By posing their opposition to "Soviet hegemonism" as part of an overall strategy that also opposes "American hegemonism," the Chinese hope to persuade Moscow of the real opportunity for a serious breakthrough in Sino-Soviet relations while still not precluding a continued dialogue with Washington.

It seems doubtful, however, that the Chinese will be able to sustain indefinitely the perception of such an independent stance if meaningful Soviet concessions are not forthcoming on one or more key issues. Improvements in the atmospherics of interstate relations can likely be sustained, since they help keep Sino-Soviet tensions at a more manageable level. More far-reaching accommodation, however, depends on Moscow's willingness to reduce its military and political presence around China's borders.

Such an accommodation, if it did occur, would pose a direct challenge to the security interests of the West. Depending on the possible context and terms of such a potential accommodation, the United States would be likely to disassociate itself further from high-level political consultation with Peking, unless any Sino-Soviet understandings were to proceed in tandem with Chinese efforts to further improve their relations with the United States. A partial accommodation between Moscow and Peking might also lead to a heightened U.S. effort to improve its relations with the Soviet Union. Although all such possibilities are admittedly somewhat conjectural, they illustrate how Chinese dealings with the Soviet Union will affect not only Sino-Soviet relations, but Soviet-American relations as well.

For the present, however, the Chinese seem to entertain few illusions about the likelihood of significant change in the near-term future in Soviet policy objectives in Asia. Despite the superficial equivalence in Chinese assertions about a world of two "hegemonic superpowers," leaders in Peking understand that their far more enduring security problems concern the Soviet Union, not the United States. Thus, any major departures in Sino-Soviet relations in the absence of clear shifts in Soviet political-military behavior toward China would violate one of the cardinal principles of Chinese strategy. Prevailing sentiment in Peking continues to insist that no significant accommodation in Sino-Soviet relations is possible without a reduction and redirection of the long-term Soviet threat to China. To do more in the absence of such change would reveal Chinese weakness and vulnerability to external pressure, now increased in Soviet eyes because of the uncertainties in Sino-American relations.

Assessing Peking's Strategic Role: Does China Really Matter?

Where does China fit within the global strategic balance of the 1980s? How important is China likely to prove in the evolution of the international strategic system? In key respects, strategic significance is in the eye of the beholder. Judgments about the importance of China's international role vary widely. Among many smaller states (especially those in Asia), the importance attributed to China by the superpowers is a source of both bemusement and concern. Although few dispute China's power potential, the modest levels of China's economic accomplishments—coupled with the rigidities of centralized economic planning and stultifying bureaucratic control—make the PRC at best a dubious candidate for major-power status. China's repeated inability to sustain a consistent political and economic course bespeaks a political system without an effective, long-term strategy. China is large, backward, and enjoys only the trappings and symbols of major power standing, not the reality. Absent China's capability to affect relations among Peking, Washington, and Moscow, China would be little more than the world's most populous society—a largely agrarian economy with neither the capability nor the inclination to exert significant influence on the direction of world politics.

Numerous states thus look upon China with a mixture of denigration and envy. They fail to attach any particular significance to China's strategic role. In this view, China's supposed power reflects a common preoccupation of the two superpowers with the PRC's political and strategic directions, and Peking's own careful cultivation of its international image. Yet they are mystified by the attention lavished upon the Chinese. Even among the disparate nations of the Third World, it is increasingly inappropriate to describe China as either a model or a putative leader. The composite perception of China among intermediate and smaller powers is highly unflattering: China enjoys the privileges and deference conceded a major world power, without possessing the requisite national capabilities and accomplishments that appear to define the term.

Thus, China clearly occupies an anomalous position among the world's major powers. Viewed in relation to many conventional measures of national power, China does not appear particularly important. China has a per capita gross national product of $410, placing it among the world's less developed states. Its most compelling problems are internal rather than external: China must rigorously control its population and find means to feed, clothe, and house its one billion people. Despite its seeming commonality with the states of the Third World, however, by circumstances, history, achievement, and intention China is very much a factor in the global power competition. China has tested and deployed intercontinental ballistic missiles, and few world capitals receive as careful scrutiny and diplomatic attention as does Peking. These observations underscore one of the paradoxes of power in the contemporary international system: China exerts international influence well beyond its material or military strength. How has it achieved such results?

China's military power is the first critical underpinning of Peking's international influence. The Chinese see no reasonable alternative to the acquisition of both conventional and nuclear weaponry. In absolute terms, China's ground forces are the world's largest; only the Soviet Union and the United States possess more ships and planes. The PRC's nuclear arsenal, though small and in most respects severely dated by superpower standards, remains a vital national priority. Even more important, China has shown little hesitancy or equivocation in employing armed force when the risks of inaction were judged greater than the dangers of action. From the Korean intervention in 1950 to the attack on northern Vietnam in 1979, the Chinese leadership proved ready to use force to defend China's national boundaries, assert claims to disputed territories, demonstrate political will, and deter adversaries contemplating the use of force against China.

Peking's record as a military power over the past three decades has gained China an international importance that it would otherwise not possess. Even in those instances when China's military performance has been judged suspect (most notably in China's border war against Vietnam), China's willingness to employ arms and sustain major losses has conferred substantial credibility elsewhere. This is most dramatically evident in other Asian capitals. Although outmoded and vulnerable by the standards of the major industrial societies, China's military forces are forbiddingly large and are thus paid careful heed. To those smaller states that live in the shadow of Chinese power, it matters little that China's weapons are based largely on production technologies of the late 1950s. The perception and credibility of such power are pivotal, and in this respect China has very much succeeded: No nation on the PRC's periphery dares contemplate military action without serious consideration of its political and military repercussions vis-à-vis China.

Even the superpowers convey a grudging but real respect for China's military fortitude. In the Korean conflict, China suffered grievous manpower losses against U.S. forces, but the PRC's intervention had a chastening effect on American political and military leaders alike. Fifteen years later, the credibility of Chinese threats to intervene in the Vietnam conflict silenced the advocates of involvement of U.S. ground forces in North Vietnam. Along the Sino-Soviet border, Soviet military planners understand the potential implications of major military hostilities initiated against Chinese forces. The prospect of a prolonged war of attrition against the PRC—not to mention potential nuclear retaliation by the Chinese—helps deter the possibility of a full-scale Sino-Soviet war. China's investment in arms has thus yielded powerful results, no matter what the costs.

China's nuclear program has had a particularly potent effect on the perception of Chinese power. The very distinctiveness of such weapons—few possess them and none dare use them—places the nuclear nations in a category apart from all others. Among the states of the nonindustrialized world, China alone has tested such weapons and developed means to deliver them. In May 1980, China entered into an even more exclusive group when it successfully tested a missile of full intercontinental range, thereby providing China a theoretical capability to reach major targets in the United States as well as the Soviet Union. In October 1982, China achieved an additional breakthrough with the successful undersea launching of a sea-based ballistic missile. Both efforts provide potent assurance that Chinese strategic power will not be slighted nor ignored. It has helped make China a credible world power, especially in the eyes of the two nuclear superpowers. Perhaps not accidentally, the five states unambiguously engaged in nuclear weapons deployment are also the five permanent members of the United Nations Security Council. No matter how unsuitable nuclear capabilities might be for use in a direct military sense, they confer prestige and international recognition, and they constitute a vivid demarcation of power in the international system.

Yet alternative paths to international power exist, along which China does not fare nearly as well. For example, a nation's level of technological and economic advancement may offer far better grounds for assessing national power than does its military might. Scientific, entrepreneurial, and management skills are judged essential to a nation's stability, prosperity, and internal cohesion and effectiveness. Japan, which offers the preeminent example of such a society, lacks almost all the natural resources needed for national self-sufficiency; its military strength is exceedingly modest when compared to its economic power; and its global political role remains tentative, equivocal, and understated. Yet Japan's prodigious economic accomplishments during the postwar era confer upon it an undeniable legitimacy and stature.

The Chinese are in no position to make comparable arguments. In the past China's pursuit of self-reliance was praised as the only viable path to autonomy and national dignity for Third World states. The Chinese now recognize that this goal was elevated to unthinking dogma, severely impeding China's economic and technological transformation. Two decades of internal political upheaval ill served the vital goals of economic growth, technological self-sufficiency, and scientific advancement. As a result, China today remains woefully short of the educational, scientific, and entrepreneurial talent needed to compete effectively in the international economic system. If there is a power of example that attaches to economic advancement, China is far from achieving it. Indeed, these arguments readily lead to the view that China lacks the assets and skills that will truly count in future global politics. According to this perspective, China is better seen as a supplicant than a leader: It needs the developed world's help more than the developed world could possibly require its involvement and cooperation.

Despite these economic shortcomings, there is an additional belief in China's national power potential. By virtue of its size, population, and past greatness as a society and civilization, China assumes international importance irrespective of the present deficiencies and shortcomings. Calculated allusions to "the one billion Chinese" effectively convey this line of reasoning; no other society can make such a claim of imputed importance. China can thus proffer (or withhold) its loyalties or affiliations as a source of power in its own right. Because of its size, its vast population, and its underutilized economic potential, China possesses international leverage beyond that of smaller, resource-poor societies. It is little wonder that China continues to represent a major asset in the global power competition, though this status is more in the realm of attributed power than usable capabilities.

Yet weapons, economic strength, and power potential alone cannot explain the imputed significance of China in a global power equation. If its strategic significance is judged modest and its economic performance has been at best mixed, this cannot account for the considerable importance of China in the calculations of both Washington and Moscow, and the careful attention paid to it in other key world capitals. The answer lies in the fact that, notwithstanding its self-characterization as a threatened and aggrieved state, China has very shrewdly and even brazenly used its available political, economic, and military resources. Toward the superpowers, Peking's overall strategy has at various times comprised confrontation and armed conflict, partial accommodation, informal alignment, and a detachment bordering on disengagement, sometimes interposed with strident, angry rhetoric. As a result, China becomes all things to all nations, with many left uncertain and even anxious about its long-term intentions and directions.

To be sure, such an indeterminate strategy has at times entailed substantial political and military risks. Yet the same strategy has lent considerable credibility to China's position as an emergent major power. China has often acted in defiance of the preferences or demands of both superpowers; at other times it has behaved far differently from what others expect. Despite its seeming vulnerability, China has not proven pliant and yielding toward either Moscow or Washington. Here as well, China has maintained its credibility and resiliency under pressure; Peking's leaders have established a record of refusing to be taken for granted. For all these reasons, China has assumed a singular international position, both as a participant in many of the central political and military conflicts in the postwar era and as a state that resists easy political or ideological categorization.

China, therefore, has achieved a "swing" value in international strategic politics, since no other state—large or small—has ever occupied as many diverse positions and alignments in relation to the superpowers. Anxieties about Chinese power compelled the United States and subsequently the Soviet Union to deploy major military forces on a second front in Asia—no doubt a somewhat dubious accomplishment from the perspective of Chinese security, but one that testifies to China's centrality to Soviet and American calculations about war and peace. Indeed, in considerable measure the burdens and complications of such a second front ultimately compelled America's strategic reassessment in Asia and toward China. The Chinese may ultimately hope for a comparable reappraisal on the part of the Soviet Union.

Both Washington and Moscow understand the unique role that China has assumed in relation to the Soviet-American rivalry. Peking's position and alignment—and the defense requirements China generated for both superpowers—have frequently had a critical influence on the polarization of the international system, and on the relative defense burden each superpower has had to bear. Indeed, in a certain sense China must be judged a candidate superpower in its own right—not in imitation or emulation of either the Soviet Union or the United States, but as a reflection of Peking's unique position in global politics. In a long-term sense, China represents a political and strategic force too significant to be regarded as an adjunct to either Moscow or Washington or simply an intermediate power. The key issues nonetheless remain: How can such strategic independence best be used to China's advantage? And what does it suggest about the long-term directions of Chinese power in the international system?

Few answers have even been suggested for these questions, nor is there any evidence that the Chinese have given them much thought. The Chinese, to be sure, have been a central participant in a global diffusion of political, economic, and military power. This is not meant to suggest that the Chinese will soon acquire capabilities analogous to those of either Moscow or Washington. The hallmarks of what Liddell Hart termed the "acquisitive approach" to grand strategy are well beyond China's technological and economic reach:[5] China still lacks extensive military forces deployed abroad on a more or less permanent basis; major alliance commitments and obligations; large, ocean-going navies; and the capacity for military intervention over great distances. China will increasingly, if selectively, acquire military power that testifies to its strategic independence, especially in nuclear weaponry and in naval forces large and sophisticated enough to assert control of China's claimed territorial waters. Yet a genuinely expansive conception of national security is a "to be or not to be" question that does not require conclusive assessment in the foreseeable future.

The critical issue for the remainder of the 1980s, therefore, will remain a variant of what has long preoccupied China's foreign policy: defining a political role in Asia that is autonomous from both superpowers, yet not in fundamental conflict with the interests of either. It is still far from certain whether this goal is feasible or realistic. China must try to persuade both Moscow and Washington of its legitimacy as a political-military power, with Peking unconstrained by extensive formal obligations to either the United States or the Soviet Union. Both superpowers, moreover, maintain a vital stake in the evolution of the Asia-Pacific region, so the Chinese can hardly expect either state to diminish its attention to the region.

In addition, numerous uncertainties attach to a more independent conception of Chinese power. Either Soviet or American policy or both could move in directions far more threatening or alluring to

5. B. H. Liddell Hart, *Strategy* (New York: Frederick A. Praeger, 1954), chap. 22.

Chinese interests, and such movement might lead some within the Chinese leadership to barter away long-sought strategic gains out of momentary need or opportunity. China's long-term modernization strategy might not generate its anticipated results, leaving China even more economically and militarily vulnerable and hence insufficiently credible within global or Asian politics. Alternatively, the prodigious tasks associated with China's internal reconstruction might prove so consuming of leadership attention and energy that China will seek a partial disengagement from the global great-power rivalries.

None of these uncertainties, however, alter an inescapable fact: China has no alternative but to work within the existing international system. The devolution of international power over the past several decades has undoubtedly been to China's advantage. The time has long since passed when any single state (or coalition of states) could exercise its power with impunity against Peking. Indeed, both Washington and Moscow recognize the need to garner additional political support for their increasingly costly and complicated global rivalry. China has thus become the object more of superpower solicitation than of criticism, coercion, or isolation.

The Chinese therefore understand that their long-term interests are not well served by an overly antagonistic or highly polarized international situation. Yet Asia has been the principal battleground of the postwar era, and China has never shrunk from using its military power, even if doing so has heightened tensions. In an ironic way, China's participation in these conflicts demonstrated China's centrality to the global strategic balance. Having conclusively established the credibility of their power in the midst of repeated crises and conflicts, China's leaders will hopefully now devote their energies to making certain that Asia's future does not resemble its past. Thus, the larger test for the Chinese will be to develop a political conception befitting Peking's role as a central participant in Asia's political stability and economic well-being. This remains a major challenge that leaders in China as well as elsewhere have barely begun to consider.

6 China's Changing Roles in the Contemporary World HARRY HARDING

Seen through Western eyes, there has been great change and volatility in Chinese foreign relations over the past thirty years. Consider the following examples:

• During the early years of the People's Republic, China and the Soviet Union had an extremely close civilian and military relationship, with the Soviet Union providing extensive assistance to the modernization of both China's economy and the Chinese People's Liberation Army. Today, the two countries have terminated their treaty of friendship and alliance, the Soviet Union has deployed fifty divisions along the Sino-Soviet frontier, and the Chinese describe the USSR as an aggressive superpower bent on global hegemony.

• For more than two decades, China and the United States were locked in confrontation. The two countries fought a long and inconclusive war on the Korean peninsula, and engaged in two dangerous clashes in the Taiwan straits. Each sought to undermine the other's position in international affairs. By the late 1970s, however, the two countries had established diplomatic relations, developed extensive commercial, scientific, and cultural exchanges, and found common ground on a wide range of international and regional issues. Some Americans—and even some Chinese—found it possible to consider Peking as very nearly an ally of the United States, Japan, and NATO in a coalition against the Soviet Union, and as a possible recipient of Western arms.

• In the early 1950s, immediately after the establishment of the People's Republic, the new Chinese government undertook a variety of measures designed to eliminate the Western economic presence in

China and to eradicate Western influence in Chinese scientific and educational institutions. By the early 1980s, however, Peking had not only begun to welcome investment, scientific cooperation, and loans from Western governments, multinational corporations, and international economic institutions but was also sending large numbers of students and scholars to study in universities and research centers in the West.

• In the early 1950s, and especially in the 1960s, China called for an upsurge in armed struggle throughout the world, directed against "reactionary" governments aligned with the United States. It held up its own experiences in revolution and development as models for leftist groups in other countries, and provided extensive rhetorical and material support to such movements. Today, China has attenuated its links with most national liberation movements, forsworn any attempt to "export revolution" to other countries, and warned that other leftist revolutionary parties can expect to receive only moral support from Peking.

Developments such as these have led most Western observers to emphasize the changes in Chinese foreign policy since 1949. In their view, China has shifted from an alignment with the Soviet Union to an alignment with the United States, from support for international revolution to indifference toward it, and from a posture of rejecting the international order to one of basically accepting it.[1] Moreover, this shift has also been viewed as one of the most fundamental transformations in the postwar era—and one of the most beneficial to the United States.[2]

Examining the same record, in contrast, the Chinese usually stress the continuities in their foreign relations. China, they say, has consistently followed a number of basic principles in its foreign affairs: It

1. Richard Wich has described China's change in alignment as a "geologic shift in the international political environment." See his *Sino-Soviet Crisis Politics: A Study of Political Change and Communication* (Cambridge, MA: Harvard University Press, 1980), p. 1. For similar views, see A. Doak Barnett, *China and the Major Powers in East Asia* (Washington, DC: Brookings Institution, 1977), esp. pp. 258–61; and Michael Yahuda, *China's Role in World Affairs* (New York: St. Martin's Press, 1978).

2. See, for example, Donald S. Zagoria, "The New Equilibrium in East Asia," in Robert B. Hewett, ed., *Political Change and the Economic Future of East Asia* (Honolulu, HI: Pacific Forum, 1981), pp. 4–5.

has opposed hegemonism, supported the process of decolonization, and opposed the remnants of colonialism in the Third World. It has fought to preserve its own sovereignty and independence and attempted to develop its economy and military strength through a policy of self-reliance. It has sought peaceful coexistence with other countries, even while expressing support, in a spirit of "proletarian internationalism," for progressive forces abroad. In short, Chinese leaders insist that their country's foreign policy has been unvarying in its basic orientation and goals. As Party general secretary Hu Yaobang put it in his report to the Twelfth Party Congress in September 1982, "China follows an overall long-term strategy, and is definitely not swayed by expediency or by anybody's instigation or provocation."[3]

The differences between the Western and Chinese perspectives invite a closer examination of the issue of change and continuity in Chinese foreign policy since 1949. The basic thesis of this chapter is that both viewpoints contain a significant element of truth. China's foreign relations have experienced both continuity and change, and understanding China's contemporary foreign relations demands attention to both the enduring and the transient. Similarly, predictions of China's future roles in international affairs require an estimate of whether the changes of the past thirty years have now ceased, or will continue; and whether the apparent continuities of past decades are enduring, or are ephemeral. To provide the basis for such assessments, it is helpful to begin with a periodization of China's changing roles in the contemporary world.

A Periodization of China's Foreign Relations

In charting the course of China's foreign relations over the past three decades and more, four dimensions seem particularly useful: (1) the degree of China's *involvement* with the rest of the world; (2) the extent of China's *alignment* with either of the two superpowers, the United States and the Soviet Union; (3) the economic, military, and

---

3. Hu Yaobang, "Create a New Situation in All Fields of Socialist Modernization," *Beijing Review,* 13 September 1982, p. 29.

political *resources* China brings to the conduct of its foreign policy; and (4) China's *objectives* in international affairs, particularly with regard to the preservation or transformation of the prevailing international order.

On this basis, it is possible to divide Chinese foreign policy since 1949 into five periods: the 1950s, when China, aligned with the Soviet Union, sought radical changes in the international balance of power; the early 1960s, when China became even more radical and asserted its independence from the Soviet bloc; the late 1960s, the most revolutionary period, when China effectively insulated itself from the rest of the world; the early and middle 1970s, when China abandoned its radical critique of the international order for a more reformist approach; and the late 1970s, when China seemed not only to accept the international status quo but also to move into alignment with the United States. In the early 1980s, China appears to be moving in new directions, which may represent a new stage in its foreign relations.

Aligned Radical State

In the 1950s, China could best be described as a country interested in defending its newly completed revolution from threats both at home and abroad. After gaining nationwide power in 1949, the most pressing tasks of the CCP were the consolidation of political control over the world's most populous country and the inauguration of a program of rapid socialist transformation and sustained economic development. Both of these goals had significant international implications. The consolidation of political power required that the new regime ensure its security against the two external forces that seemed determined to eliminate it: the Nationalist government on Taiwan, and the Nationalists' ally in Washington. Socialist transformation and economic development required that Peking seek capital, technology, and advice from abroad, particularly from the more advanced Communist nations. Both these imperatives led China into an alliance with the Soviet Union, as embodied in the Treaty of Friendship, Alliance, and Mutual Assistance of February 1950.

In the economic realm, the 1950s saw extensive economic and technological cooperation between China and the Soviet Union. Moscow played a major role in the formulation of China's First Five

Year Plan (1953–57). It granted China about $1.5 billion in loans and credits, which allowed Peking to make extensive purchases of Soviet military and civilian equipment. China imported more than two hundred complete industrial plants from the USSR and Eastern Europe and received assistance from the socialist bloc in the renovation and expansion of still others. China sent eleven thousand students, and thousands more midcareer scientists, technicians, and officials, to the Soviet Union for training. And Moscow dispatched more than ten thousand advisers to China to help design and manage virtually every sector of Chinese society. This program of Soviet assistance to China has been described by one American scholar as "the most comprehensive technology transfer in modern history."[4]

China's foreign trade patterns in the 1950s fully reflected Peking's alignment with the Soviet Union. In 1950, China's trade with non-Communist countries was still two and a half times that with the Communist bloc, reflecting the fact that, under the Nationalist regime, most of China's economic intercourse had been conducted with the West. By 1959, in contrast, China's trade with the socialist bloc had risen to a level twice that of its trade with the West. In part, this was due to China's desire for assistance and advice from more advanced Communist countries. But it was also the result of the economic embargo against China that was imposed during the Korean War by the United States and many of its European allies and maintained by Washington even after the Korean armistice had been signed.

In the security sphere, the Sino-Soviet alliance involved extensive military cooperation between the two countries. Moscow extended its nuclear umbrella over China, exported both weapons and military doctrine to help modernize the Chinese armed forces, and helped develop China's capacity to produce its own conventional weapons. The degree of trust between the two countries at the height of their alliance was reflected in a 1957 agreement on nuclear cooperation in which the Soviet Union promised to assist China in developing nuclear weapons, and may even have agreed to provide the PRC with

4. Hans Heymann, Jr., "Acquisition and Diffusion of Technology in China," in U.S. 94th Congress, 1st Session, Joint Economic Committee, *China: A Reassessment of the Economy* (Washington, DC: U.S. Government Printing Office, 1975), p. 678.

a sample atomic bomb and the technical data concerning its manufacture. In return, Peking agreed to identify China with the socialist camp, to acknowledge (and, at crucial points, promote) the Kremlin's leadership of that camp, and to coordinate China's foreign policy with that of the Soviet Union.

Developments throughout the 1950s provided China with substantial evidence to confirm its initial judgment that the United States presented a significant threat to its security. The outbreak of the Korean War in June 1950 saw Washington reverse its policy of disengagement from the Chinese civil war and interpose the U.S. Seventh Fleet between Taiwan and the Mainland. A few months later, in disregard of explicit Chinese warnings, American forces began to advance into North Korea in order to reunify Korea under non-Communist rule—a decision that led to Chinese intervention in the conflict. General Douglas MacArthur proposed American military action against the Chinese mainland, and President Dwight Eisenhower later threatened to employ nuclear weapons against China if the conflict was not brought to an end. During both the Truman and the Eisenhower administrations, the United States began to construct a network of bilateral and multilateral alliances in Asia, including a mutual defense treaty with Taiwan, that were intended to encircle and "contain" China. And Secretary of State John Foster Dulles described American policy toward China as nothing less than an attempt to "hasten the passing" of Communist rule on the Mainland.[5]

Given this situation, it might have seemed only logical for China to maintain its alliance with the Soviet Union as a counterweight against the United States. And yet, China never seemed completely comfortable with the arrangement. For one thing, a close and exclusive alignment with the Soviet Union had not been the first choice of a number of leaders of the CCP, including both Zhou Enlai and, at least for a time, Mao Zedong. The relationship between Moscow and the Chinese Communists during the CCP's struggles against the

5. John Foster Dulles, "Our Policies toward Communism in China," *Department of State Bulletin,* 37: 942 (15 July 1957): 95.

warlords and the Nationalist government had been quite strained, with Stalin repeatedly giving his Chinese comrades unwise and self-serving advice on how to conduct their revolution. By the mid-1940s, as a result, some Chinese Communist leaders were hoping for an accommodation with the United States that would allow a victorious Communist movement to take a more balanced position between Washington and Moscow, gain access to American capital and technology, and reduce the chances that the United States would take a hostile position toward a Communist government in China.[6]

Furthermore, while the Soviet Union was generous to China in many ways—particularly in its willingness to assist the PRC in developing nuclear weapons—Moscow also struck a hard bargain in its relations with Peking. In exchange for the military alliance of 1950, Stalin demanded, and received, continued privileges in China, including the formation of four joint-stock companies and the retention of Soviet port facilities and naval bases in Dairen and Port Arthur. During the First Five Year Plan, the Chinese complained, the Soviet Union insisted that Peking pay for all the economic and military assistance it received, interfered with China's economic planning, exported a model of development that was unsuited to China's needs, and sought to integrate the PRC into a "socialist international division of labor." And once Nikita Khrushchev began to speak of "peaceful coexistence" with the United States at the Twentieth Party Congress in 1956, Peking began to worry that Moscow might choose to sacrifice Chinese interests for the sake of improving its relations with the United States.

Thus, even during this period of Sino-Soviet alliance, China gradually began to stake out a somewhat more independent foreign policy. For a brief period in the mid-1950s, China issued a series of overtures toward the United States, in an attempt to reduce its economic and strategic dependence on the Soviet Union. At various times, Peking

---

6. On relations between the CCP and the United States in the 1940s, see James Reardon-Anderson, *Yenan and the Great Powers: The Origins of Chinese Communist Foreign Policy, 1944–45* (New York: Columbia University Press, 1980); and Dorothy Borg and Waldo Heinrichs, eds., *Uncertain Years: Chinese-American Relations, 1947–1950* (New York: Columbia University Press, 1980).

proposed trade and exchanges with the United States, suggested a conference between the foreign ministers of the two countries, and even took a relatively conciliatory position on the Taiwan issue. But Peking's initiatives met with little interest in Washington, where they were seen merely as self-serving attempts to split the United States from its Nationalist ally in Taipei.[7]

For most of the 1950s, therefore, China's independent leanings were reflected in its attempts to weaken the American strategic position in Asia by undermining U.S. ties with the smaller developing states in the region. In the early 1950s, Peking did so by supporting national liberation movements in Asian countries aligned with the West and by providing large amounts of military and economic assistance to Viet Minh forces in French Indochina and rhetorical support and small amounts of material aid to Communist movements in Thailand, Burma, Malaya, and the Philippines. Later in the decade, China sought to improve its relations with virtually all independent Third World governments, in the Middle East as well as in Asia. Through this "Bandung line," named after the conference of Asian and African governments in Indonesia at which it was announced, China tried to persuade Third World governments to adopt a neutral position in cold war rivalries, in order to attenuate their political and military ties with the United States.

These actions, however, did not make China a truly revolutionary state in the 1950s. Chinese foreign policy during this period was essentially defensive: It aimed at discouraging the smaller countries of Asia from participating in the American design for the diplomatic isolation, economic embargo, and military encirclement of China. China certainly did not accept the international status quo, but it had not yet launched a frontal challenge against it, as it would begin to do in the early 1960s.

Independent Radical State

By the end of the 1950s, serious tensions had emerged in Sino-Soviet relations. The Chinese had become convinced that the model

7. Robert Sutter, *China-Watch: Toward Sino-American Reconciliation* (Baltimore: Johns Hopkins University Press, 1978).

of development they were importing from the Soviet Union was inappropriate to Chinese conditions; but their attempt to break away from the Soviet model, through the Great Leap Forward, led the Kremlin to order the withdrawal of Soviet advisers from China. A Soviet proposal in 1958 for a joint naval fleet in the Western Pacific confirmed Chinese suspicions that Khrushchev wished to establish control over the Chinese armed forces. And lukewarm Soviet support for China in the Quemoy crisis of 1958 along with the Kremlin's indecisiveness in the Sino-Indian border conflict of 1959 also seemed to testify that the Soviet Union would compromise its support of basic Chinese territorial interests for the sake of avoiding conflict with the United States or improving its relations with nonaligned states such as India.

While the formal Sino-Soviet alliance would remain in effect until its expiration in 1980, the actual relationship between the two countries attenuated rapidly. Trade between the two countries dropped markedly; the Chinese accepted no further credits from Moscow and spared no effort to pay off their outstanding debts ahead of schedule. Although the Soviet Union continued for a time to sell some conventional military equipment to China, Khrushchev renounced his earlier agreement to help China develop its own nuclear weapons.

The main arena for the Sino-Soviet split, however, was the exchange of polemics between the two Communist parties. Even though both countries continued to claim membership in a common socialist bloc, they began to express vehement opposition to each other's domestic and foreign policies. Peking warned that Khrushchev's domestic programs were leading the USSR down the road to capitalism and charged that his policy of peaceful coexistence with the United States was nothing less than a cleverly disguised attempt to share global hegemony with the United States. The Soviet Union, in turn, accused the Chinese of exaggerating the need for continued class struggle at home, favoring violent revolution abroad, and willfully ignoring the devastating consequences of a nuclear war between East and West. Each side attempted to gain international support for its position: the Soviets attempting to write China out of the Communist camp and to combat Peking's influence in the Third World; the Chinese trying to form splinter Maoist parties and to exclude the Soviet Union from conferences of Third World nations.[8]

Yet the emergence of the Sino-Soviet dispute did not produce a rapprochement between China and the United States. Throughout the 1960s, and particularly as American involvement in the Vietnam conflict grew, Peking still regarded Washington as the principal threat to Chinese security. Moreover, since Peking was criticizing Moscow for advocating peaceful coexistence between socialism and capitalism, consistency demanded that China's relations with the United States remain frozen. To be sure, the two countries were able, through an ongoing series of ambassadorial negotiations at Warsaw, to avoid any major crises in their relations comparable to their two confrontations in the Taiwan straits in the 1950s. But while this development provided greater predictability and stability in Sino-American relations, it did not represent any significant reduction in tension between Peking and Washington.

Thus, instead of shifting its alignment from the Soviet Union to the United States, China pursued an independent foreign policy during the early 1960s. With relations with the United States frozen, and those with the USSR in decline, China began to increase its import of technology from Europe and Japan and to develop diplomatic ties with Western Europe. Peking achieved dramatic victory in this regard in 1964 when it established formal relations with Gaullist France—the first European nation to recognize the People's Republic since the early 1950s. In the security sphere, Peking convinced itself that it could take on both superpowers simultaneously by making preparations to fight a people's war against foreign invasion and by developing its own independent nuclear capability, which it achieved in minimal fashion with the explosion of its first atomic bomb in 1964.

But the main theme of Chinese foreign policy in this second period

8. For overviews of the early years of the Sino-Soviet dispute, see Donald S. Zagoria, *The Sino-Soviet Conflict, 1956–61* (Princeton, NJ: Princeton University Press, 1962); John Gittings, *Survey of the Sino-Soviet Dispute* (London: Oxford University Press, 1968); and William E. Griffith, *The Sino-Soviet Rift* (Cambridge, MA: MIT Press, 1967).

was Peking's attempt to mobilize the Third World to join an international united front against the two superpowers and the international system that they allegedly dominated. China encouraged Third World countries to support Indonesia's call for the creation of a new United Nations organized around the "newly emerging forces" of the developing world; to take Djakarta's side in its "confrontation" with Malaysia; to refuse economic assistance from the Soviet Union and the United States; to support national liberation movements working against the remaining colonial and apartheid regimes in Africa; and to oppose the nuclear test ban treaty of 1963. China also began to provide greater rhetorical—and, in some cases, material—support to revolutionary movements in countries whose governments refused to recognize the PRC, voted against Peking's admission to the United Nations, or maintained close military and political ties with the United States.[9]

All this represented a much more strident and disruptive policy than the Bandung line of the 1950s. Where Chinese leaders had once tried to form an alignment with moderate Third World leaders such as Nehru, Nasser, and Tito, they now restricted participation in their united front to the more radical regimes of the Third World. Where Peking had once been satisfied with neutralism in Asia and Africa, China now seemed to demand Third World adherence to a very radical set of policies. The China-India-Egypt alignment of the mid-1950s was replaced by the so-called Peking-Djakarta-Hanoi-Pyongyang axis of the mid-1960s.

Not surprisingly, this new Third World policy failed to yield many results. China had neither the military nor the economic capability to provide large amounts of assistance to revolutionary movements, except the one in Vietnam. And the issues around which Peking chose to construct its united front—opposition to the United States, the Soviet Union, and all pro-Western developing countries—were not attractive to many Third World governments. The failure of China's initiatives toward the Third World in the early 1960s was symbolized by three events: Zhou Enlai's ill-fated tour of Africa in

9. Peter Van Ness, *Revolution and Chinese Foreign Policy* (Berkeley: University of California Press, 1971).

1964, in which he unwisely declared the "revolutionary prospects" on the continent to be "excellent"; the cancellation of a second Bandung conference in Algiers after a military coup in Algeria in 1965; and the overthrow of the friendly Sukarno government in Indonesia by another military coup later that same year.

Isolationist Revolutionary State

With the outbreak of the Cultural Revolution in late 1966 and early 1967, Chinese foreign relations underwent a further radicalization, reflecting the heightened radicalism of Chinese domestic politics. That radicalization, which was reinforced by the chaos of China's foreign affairs bureaucracy, produced a nearly complete break of China's international diplomatic and economic relations. In the early part of the decade, China was independent from the two superpowers but actively involved in world affairs; at the height of the Cultural Revolution, China turned almost completely inward, isolating itself from the rest of the world.

At home, the Cultural Revolution reflected the resurgence of the utopian populist and egalitarian impulses that have traditionally provided a counterpoint to the predominantly hierarchical and authoritarian cast of Chinese politics and society. In international affairs, the Cultural Revolution represented the revival of yet another submerged strain of thought: a strongly xenophobic Chinese nativism, similar in some respects to the antiforeignism of the Boxer Rebellion of the turn of the century. The avowed domestic purpose of the Cultural Revolution was to prevent the institutionalization of privilege and elitism; in foreign affirs, it was to protect the country against corrosive influences from abroad. The recall of every Chinese ambassador, save one, during the Cultural Revolution was, in part, occasioned by the organizational chaos within the Ministry of Foreign Affairs. But, to an equally significant degree, it was also a symbol of the radicals' desire to insulate China from the corruption of contact with foreigners. So, too, was the decline in China's trade with the outside world, which fell from $4.2 billion in 1966 to $3.8 billion in 1968.

The xenophobia and nativism of the Cultural Revolution was reflected in other ways, as well. Red Guards surrounded the Soviet

Embassy in Peking, submitting it to a constant barrage of revolutionary rhetoric broadcast from makeshift loudspeakers. The dependents of Soviet diplomats, seeking to leave China for home, were forced to crawl on their knees to the airplane waiting for them at Peking airport. The British legation in Peking was burned to the ground; and a Reuters correspondent was seized and placed in solitary confinement. The rhetorical tone of the period was evident in an anti-Soviet editorial in *Renmin Ribao,* the official Party newspaper, which was headlined, "Hit Back Hard at the Rabid Provocations of the Filthy Soviet Revisionist Swine."[10]

Chinese policy toward the Third World was also redefined in ways that made the qualifications for membership in the united front against the United States and the Soviet Union even more restrictive than in the early 1960s. Peking virtually ceased making appeals to established Third World governments, choosing to regard all of them as little more than political instruments of American imperialism or Soviet revisionism. Even relations with North Korea became strained, as China accused Kim Il-sung of revisionism. About the only governments with which China remained friendly were those of Albania and North Vietnam. Peking encouraged Maoist insurgents to carry out armed struggle against the governments of virtually every developing country, thus creating "storm centers of world revolution" throughout the Third World.[11] In an analogy to China's own Communist revolution, and in accordance with the Maoist doctrine reemphasized by Lin Biao in 1965 in his "Long Live the Victory of People's War," armed insurgents were to seize control of the "countryside" of the world, surround the developed "cities," and thus cause the collapse of both the Soviet Union and the West.[12]

Semi-aligned Reformist State

By the end of the 1960s, however, the Chinese had concluded that the international isolation produced by the Cultural Revolution

10. "Hit Back Hard at the Rabid Provocations of the Filthy Soviet Revisionist Swine," *Renmin Ribao,* 27 January 1967, in *Peking Review,* 3 February 1967, p. 23.

11. "Excellent Situation: East Wind Prevails over the West Wind," *Renmin Ribao,* 30 September 1967, in *Peking Review,* 20 October 1967, pp. 26–28.

12. Lin Piao [Lin Biao], *Long Live the Victory of People's War* (Beijing: Foreign Languages Press, 1965).

was becoming increasingly dangerous. Throughout the latter part of the decade, both China and the Soviet Union had reinforced the military forces deployed along their common frontier, thus introducing a military element into what had originally been a political and polemical conflict. Ultimately, in 1969, the two sides engaged in serious armed clashes over several small islands in the Ussuri River, which separates Chinese Manchuria from Soviet Siberia, as well as at other points along their disputed frontier. Those clashes, plus the precedent of the Soviet intervention in Czechoslovakia in August 1968, raised the possibility of a large-scale Soviet attack against China in the name of preserving socialism in Peking.

At the same time, the Chinese also concluded that the changing fortunes of the Vietnam War had produced a major shift in the international balance of power away from the United States and toward the Soviet Union. By late 1968, it was clear to the Chinese leadership that the United States was losing its struggle in Vietnam and had decided to disengage from the conflict. And a new American administration, under Richard Nixon, seemed willing to seek an accommodation with Peking as a means to bolster its deteriorating strategic position.

In this context, China began to redefine its foreign policy, taking three initiatives in the early 1970s that departed sharply from the isolation and radicalism of the Cultural Revolution. First, over the opposition of some of China's military commanders, as well as the radicals who had come to prominence during the Cultural Revolution, Mao Zedong and Zhou Enlai began to explore the possibility of improved relations with the United States, in order not only to stabilize the situation along the Sino-Soviet frontier but also to create a new global alignment to contain a Soviet Union that was rapidly becoming more ambitious and more powerful. The Sino-American rapprochement, symbolized by President Nixon's visit to Peking in February 1972, was hindered by remaining differences between the two countries over Taiwan, and by disagreements over the desirability of détente with the Soviet Union. Nonetheless, while China continued to describe the United States as a "hegemonic" and an "imperialist" power, it in fact began to tilt toward Washington in a partial alignment against the Soviet Union.[13]

Second, again over the opposition of radical leaders at home, Peking abandoned the radicalism that had served it so poorly throughout the 1960s in favor of a kind of international reformism more in harmony with the thinking of most Third World governments. China greatly reduced—although it did not yet completely eliminate—its support for leftist insurgencies and revolutionary movements abroad, even going so far as to condemn some of them as reflecting ultraleftist, "Trotskyist" tendencies. Instead of an international revolution, Peking began to support Third World demands for a "New International Economic Order" and expressed its willingness to work with established governments in the developing world to achieve such reforms. Rather than denouncing the United Nations, as it had done in the 1960s, China accepted its seat in 1971 quickly and with expressions of gratitude.[14]

Third, China rejected the economic autarky characteristic of the Cultural Revolution and began to resume active commercial transactions with the rest of the world, particularly with the West. But, largely because of the concern of radical leaders with the danger of economic dependence on foreigners, the types of economic relationships in which China was willing to engage remained severely limited. As late as 1977, even after the purge of the Gang of Four, Peking was still providing a rather restrictive account of its commercial transactions with the rest of the world: It would not allow foreigners to "dump" their consumer goods on its domestic market, would not accept foreign loans, would not "mortgage its natural resources" so as to import foreign technology, would never allow foreign invest-

13. On the domestic debate over the accommodation with the United States, see Thomas M. Gottlieb, *Chinese Foreign Policy Factionalism and the Origins of the Strategic Triangle,* R-1902-NA (Santa Monica, CA: Rand Corporation, November 1977).

14. On the debate over the abandonment of radicalism in favor of a more reformist approach to the international order, see Harry Harding, "The Domestic Politics of China's Global Posture, 1973–1978," in Thomas Fingar and the *Stanford Journal of International Studies,* eds., *China's Quest for Independence: Policy Evolution in the 1970s* (Boulder, CO: Westview, 1980), pp. 93–146.

ment in China, and would not permit foreigners to "meddle in the management" of Chinese enterprises.[15]

Chinese foreign policy during this period was summarized in the "theory of the three worlds," first formulated by Mao Zedong in February 1974 and presented publicly by Deng Xiaoping in a speech before the United Nations General Assembly two months later. According to that doctrine, the main characteristic of international affairs was the growing resistance of the developing countries (the Third World), supported by the more developed countries of Eastern and Western Europe and Japan (the Second World), against the economic and political hegemonism of the United States and the Soviet Union (the First World). All Second and Third World countries, regardless of their social or political systems, were welcome to join Peking in a united front against the two superpowers. Opposition to hegemonism, rather than "people's war" or "armed struggle," was now viewed as the essence of a "progressive" foreign policy.[16]

Theoretically, therefore, China still considered both the United States and the Soviet Union to be its adversaries. But Peking subtly incorporated its partial alignment with the United States into its formal foreign policy doctrine, first by reversing the order in which the two superpowers were listed so that the Soviet Union always appeared before the United States, and then by explicitly declaring that the Soviet Union represented the more "ferocious" and "treacherous" of the two.[17]

Aligned Conservative State

Developments both at home and abroad caused further moderation of Chinese foreign policy in the late 1970s. The purge of the

15. For representative press accounts stressing these limits, see Radio Peking, 15 February 1977, in *Foreign Broadcast Information Service Daily Report: People's Republic of China* [hereafter cited as *FBIS*], 9 March 1977, pp. E9–14; and *Peking Review,* 25 February 1977, pp. 16–18.

16. "Speech by Teng Hsiao-ping [Deng Xiaoping], Chairman of Delegation of the People's Republic of China," *Peking Review,* 12 April 1974 (Supplement).

17. See, for example, the most authoritative exegesis of the theory of the three worlds: Editorial Department of *Renmin Ribao,* "Chairman Mao's Theory of the Differentiation of the Three Worlds is a Major Contribution to Marxism-Leninism," *Peking Review,* 4 November 1977, pp. 10–41.

Gang of Four in October 1976, one month after the death of Chairman Mao, removed the leaders of the opposition to alignment with the United States and greater economic relations with the West. The establishment of formal diplomatic relations between Peking and Washington in December 1978 seemed, at least temporarily, to eliminate the Taiwan issue as an obstacle to the further improvement of Sino-U.S. relations. And continuing expansion by the Soviet Union and its allies—exemplified by the Vietnamese invasion of Cambodia in December 1978 and the Soviet invasion of Afghanistan one year later—raised the threat of a Soviet diplomatic and military encirclement of China. As a result, Chinese leaders introduced significant modifications into each of the three initiatives they had adopted in the early and middle 1970s, in ways that produced a closer alignment between China and the United States and that gave the impression that China had become, for all practical purposes, a status quo power.

By the end of the 1970s, for example, references to the New International Economic Order had virtually vanished from Chinese pronouncements on world affairs. Instead, Peking seemed more concerned with preserving the existing international strategic balance against the threat posed by the Soviet Union. Some Chinese scholars said privately that sweeping international economic reform was both unnecessary and impractical, and the Chinese press repeatedly argued that the main focus of Third World foreign policy should be resistance to Soviet expansionism, rather than creation of a New International Economic Order.

Moreover, China dropped the United States from its list of hegemonic powers, leaving in that category only the Soviet Union and such proxy states as Cuba and Vietnam. While Peking never said so formally, some Chinese scholars implied that the United States had, in effect, been so weakened by its experience in Vietnam that it was no longer an active imperialist power but had fallen, like Britain and France before it, into the ranks of the Second World.[18]

18. For one full exposition of this view by a Chinese scholar then in the United States, see Hua Di, "Chinese Comprehensive Strategic Doctrine," in *The Role of Technology in Meeting the Defense Challenges of the 1980s* (Stanford, CA: Northeast

This reassessment of American intentions and capabilities enabled China to move into closer alignment with the United States. After the normalization of Sino-U.S. relations in 1978, therefore, the strategic relationship between the two countries began to expand along a number of dimensions. Peking and Washington started to consult on a wide range of regional and global questions of common concern and began to devise parallel or coordinated policies on such issues as Indochina and Afghanistan. They began a limited cooperation on security matters, with the United States relaxing its restrictions on the export of military technology to China and China agreeing to establish a joint surveillance facility to monitor Soviet missile tests. The United States stated its interest in a "secure and strong" China, and Deng Xiaoping, just before his visit to the United States in early 1979, called for a strong anti-Soviet partnership among China, the United States, Japan, and Western Europe.[19]

Neither side expressed any interest in creating a formal military alliance comparable to the Sino-Soviet alliance of 1950. Instead, they seemed satisfied to remain, in the words of the Carter administration, "friends, rather than allies."[20] But the two countries began increasingly to speak of their parallel international objectives and common foreign policy interests and worked to narrow (or at least to understate) their remaining points of disagreement. All this amounted, if not to an alliance, at least to a reasonably close alignment between Peking and Washington.

Finally, in the economic sphere, China greatly relaxed the restrictions on its commercial relations with the West that had prevailed throughout the 1970s, concluding that its economic and scientific modernization could be promoted better by cooperation with the West than by pure self-reliance. The Chinese therefore began to explore a variety of economic relationships with the West that had previously been proscribed, including joint ventures with foreign

Asia-United States Forum on International Policy, Stanford University, November 1981), pp. 67–104.
  19. *Time,* 5 February 1979, p. 34.
  20. Richard C. Holbrooke, "China and the U.S.: Into the 1980s," *Current Policy,* no. 187 (Washington, DC: Bureau of Public Affairs, U.S. Department of State, 4 June 1980), p. 3.

investors, management consulting contracts and licensing agreements with foreign firms, technical assistance from intergovernmental organizations, and loans from commercial banks, foreign governments, and international financial institutions. By 1981, Peking's foreign trade bill was $37.6 billion, nearly ten times what it had been a decade earlier. China had gained access to nearly $30 billion in credit from Western financial institutions. Moreover, Peking had invited a sizable contingent of foreign experts to teach at Chinese universities and had dispatched a large number of students and scholars to universities and research institutions abroad.

Independent Reformist Leanings

By the end of 1982, however, this policy of "aligned conservatism" had undergone considerable modification. Every available indication suggested that the foreign policy orientation that China had adopted between 1979 and 1981 might be the shortest-lived of all of Peking's foreign policies—more transient even than the disastrous radicalism of the Cultural Revolution.

First, there were serious strains in Sino-U.S. relations. The immediate cause of the problem, of course, was the reemergence of the Taiwan issue to complicate the relationship between Washington and Peking. The Chinese suspected the Reagan administration of wishing to upgrade American relations with Taipei, and of following what was tantamount to a two-China policy. What is more, Peking was also disappointed that neither the normalization of Sino-American relations in late 1978, nor the publication of its position on the reunification of Taiwan and the Mainland, nor the termination of the U.S.-Taiwan Mutual Defense Treaty a year later, had persuaded Taipei to begin negotiations with Peking over the future of the island. Thus, in the fall of 1981, China demanded that the United States agree to a timetable for halting the sale of all weapons to Taipei, seeing such a demand as a way of both testing American policy toward Taiwan and placing greater pressure on the Nationalists to negotiate.

The Reagan administration's response to Peking's demands was quite conciliatory. In early 1982, it announced that it would not sell an advanced fighter aircraft, the so-called F-X, to Taiwan. And in

August 1982, Washington pledged, in a joint communiqué with Peking, that its future arms sales to Taiwan would not exceed, in quality or quantity, the level since normalization, and that it intended gradually to reduce those sales over an unspecified period of time. For their part, while still refusing to renounce the use of force against Taiwan, the Chinese described their proposals for a peaceful reunification of Taiwan and the Mainland as representing a "fundamental policy."[21]

But these conciliatory gestures did not produce a second honeymoon in Sino-American relations. One reason was the continued expression of U.S. support for the Nationalists, leading Peking to conclude that the two countries were still far from a basic agreement in principle on the Taiwan question. Another was a series of small irritants in U.S.-PRC relations: the defection of the Chinese tennis star Hu Na, delays in the approval of licenses for the export of American technology to China, failure to agree on quotas for the import of Chinese textiles to the United States, a court judgment that the Chinese government would have to pay principal and interest to American holders of some obscure railway bonds issued in the waning months of the Qing dynasty, and the decision by Pan American World Airways to resume flights to Taiwan that had been suspended when it began service to the Mainland.

None of these incidents was, in itself, a major issue. But together they reflected some deeper problems in the Sino-American relationship. In essence, each side was becoming increasingly conscious of the limits on its relationship with the other. American business was becoming aware of the limits on trade with China; American bankers were starting to realize that China sought to minimize its foreign indebtedness; and the American academic community was becoming ever more cognizant of the limits on scholarly research in China. Chinese leaders, in turn, were concerned with the effects of rising protectionist sentiments in the United States on the future of Chinese exports to America and with the remaining controls on the export of advanced American technology. And on issues ranging from the

21. "U.S.-China Joint Communiqué," *Current Policy*, no. 413 (Washington, DC: Bureau of Public Affairs, U.S. Department of State, August 1982).

Polish crisis to the stalemate on the Korean peninsula, both governments were understanding more clearly that there remained important differences in their national interests. As a result, the August communiqué on arms sales to Taiwan failed to restore much momentum to Sino-American relations. The spirit of euphoria that had characterized the relationship in the previous decade was replaced by a sense of mutual disenchantment.

A second factor also contributed to China's reassessment of its foreign policy in 1981–82. Many Chinese appear to have concluded that the momentum that the Soviet Union had established in the mid-1970s was now fading. In the Chinese analysis, the Soviet Union's difficulties in Afghanistan and Eastern Europe, its economic and administrative inefficiency, and the resurgence of American military power under the Reagan administration meant that Moscow was not likely to achieve the strategic breakthrough vis-à-vis the United States that Peking had been predicting in the late 1970s. What is more, conciliatory Soviet gestures to China during the last months of the Brezhnev era and the beginning of the Andropov period suggested to Peking that an improvement in Sino-Soviet relations was no longer inconceivable.

Finally, Chinese leaders may well have become uneasy about their country's growing reputation as a status quo power closely aligned with the United States. In part, Chinese leaders may have realized that their country was beginning to lose support in the Third World as it reduced its support for the New International Economic Order, ordered its foreign policy around the single issue of opposition to the Soviet Union, and downplayed its differences with Washington on international issues. In part, too, leaders critical of Deng Xiaoping's ambitious program of domestic economic and political reform may have found that China's quasi-alliance with the United States was a convenient issue on which to express their dissatisfaction with Deng's leadership.

As a result of these considerations, signs of a major reorientation of Chinese foreign policy appeared in late 1981 and throughout 1982. To begin with, Chinese leaders made repeated assertions of dissociation from Washington. In a clear reference to the United States, General Secretary Hu Yaobang declared in his report to the Twelfth

Party Congress in September 1982 that China "never attaches itself to any big power or group of powers, and never yields to pressure from any big power."[22] Comprehensive descriptions of Chinese foreign policy began to refer to the United States once again as a hegemonic power, and to list examples of American hegemonism (South Africa, Central America, and the Middle East) alongside those attributed to the Soviet Union (Afghanistan and Cambodia). And Chinese press accounts implied that China now regarded South Africa and Israel to be "regional hegemonists" linked to the United States, just as Peking had long considered Cuba and Vietnam to be regional hegemonists linked to the Soviet Union.[23]

China also resumed its official dialogue with Moscow, suspended since the Soviet Union's intervention in Afghanistan in late 1979. China still insisted on major Soviet concessions as a prerequisite for progress in the negotiations, including reduction of Soviet forces along the Sino-Soviet frontier, Soviet withdrawal from Afghanistan, and an end to Soviet support for the Vietnamese invasion of Kampuchea. But the atmosphere that surrounded the Sino-Soviet dialogue was more relaxed than on previous occasions. The Chinese ceased their criticism of the Soviet Union's domestic affairs, and Hu Yaobang suggested that the two countries look ahead toward the future rather than concentrate on the "minute details" of historical questions. Vice Foreign Minister Qian Qichen, China's chief negotiator, suggested that the Soviet Union need not make concessions on all Peking's demands at once. "Even if there were changes with respect to one or another item," Qian was quoted as saying, "this would lead to an improvement of relations."[24]

These developments in Sino-U.S. and Sino-Soviet relations were designed to permit Peking to strike an "independent" position—between the two superpowers. As one Chinese journal summarized the PRC's new policy, China would

22. Hu, *Create a New Situation,* p. 29.
23. Ibid. See also then-foreign minister Huang Hua's speech to the 1982 session of the United Nations General Assembly, "China's Position on Current World Issues," *Beijing Review,* 11 October 1982, pp. 14–18.
24. Xinhua [New China News Agency], 17 October 1982, in *FBIS,* 18 October 1982, pp. C1–2; *Die Presse* (Vienna), 7–8 December 1982, in *FBIS,* 7 December 1982, p. C1.

totally oppose hegemony, no matter who seeks it or where it is sought. . . . On the Afghan and Kampuchean issues, both China and the United States oppose the Soviet Union and Vietnam. . . . In another case, both China and the Soviet Union oppose the United States in supporting Israeli aggression and the South African apartheid rule. This does not mean that China "allies" with the United States under some circumstances, or becomes a Soviet partner under other circumstances. [Instead,] this precisely proves that . . . China is independent of all the superpowers.[25]

In place of the United States and the West, China now stressed its identification with the Third World. "Socialist China," Hu Yaobang said in his report to the Twelfth Party Congress, "belongs to the Third World," for it has "experienced the same sufferings as most other Third World countries, and . . . is faced with similar problems and tasks."[26] Media accounts of Chinese foreign relations began once again to emphasize problems of Third World development and to state China's support for a restructuring of the international economic order. To symbolize China's identification with the Third World, Peking began to describe the Taiwan question as an example of the broader process of superpower intervention in the developing world: a case of American infringement on the sovereignty of a Third World country.

Thus far, however, Chinese foreign economic relations have undergone less change than its geopolitical posture has. To be sure, Chinese leaders have become increasingly concerned about the "spiritual pollution" produced by contact with the West. They blame the rise of political dissent, defections of Chinese to foreign countries, growing corruption within the Chinese bureaucracy, and even an increase in the crime rate, at least partially on China's wider relationship with the rest of the world. But they still seem eager to reap the benefits of China's new "open door." Although it has placed increasing restrictions on unofficial and informal contacts between Chinese

25. *Liaowang,* quoted in Xinhua [New China News Agency], 20 October 1982, in *FBIS,* 21 October 1982, pp. A1–2.
26. Hu, *Create a New Situation,* p. 31.

and foreigners and reduced some opportunities for Chinese to study abroad, Peking has not limited the wide range of economic and commercial transactions with the West that were inaugurated in the late 1970s. While increasing its trade with the Soviet Union and Eastern Europe, China has continued to place much higher priority on maintaining its economic relations with the United States, Western Europe, and Japan. To a degree unknown since the 1950s, in other words, Chinese foreign policy has been marked by a separation of politics and economics.

What is more, it remains to be seen whether China will seek true equidistance between the United States and the Soviet Union or whether, as is more likely, it will continue to have better relations with Washington than with Moscow. Much will depend on the policies that the United States and the Soviet Union adopt on issues of interest to the Chinese—specifically, the positions that the United States takes on arms sales to Taiwan and the export of advanced technology to the PRC, and the response that Moscow makes to China's conditions for an improvement in Sino-Soviet relations. In addition, China will calculate the overall strategic balance between the two superpowers, feeling freer to assert its independence when the United States and the USSR enjoy rough strategic parity, and obliged to tilt toward one and against the other should the superpowers' strategic relationship become disequilibrated.

These new directions in Chinese foreign relations, therefore, might tentatively be summarized as a kind of "independent reformism," in which Peking renews its support for the reform of the international political and economic order and stresses its independence from both superpowers. In so doing, Chinese foreign policy both contains echoes of the past and strikes off in new directions. China's identification with other developing countries, its criticism of hegemonism of both superpowers, and its resurrection of the "theory of the three worlds"—all are highly reminiscent of the foreign policy of the mid-1970s. Peking's relations with the two superpowers, however, may have little precedent. To a greater degree than in the 1970s, China is seeking to avoid any implication that it is "aligned" with, or a partner of, the United States. But China's statements of nonalignment do not mark a return to the foreign policy of the early 1960s, the last time that China asserted its independence from both the United States and the Soviet Union. Then, China's position was to oppose vigorously the initiatives of both superpowers. Now, China may feel it possible to pursue parallel policies with the Soviet Union on one set of issues and still join with Washington on another. As one Chinese writer has described this possibility,

> [I]n the struggle between the Soviet Union and the United States for world hegemony, China may adopt a similar attitude with this or that superpower on this or that issue, and have a certain "point of meeting." But its point of departure [in determining its position] is different.[27]

China, in other words, will be actively engaged in dialogue with both superpowers but will be completely aligned with neither one.

Changes

In the introduction to this chapter, we identified four dimensions that provide a useful way of analyzing China's evolving foreign policy since 1949: (1) the degree of China's *involvement* with the rest of the world; (2) the extent of China's *alignment* with either of the two superpowers, the United States and the Soviet Union; (3) the economic, military, and political *resources* China brings to the conduct of its international affairs; and (4) China's *objectives* in international affairs, particularly with regard to the preservation or transformation of the prevailing international order. This brief overview of the complex history of contemporary Chinese foreign relations suggests that there has indeed been change in each of these four dimensions.

The level of China's involvement with the rest of the world has displayed a gradual cyclical pattern since 1949. China was closely integrated with the socialist bloc through most of the 1950s, began to turn inward in the early 1960s, shut itself off from the rest of the world at the height of the Cultural Revolution, revived its basic trading and diplomatic relationships in the early 1970s, and then

---

27. *Liaowang,* quoted in Xinhua [New China News Agency], 20 October 1982, in *FBIS,* 21 October 1982, pp. A1–2.

developed a wide panoply of economic partnerships later in the decade.

This cyclical pattern can be traced to the continuing impact of one of the most intense and enduring domestic political controversies in modern Chinese history. Here, more than in any other dimension of China's international behavior, there is a direct and immediate connection between China's domestic politics and its foreign policy. In essence, the rise and fall of Chinese autarky and isolation in the 1960s and early 1970s is the story of the rise and fall of radical nativism and utopianism in Chinese domestic affairs.

Ever since the mid-nineteenth century, there has been vigorous debate among Chinese leaders and intellectuals over the degree to which modernization (or, to use the original Chinese term, "self-strengthening") required China to import technology, institutions, and values from abroad. To some during the late Qing dynasty, such relations with the outside world were necessary if China was to strengthen itself to the point that it could resist foreign encroachment and regain its national dignity. To others, economic and cultural relations with foreigners would only contaminate Chinese society, disrupt the internal Chinese political order, and reduce China's independence and sovereignty. It would be better, this second group argued, to keep the foreigners away altogether and rely upon the restoration and rejuvenation of traditional Chinese culture and society to save the country.[28]

This nineteenth-century debate between "cosmopolitans" and "nativists" has had its counterpart in the People's Republic as well. More radical leaders, such as the Gang of Four in the late 1960s and early 1970s and, to a degree, Mao Zedong himself in certain periods of his life, have feared that economic relations with the West—or even with the Soviet Union, as a "revisionist" country—would bring with them "bourgeois" values and concepts that would gradually erode China's commitment to pure, revolutionary socialism. When radicals have been in power, as in the Cultural Revolution, they have implemented a policy of economic autarky and self-reliance. In addition, they have

28. For an overview of this long-standing dispute, and its continuing impact on the present, see Michel Oksenberg and Steven Goldstein, "The Chinese Political Spectrum," *Problems of Communism* 23:2 (March–April 1974): 1–13.

also tended to emphasize a militant and rigid posture toward China's adversaries, in the belief that such a stance would help maintain the levels of internal mobilization and commitment necessary to combat ideological decay.

More moderate leaders, in contrast, have considered economic cooperation with more advanced countries to be a prerequisite for the rapid modernization of China's industry, agriculture, and military forces, and thus for ensuring China's security and sovereignty in a threatening world. They believe, moreover, that a strong central government can enable China to avoid becoming dependent on any foreign power and to resist cultural contamination from abroad. When more moderate leaders have been in power, as in the early 1950s, the late 1970s, and the early 1980s, they have been willing to see China actively import technology, capital, and even institutions and culture from abroad.

A second change in China's foreign relations over the last thirty years has been Peking's shift of alignment from East to West, from alliance with the Soviet Union in the 1950s to alignment with the United States, Western Europe, and Japan in the late 1970s. Although more recent developments have partially reversed this transformation, even today China's interests lie much more with the West than with the Soviet Union.

This reorientation of China's global posture occurred, as we have seen, in both the economic and the political spheres, involving not only the redefinition of China's friends and adversaries but also fundamental shifts in Chinese trading patterns. In the 1950s, Peking not only was engaged in close military and strategic cooperation with the Soviet Union but also conducted, by the end of the decade, about two-thirds of its trade with the socialist bloc. In the late 1970s, similarly, China linked itself both strategically and economically with the West. Just as Chinese leaders stressed their common security interests with the United States and its allies, so too did they direct more than 90 percent of their trade to the West.

But China did not move smoothly from alliance with the Soviet Union to alignment with the United States. Instead, it passed through a long intermediate period, corresponding to the decade of the 1960s, in which it asserted its opposition to both superpowers and identified itself with the Third World, before engaging in rapprochement with the United States in the early 1970s.

Peking's changing position vis-à-vis the two superpowers was, in part, a response to the changing policies of the Soviet Union and the United States toward China. The creation of the Sino-Soviet alliance in 1950 was largely a reaction to signs of American hostility to the CCP: Washington's refusal to respond positively to Communist overtures in the middle and late 1940s, its economic and military assistance to Chiang Kai-shek in the final stages of the Chinese Civil War, and its continued recognition of the Nationalist government even after it had been driven off the Mainland. The Sino-Soviet split, in turn, was a response to what the Chinese perceived as the strategic and economic unreliability of the Soviet Union in the late 1950s. And the Sino-American accommodation was the result of the military confrontation between China and the Soviet Union in 1969, as well as the overtures made to Peking both publicly and privately by the Nixon administration over the following months.

Although Peking's international realignment was clearly a reaction to these specific developments in its relations with the Soviet Union and the United States, it can also be understood as a reflection of the changing international balance of power since World War II. In the early postwar years, the United States enjoyed both economic and military preeminence and sought to use that power to contain and encircle its adversaries in Moscow and Peking. That unequal distribution of power was one reason why China and the Soviet Union drew closer together in the early 1950s.

By the end of the decade, however, China had concluded that the international balance had begun to shift. The launching of the Soviet sputnik led Mao Zedong to the conclusion that, as he put it in late 1957, the "East Wind" was prevailing over the "West Wind"; and the emergence of a large number of newly independent countries in Asia and Africa in the late 1950s and 1960s presaged the emergence of a potentially powerful counterweight to both superpowers. When Peking and Moscow proved unable to agree on the significance of these two developments, the Chinese were confident that the emerging parity between the United States and the Soviet Union, and the rise of an assertive and independent Third World, would allow them to assume a posture of hostility toward both superpowers through most of the 1960s.

The shifting military balance between the Soviet Union and the United States since that time can also explain China's alignment with the West in the late 1970s, and the signs of greater independence from the United States more recently. Following the Cuban missile crisis of 1962, the Soviet Union launched a determined program to bring its strategic and conventional forces to a level of equality, if not supremacy, vis-à-vis the United States, and then sought to use its greater military power to expand its influence in the Third World in the 1970s. The agony of the Vietnam War produced a general revulsion in the United States against foreign military involvement and led to substantial reductions in American defense spending in the 1970s. These developments caused China to conclude that some sort of Sino-Western alignment would be required to restore the international balance against a rapidly expanding Soviet Union, and thus encouraged Peking to seek first a rapprochement, and then a degree of alignment, with the United States in the 1970s. More recently, however, the Chinese have judged that the international and internal difficulties of the Soviet Union, coupled with the increases in defense spending in the United States, have somewhat redressed the strategic imbalance. Accordingly, they perceive the international situation as being more conducive, once again, to a posture of independence from both superpowers.[29]

A third change in China's foreign relations since 1949 has been a marked increase in the resources, both material and diplomatic, that China brings to its international affairs. In 1949, Mao Zedong could accurately describe China as a "semi-colony," whose strength had been sapped by decades of revolution, civil war, and foreign invasion. From that position of weakness three decades ago, China has now become, in Jonathan Pollack's useful phrase, a "candidate superpower" whose voice is heard on a wide range of international

---

29. Xinhua, 20 December 1982, in *FBIS,* 20 December 1982, pp. A2–3; and Xinhua, 23 December 1982, in *FBIS,* 23 December 1982, pp. A1–3.

issues, and which plays a significant role in the global strategic balance.[30]

Consider first China's diplomatic posture. Through the early 1950s, for example, China enjoyed formal diplomatic relations with only twelve countries outside the socialist camp and was excluded from the United Nations. In the 1960s, however, many of the newly independent nations of the Third World chose to recognize Peking rather than Taipei, so that by the fall of 1971, the People's Republic was able to gain a seat in the United Nations. By the end of 1982, Peking had diplomatic relations with 125 other nations and was a member of most major international economic organizations.

The expansion of China's diplomatic ties overseas has been accompanied by the globalization of Peking's foreign policy. In the early 1950s, China was preoccupied primarily with its relations with the two superpowers, with Asia, and, to a lesser degree, with the other Communist states. Later in the decade, Peking showed a growing interest in the newly emerging countries of Africa and the Middle East. In the early 1960s, as its split with the Soviet Union widened, China began to devote its attention to improving relations with Western Europe and Japan. Today, Peking has begun to show some interest in Latin America and the Caribbean—the part of the world that is most distant from China, and thus most remote from China's security concerns. In this way, the focus of China's foreign policy has steadily spread outward from Asia to include most of the world. In material terms, China may remain only a regional power, but its foreign policy has acquired global scope.

There has been a similar increase in China's economic activity. Since 1970, China's trade has been rising rapidly, both in absolute terms and as a proportion of the PRC's gross national product. In the 1970s, China's two-way trade increased nearly tenfold, from around $4 billion to about $40 billion in current prices. Over the same decade, trade also rose from an estimated 3.5 percent of China's GNP to approximately 9.4 percent. Moreover, as its trade has grown, the PRC has become a significant trading partner of an

30. Jonathan D. Pollack, "China's Potential as a World Power," P-6524 (Santa Monica, CA: Rand Corporation, July 1980).

increasing number of states. In 1981, China became the third largest importer of American goods in Asia, following Japan and South Korea. That same year, it was Japan's fifth largest trading partner, after the United States, Saudi Arabia, Indonesia, and Australia.

How has China been able to transform itself from relative weakness to relative strength in the space of thirty years? In part, it is the result of China's sheer size and population, which help give the PRC the world's largest standing army, its third largest navy, and its third largest air force. In part, it is due to the substantial economic development that has occurred since 1949, giving China, at about $400 billion, the world's sixth largest GNP, an industrial sector equal to that of Japan in the early 1960s, and the world's third largest strategic nuclear force. Moreover, these resources are at the command of a powerful central government, in sharp contrast to the political fragmentation that characterized the country before 1949.

In addition, Chinese leaders have employed their available material resources with great skill. They have, beginning in the mid-1950s, undertaken a surprisingly large foreign aid program, in some cases providing economic and technical assistance to countries whose per capita income was higher than China's. Through the clarity and self-assurance of their foreign policy doctrine and their ability to impress and persuade both official and unofficial visitors, Chinese leaders have made their country a major commentator on world developments. On numerous occasions—in Korea, in the Taiwan straits, along the Sino-Soviet and Sino-Indian frontiers, and in Vietnam—they have shown that they are willing to use their limited conventional military resources in active support of their foreign policy goals, even against more powerful adversaries. And it is widely believed, both in Asia and in other parts of the world, that China is likely to become an increasingly significant force in world politics over the rest of the century.

These trends, to be sure, should not be overstated. By most measurements of national power, China remains a poor country, with a low GNP per capita, obsolescent industrial technology, and relatively primitive weaponry. There are, as well, real limits to the speed with which China can develop its economy and modernize its armed forces. For the foreseeable future, China will remain an Asian, rather

than a global, power. Nonetheless, China has been able to attain—
and is likely to maintain—a degree of influence in world affairs far
beyond that which might have been predicted from its present-day
material resources alone.

The rise in China's international status helps explain the final
change in China's foreign relations: its transformation from a revolutionary power to a reformist—even, for a brief period, a conservative—state. For most of its first two decades, China adopted a radical
foreign policy. During the 1950s, it sought to force its way into the
international system controlled by the United States; during the
1960s, it tried to mobilize a coalition of revolutionary regimes and
movements to destroy that system. With the end of the Cultural
Revolution, however, China quickly emerged from its self-imposed
isolation. During the 1970s, China fully integrated itself into the
postwar international order. The first part of the decade marked
Peking's full entry into the international political system, as indicated
by its membership in the United Nations and its related agencies and
the expanding roster of countries with whom it enjoyed formal
diplomatic relations. By the end of the decade, China had become an
active participant in the international economic order as well, thereby obtaining access to foreign capital, technology, and markets.

Writing in *World Politics* in April 1974, the political scientist Tang
Tsou suggested two preconditions for the deradicalization of the
foreign policy of a revolutionary state such as China: First, it would
have to come to perceive the existing international order as strong
and enduring; and second, it would have to believe that it had
acquired a "fair stake and a proper place" in that order.[31] China has
now met both of those conditions. The very endurance of the postwar
system—despite the emergence of the newly independent states of
the Third World, despite the expansionism of the Soviet Union,
despite the growing fatigue of the United States, and despite the
endeavors of radical forces opposed to that order—has doubtless
convinced Peking that it is likely to be around for a few more
decades. And China's rising international status has also assured

31. Tang Tsou, "Statesmanship and Scholarship," *World Politics* 26:3 (April
1974): 428–50.

most of its leaders that Peking has finally earned the place in the international order that it deserves.

This is not to say that the People's Republic will be a status quo power. The tentative and abortive experimentation with such an approach in the late 1970s demonstrates that it enjoys little support in Peking. As a developing country committed to a progressivist international doctrine, China will find much to be reformed in international relations. But Peking's growing integration into the world community explains why Chinese foreign policy is not as radical or disruptive as it was in the past. China may seek to remake international politics, but it is doing so from within, rather than from without.

Continuities

As noted earlier, Chinese spokesmen tend to emphasize continuity, rather than change, in the PRC's foreign relations since 1949. And indeed, despite all the transformations that have occurred over the last thirty years, some fundamental continuities are apparent. Here, we will consider several such enduring themes—themes that may have been submerged by events on occasion but nonetheless have dominated the overall record of Chinese foreign policy.

Of these continuities, none is more important than China's concern with its security and sovereignty. Protecting China against foreign attack and warding off attempts at encirclement have been Peking's paramount foreign policy goals since 1949. Nearly equal importance has been assigned to issues of sovereignty and status, such as gaining diplomatic recognition from the United States, securing representation in the United Nations, renegotiating China's borders with its neighbors, reunifying Taiwan with the Chinese mainland, and recovering Chinese sovereignty over Hong Kong.

To a very large degree, these concerns are the understandable product of the modern history of China: China, after all, was the victim of repeated military pressure from foreign powers from the Opium Wars of the 1840s and 1850s through the Sino-Japanese War of the 1930s and 1940s. Over the course of a century, this pressure resulted in the opening of increasing numbers of Chinese ports to foreign trade, the extension of extraterritorial privileges to foreigners, the steady loss of territory around the periphery of China, the opening of China to foreign investment and missionary work, the cession or lease of ports along the Chinese coast to foreign countries, and the division of China into informal "spheres of influence." Ultimately, the pressure culminated in all-out war with Japan, as Japanese troops invaded first Manchuria and then China proper, in an attempt to turn China into a semicolony. This searing experience leads many Chinese to assign high priority to overcoming what they see as the "national humiliation" of the past.

Since 1949, China has continued to see good reasons for concern about preserving its security and sovereignty. Territories that were once part of China, including Taiwan, Hong Kong, and Macao, presently lie beyond the formal authority of the government in Peking. The two superpowers have, in succession, attempted to construct networks of bases and alliances in order to encircle China militarily and isolate it diplomatically: first the United States, through the system of bilateral and multilateral alliances discussed earlier; and then the Soviet Union, through its military relationships with Afghanistan, Outer Mongolia, and Vietnam, and through its political ties to India. China has, at various times, faced direct threats to its security from all four points of the compass: from Taiwan and the United States to the east, the Soviet Union to the north, Vietnam to the south, and India to the west. Few other major powers have felt as threatened, for such a long period of time, and by such powerful adversaries, as China has.

China's concern with its own security has not, however, led Peking to seek more powerful allies or protectors in a continuous or unquestioning way. Indeed, a second continuity in Chinese foreign policy, and one that we have already touched upon at several points in this essay, is China's ambivalence about turning abroad for economic assistance, advanced technology, or modern institutions. Even those who have advocated doing so have often warned that China might lose its traditional cultural values, or become economically and culturally dependent upon its foreign patrons. In the same way, despite the ancient tradition of "using barbarians to control barbarians," modern Chinese have often been skeptical about the reliability of using one foreign power as a diplomatic counterweight against another. As a result, China has tended to be a somewhat querulous ally, suspicious that its major protector might decide to reach its own accommodation with their common enemy, sacrificing China's national interests in the process.

Thus, while China has undergone cycles of alignment and isolation, reflecting its ambivalence toward interaction with the West, the center of gravity of its modern politics is a commitment to strategic independence and economic self-reliance. These principles require that China take care to preserve the initiative, protect its sovereignty, and ensure its own independence of action when engaging in economic and strategic relationships with stronger powers. As one overview of Chinese foreign policy in late 1982 put it, "Our right to maintain independence and keep the initiative in our own hands is the fruit from ground irrigated with the blood of numerous martyrs. It is the most precious thing in the world. No one can damage it."[32] Now that China's economic, military, and political resources are greater than at any time in its history, this goal of international independence appears finally within reach.

A third continuity involves the conceptual framework that Chinese policymakers have brought to their analysis of international affairs. In their view, global politics is the story of the rise and fall of hegemonic powers: the emergence of nations with enough resources to seek global domination, the rise of leaders committed to a strategy of international expansion, the initial success of that hegemonic strategy, the gradual formation of a united front of weaker powers against it, the eventual overextension of the expansionist nation as it encounters the determined resistance of the opposing united front, and its gradual decline into passivity.[33] In Chinese eyes, this pattern has been repeated at least five times in modern world history, with the role of would-be world hegemon played at various times by Spain and Portugal, Britain and France, Germany and Japan, the United States, and, most recently, the Soviet Union.

32. Radio Beijing, 30 November 1982, in *FBIS,* 9 December 1982, p. A5.
33. The best analysis of the Chinese world view can be found in Davis B. Bobrow, Steve Chan, and John A. Kringen, *Understanding Foreign Policy Decisions: The Chinese Case* (New York: Free Press, 1979).

This view of the world has encouraged Chinese leaders to place their own security and sovereignty in a global context. Rather than viewing their security concerns purely in local terms, they have tended to see them in relation to the broader global strategy of the hegemonic power of the moment. Thus, when the United States undertook to "contain" China in the 1950s, it did so as part of its attempt to maintain hegemony over the rest of Asia. Once that bid was irretrievably lost, in the Chinese analysis, Washington was forced to come to terms with Peking. Similarly, the Soviet threat to China in the late 1970s was not viewed in isolation, but rather as part of a global strategy: three "southward thrusts" into the Middle East, Africa, and Southeast Asia that were designed to isolate China and place a stranglehold on the flow of strategic materials to Japan and Western Europe. And signs of Soviet flexibility toward China in the early 1980s are seen as evidence that Moscow has lost the initiative that it enjoyed only a few years earlier.

China's view of international politics as a worldwide struggle against imperialism has also led Peking to consider itself as a leader of the world's "progressive" forces, which it encourages to join China in a united front against the hegemonic powers of the day. On occasion, as during the Cultural Revolution, Peking has defined "progressivism" extremely narrowly, to include only a handful of radical Maoist insurgency movements. More commonly, China has believed all (or at least most) Third World governments to constitute this international progressive force. This reflects not only China's reading of Marxism-Leninism but also its sense of a common history with the other developing countries of Asia, Africa, and Latin America.

And yet, China has often appeared to be somewhat aloof and detached from these progressive undertakings. Even during the radicalism of the 1960s, Peking assigned relatively few resources to the support of friendly revolutionary movements abroad. As part of its support for a New International Economic Order in the 1970s, it promoted the formation of producers' cartels and cooperation among Third World countries, but it simultaneously refused to join either OPEC or the Group of Seventy-seven. China explains its reticence by reference to its limited material resources and its desire to avoid detailed involvement in contentious issues that might split the united front that Peking wishes to form. But perhaps the deeper explanation is China's underlying desire for independence of action. The same force that prevents Peking from engaging in too close an alignment with either superpower has also prevented it from forging too close a relationship with the Third World.[34]

Thus, the approach to international affairs taken by Chinese leaders is shaped by a number of fundamental assumptions: that their foreign policy is rooted in a systematic, scientific, and correct body of doctrine; that global politics is characterized by the Manichaean struggle between imperialism and progressivism; that China has, for the last two hundred years, been a victim of imperialist expansion and pressure; and that China's foreign policy represents the interests not only of the Chinese people but also of the "peace-loving" and "progressive" forces of the rest of the world. This helps produce a final continuity in China's foreign relations: the self-confidence and moralism so characteristic of much of Peking's international behavior.

China's self-confidence is particularly evident in a number of aspects of its foreign relations. It is one of few countries that has been willing to declare its open opposition to both the United States and the Soviet Union. While showing flexibility in its day-to-day diplomacy, it has displayed a rigid attachment to its basic principles and goals. It states forceful and well-articulated positions on virtually every major international issue, from Soviet-American relations to regional conflicts within the Third World. Whether this reflects a pride in China's history and culture, a faith in the innate strength of a billion people, or a confidence in the accuracy of judgments made in accordance with official Marxist-Leninist doctrine, Chinese leaders have usually conveyed a sense of determination and certitude that few other countries have matched.

Chinese policymakers also view international affairs in moralistic terms, with an intensity that occasionally verges on self-righteousness. In their eyes, much of their foreign policy agenda involves

34. On China's aloofness from the Third World, see Samuel S. Kim, *China, the United Nations, and World Order* (Princeton, NJ: Princeton University Press, 1979), chap. 9.

overcoming the legacy of China's unjust and unequal treatment at the hands of the major powers. China's international behavior, therefore, does not reflect simply the rational pursuit of calculated national interest. It also embodies the widely and deeply shared commitment to overcome humiliation, secure redress of past grievances, and achieve a position of equality with all other major powers. "We do not tolerate any encroachment on China's national dignity or interests," Hu Yaobang stated in September 1982. "Having suffered aggression and oppression for over a century, the Chinese people will never again allow themselves to be humiliated as they were before."[35]

Prospects

Chinese foreign policy since 1949, then, has contained elements of both change and continuity. In this essay, we have emphasized four dimensions of transformation: China's involvement with the rest of the world, its position in the ongoing confrontation between the Soviet Union and the United States, its international status and influence, and its satisfaction with the present international system. On all these dimensions, China's international relations have undergone significant change over the last thirty-odd years. At the same time, however, many of the fundamentals of China's foreign policy have remained relatively constant. China's leaders have regularly viewed international politics as a struggle for hegemony among superpowers, have maintained an abiding concern with their security and sovereignty against threats from abroad, have sought to preserve a high degree of independence and initiative in their international conduct, and have tended to identify their country with the developing nations of the Third World, rather than with either of the two superpowers. In a word, the major transformation is China's gradual emergence as a world power, increasingly engaged in the international community; the principal continuity is Peking's desire to overcome the national humiliation of the nineteenth and early twentieth centuries.

In attempting to assess the future of China's foreign policy, it

35. Hu, *Create a New Situation*, pp. 29–30.

seems appropriate to begin by asking whether the four transformations that have marked China's emergence as a major power will continue, or be reversed. Then, we will consider whether the continuities of outlook, objectives, and style that link past and present in China's foreign policy are likely to change.

Will China Again Turn Inward?

China's degree of involvement with the rest of the world has, as we have seen, varied substantially over the last thirty years. Some of the change can be traced to international developments over which China had incomplete control, such as the American embargo of commercial relations with China in the 1950s and 1960s, and the disintegration of the Soviet bloc in the 1960s. But the single most powerful explanation of the cyclical pattern of engagement and isolation in Chinese foreign policy has been the rise and fall of radicalism in the PRC's domestic affairs.

The level of China's international involvement over the rest of the century thus very much depends on the fate of radicalism in China's internal politics. Most observers, both Chinese and Western, doubt that China will ever experience a resurgence of radical xenophobia on the scale of the Cultural Revolution. They therefore do not expect that China will ever again isolate itself as completely from the rest of the world as it did in the late 1960s. But China is expected to remain ambivalent about its ties with the outside world. The international system will continue to be regarded both as a source of valuable technology and capital and as a source of ideas and values that subvert China's established political and cultural order. What is more, the pattern of China's international dealings is likely to be uneven, with increasing suspicion between those localities, organizations, and individuals who have extensive contact with foreigners and those that do not.

As a result of these pressures, the cyclical pattern of engagement and isolation that characterized the first thirty years of the People's Republic is likely to continue, but to be dampened. We may well see periods in which the restrictions on the range and scope of contacts between Chinese and foreigners are relaxed, followed by periods in which the same constraints are tightened. And, as in the past, this process will be closely linked to an ongoing political struggle between those who would seek to modernize China by liberalizing its political and economic institutions and those who believe that China will fall into disorder and instability unless firm political control is maintained. Each period of restriction may produce some irritation in China's relations with foreigners, but is unlikely to cause any fundamental unraveling of the growing web of commercial, diplomatic, educational, and cultural activities that binds China to the rest of the world.

Will China Alter Its Alignment in the Strategic Balance between East and West?

The second variation in China's foreign policy has been Peking's shift from alignment with the Soviet Union in the 1950s to a loose alignment with the United States in the 1970s. As we have seen, the PRC's position in the ongoing Cold War between Moscow and Washington has been determined by China's assessment of the shifting international balance of power, as well as by the specific policies which the two superpowers have adopted towards Peking.

On this score, there is every reason to expect that, for the foreseeable future, China will maintain the relatively independent posture that it adopted in the early 1980s. China will, in other words, maintain an active dialogue with each superpower, avoid confrontation with both, and be completely aligned with neither. Such a policy seems well suited to an international environment that is gradually becoming more multipolar in character. It also fits well with China's long-standing desire to achieve and secure a high degree of independence and initiative in its foreign affairs. But having sketched out the broad outlines of its policy, China must still fill in the details. It must decide whether it will seek a rough equidistance between Moscow and Washington, or whether it will maintain closer relations with the United States than it does with the Soviet Union. This decision will obviously be highly dependent upon the policies that the two superpowers adopt toward China in the years to come.

Maintaining its present course is, of course, not the only possibility for China in its policy toward the United States and the Soviet Union. A dramatic change in the relative power of the two superpowers might well encourage Peking to forge a closer alignment with the weaker against the stronger. Alternatively, a turn toward radicalism at home would probably lead China to resurrect the "dual adversary" policy of the 1960s, at the expense of its ongoing dialogue with both Washington and Moscow. But neither of these is a particularly likely development. On balance, we can expect China to remain independent of the Soviet Union but also somewhat aloof from the West.

Will China's International Status and
Influence Continue to Increase?

The third change in China's foreign policy since 1949 has been the rise in China's international standing, from its rather isolated and beleaguered position in the early 1950s to its present role as a "candidate superpower." Much of the change is attributable to the real increases in China's military and economic resources, and the skill with which Chinese leaders have employed them. But there has also been a tendency for foreign observers to exaggerate the strength of the PRC, as they overlook the limitations on China's present resources and emphasize its future potential.

China's real resources are almost certain to increase markedly over the rest of the century. Chinese leaders project a growth rate of about 7 percent a year until the year 2000, such that China's gross national product at the end of the century will be quadruple what it was in 1980. China's ability to attain those ambitious targets will depend on the success of the current efforts at economic reform and readjustment and on the fate of the country's ambitious program of population control. And the effect of economic development on China's military capabilities will obviously further depend on a number of fundamental political and strategic choices that have yet to be made, such as the appropriate level of military spending and the mission and structure of the armed forces. But even if China's growth rate is slower than 7 percent (say, the 5 percent projected in the chapter by Bruce Reynolds), and even if a relatively small proportion of national resources are channeled into the military, one can expect that China will, in material terms, become significantly more powerful over the next two decades.

Ironically, however, China's influence in international affairs may not increase as rapidly as its material resources. For one thing, as foreigners have gained greater access to China, they have gained greater familiarity with China's weaknesses as well as its strengths. For another, much of the projected progress in China's economic development and military modernization has long been anticipated by the PRC's neighbors. China's prospects are thus undergoing a process of demythologization, with the somewhat paradoxical result that an effectively modernizing postrevolutionary China looms smaller in most countries' strategic calculations than did a less effectively modernizing revolutionary regime.

Will China Once Again Challenge the Legitimacy of the International Order?

The final transformation of China's foreign policy identified in this essay has been the change in the PRC's orientation toward the international system. In the 1950s, China was a radical state, seeking to break into the international order dominated by the United States; by the 1960s, it had become a revolutionary state, seeking to break up that same pattern of power and influence. The change in American policy toward China helped China to enter the international system it had struggled against for so long. Since then, it has sought only moderate reforms in the international order, largely by supporting Third World demands for a New International Economic Order.

Thus China is no longer an outsider in international politics. Rather, it has earned a position of some stature in the international system. Short of a cataclysmic change in China's domestic affairs, it is very improbable that China will seek to challenge the prevailing international order in the same way that it did in the 1960s, or even the early 1970s. But China's commitment to what it regards as progressive principles, and its remaining differences of interest with the two superpowers, also makes it unlikely that Peking will, over the long run, fully accept the legitimacy of the present international system. For the foreseeable future, China will continue to identify itself with those smaller and weaker countries who seek at least a modicum of change in the international status quo.

But if China feels most comfortable in its role as reformer, it remains to be seen how actively it will actually play the role. As the events of the last decade have illustrated, international reformism conflicts with a number of other goals and orientations that Peking holds dear. Sponsorship of international reform requires China to choose to support some Third World initiatives over others, and thus forces Peking to become more actively engaged in Third World politics at a time of increasing diversity and division within the developing world. Aggressive promotion of international reform might also strain China's political and commercial relations with its major trading partners in the developed world. And yet there is a ready solution to this dilemma: International reform may continue to be a major part of China's foreign policy rhetoric, but, in the final analysis, Peking will probably choose to devote relatively few of its scarce resources to achieving it.

So much for the transformations of the past thirty years. What of the elements of Chinese foreign policy that have remained relatively constant over the last three decades? Are these continuities likely to be enduring, or will they, too, undergo change?

Here, three questions appear particularly relevant to a forecast of China's future foreign policy. First, as China's post-Mao leaders gradually cast aside the constraints of doctrine and move toward greater pragmatism at home, will the basic organizing principles of the foreign policy of the Maoist era—opposition to hegemonism, identification with the Third World, and creation of united fronts against expansionist superpowers—also be modified in favor of a less rigid conceptualization of international affairs? China's foreign policy today is indeed something of an anomaly: It is one of the few areas of life in which the Maoist (and, indeed, the Leninist) imprint remains fully intact. As China becomes increasingly engaged in a broader range of dealings with a wider range of countries, there will be pressure to deal with each issue on its merits, without attempting to portray it as a reflection of an international Manichaean struggle of good against evil.

Nonetheless, doctrinalism is deeply rooted in Chinese culture. The faith in official orthodoxy as a means of providing coherence to policy, discipline to organization, and unity to society is not likely to disappear rapidly. Indeed, it is probably wiser to predict a redoctrinalization of Chinese domestic affairs than a total dedoctrinalization of Chinese foreign policy. To be sure, ideological categories may, in both foreign and domestic matters, come to play a lesser role in the future than in the past. A wider range of issues may be considered on purely pragmatic grounds, independent of their doctrinal implications. But the fundamental directions of Chinese foreign policy are likely to be debated in much the same terms as they were during the Maoist years, or indeed as they are today.

Second, now that China has attained substantial international status, achieved greater military power than at any time in its history, and assumed a more active role in the international economy, will its obsession with matters of security and sovereignty gradually decline? In several respects, China can now afford to take a more relaxed view of these issues than in the past. It no longer needs to fear that the Soviet Union and the United States will form a coalition against it. It has achieved an impressive degree of both strategic and conventional deterrence against Moscow. Its relations with Southeast Asia and Japan are, on balance, the best in thirty years. Its relations with India, while still strained, are likely to improve. China could easily be excused, therefore, if it decided that its security position today was vastly superior to that in the fifties, sixties, or seventies.

Nonetheless, there remains a wide range of unresolved issues that will continue to be regarded in Peking as challenges to China's security and sovereignty. These include the continuing American ties to Taiwan, the disputed borders with India and the Soviet Union, the remaining foreign control over Hong Kong and Macao, the festering conflict with Vietnam, the Soviet presence in Afghanistan and Outer Mongolia, the uncertain leanings of Pyongyang, and the latent disputes with a number of Asian neighbors over the limits of China's territorial sea. What is more, even if these particular issues can be resolved, China will always be in the somewhat discomfiting position of being nearly surrounded by major global and regional powers to the north (the Soviet Union), the east (Japan), and the south (India).

The key question is the impact that these factors, in combination, will have on China's foreign policy. Will the steady increase in its power and status enable Peking to reduce its concern with security and sovereignty and concentrate its energies on domestic developments? Will the unresolved issues mentioned above compel China to remain ever-vigilant, and even to develop and maintain a higher level of military preparedness? Or will China choose to supplant the generally defensive goals of the past with a more assertive, even expansionist, posture toward the rest of Asia? No one can tell with certainty, but perhaps the most persuasive scenario is that China will continue to view its security environment with a degree of distrust and defensiveness but will not feel compelled to depart significantly from a line of policy that assigns distinctly greater priority to domestic economic development than to military modernization.

Finally, a new generation of leaders is slowly coming to power in China—leaders who were born during the revolution but reached maturity after the establishment of the People's Republic. Will these new leaders maintain the same style as their predecessors: the same mistrust of stronger allies, the same obsession with initiative and independence, the same ambivalence about forging close relations with the rest of the world? The experience of the other Sinic civilizations in Asia suggests that these cultural problems may gradually decline over time. In Japan, Korea, Taiwan, and Singapore there has slowly emerged what might be described as a new cultural center of gravity, one that synthesizes Western technology, values, and institutions with important elements of traditional culture, and that allows these societies to interact with the West with greater self-confidence. The emergence of such a synthesis mitigates the conflict between those who would emulate the West completely and those who would attempt to exclude its influence entirely.

Similar developments may also occur in China, in time. But there are powerful forces working against them. Ambivalence about the West, while in no way unique to Peking, is probably more intense in China than in any of its neighbors. What is more, that ambivalence is sustained by two fundamental facts: first, that the overwhelming majority of China's population is rural, and has relatively little contact with foreigners; and second, that the Chinese leaders of the new generation, who reached political maturity in the 1950s, lack the formative exposure to Western ideas and institutions that their predecessors enjoyed in the 1930s and 1940s. Bridging the gap between nativism and cosmopolitanism will therefore be vastly more difficult in China than in Korea or Taiwan. And the task will only be

complicated by the fact that, as indicated above, the divisions between those who deal with foreigners and those who do not are likely
to widen, not narrow, over the rest of the decade.

Given the volatility of China's international relations in the recent
past, it is not surprising that most projections of China's future
foreign policy take the form of rather extreme scenarios. In Japan,
one widely shared image is of a China in collapse: a country whose
attempts at economic modernization have failed, whose political and
social order is in chaos, and which represents little more than a
geopolitical vacuum in the heart of East Asia, inviting intervention
by the major powers. In India and Southeast Asia, the prevailing
view is of a dragon rampant: a China whose attempts at economic
modernization have succeeded and which is deploying its augmented
stock of military, economic, and political resources to assert a degree
of hegemony over the rest of Asia. In the United States, there is the
expectation—perhaps now only a hope—that the historical relationship between the American and Chinese peoples can finally be
translated into a close economic partnership and an intimate strategic
alignment against the Soviet Union. In the Soviet Union, strategists
dream similar dreams, but with the roles reversed.

What this analysis suggests, however, is that the future of China's
foreign relations is likely to reflect less extreme changes. To be sure,
there will be some important transformations. China's resources are
likely to increase; the role of ideology in its foreign policy is likely to
decline. The restrictions on foreigners seeking to teach, work, learn,
and profit in China may rise and fall. China's policies toward specific
issues and its relationships with particular countries will doubtless
change over time.

But these changes are likely to be relatively modest in comparison
with the more sweeping and fundamental transformations of the past.
Instead, it is the continuities that will be impressive. China will most
likely try to maintain an independent posture vis-à-vis both superpowers. It will continue to assert its identity with the rest of the Third
World, without adopting a confrontationist stance toward the more
developed nations. It will remain ambivalent about its economic and
cultural relationships with the rest of the world, but it will not try to

break them. Its principal foreign policy concerns will remain the preservation of sovereignty, security, and independence in a world characterized by an ongoing struggle against international hegemonism. Failing a major (and unlikely) change in the international balance of power, in other words, the pattern of foreign relations that China has established in the early 1980s is likely to continue for the foreseeable future.

Contributors

Harry Harding is a Senior Fellow in the Foreign Policy Studies Program at The Brookings Institution in Washington, D.C. He did his undergraduate work at Princeton, and received his Ph.D. in political science at Stanford in 1974. He taught for one year at Swarthmore College, and for twelve years at Stanford, before joining the Brookings staff in the fall of 1983. He is the author of *China and the U.S.: Normalization and Beyond* (1979) and *Organizing China: The Problem of Bureaucracy, 1949–1976* (1981), as well as many other works on Chinese domestic politics, foreign policy, and U.S.-China relations.

Michael H. Hunt is presently Professor of History at the University of North Carolina at Chapel Hill. He received his Ph.D. from Yale in 1971. His publications include the prize-winning *Frontier Defense and the Open Door* (1973), a wide range of articles on Sino-American relations, and most recently *The Making of a Special Relationship: The United States and China to 1914* (1983). He is now completing a general interpretive work on the ideology of U.S. foreign policy and pursuing research on Chinese foreign policy in the 1940s and 1950s.

Steven I. Levine is Associate Professor in the School of International Service at The American University in Washington, D.C. He received his undergraduate education from Brandeis, and his Ph.D. from Harvard in 1972 in political science and Far Eastern languages. A student of East Asian politics and international communist affairs, he has written extensively on Chinese foreign policy, especially Sino-Soviet and Sino-American relations. He is the author of a forthcoming study of the Chinese revolutionary civil war of the 1940s, entitled *World Politics and Revolutionary Power in Manchuria*.

Kenneth Lieberthal is Professor of Political Science at the University of Michigan. A graduate of Dartmouth College, he received his Ph.D. from Columbia University in 1972. He is the author of *A Research Guide to Central Party and Government Meetings in China, 1949–1975* (1976), *Revolution and Tradition in Tientsin, 1949–52* (1980), and many articles and monographs on Chinese domestic and foreign affairs. Before assuming his present position at Michigan in the fall of 1983, he served for twelve years as a member of the political science faculty at Swarthmore College.

Robert B. Oxnam is President of the Asia Society. He received his Ph.D. in Chinese history from Yale University. He is the author of *Ruling from Horseback* (1975), a study of the Manchu conquest of China, and is the co-editor, with Michel Oksenberg, of *Dragon and Eagle: United States-China Relations, Past and Future* (1978). After serving on the faculty of the Department of History of Trinity College, he became the first Director of the China Council of the Asia Society in 1975, and President of the Asia Society in 1981.

Jonathan D. Pollack is a member of the professional research staff of the Political Science Department of the Rand Corporation. His research interests include Chinese strategic affairs and foreign policy decision making, U.S.-Chinese relations, Sino-Soviet relations, Chinese technological development, and U.S. security policy in the Western Pacific. A graduate of Rutgers University, he received his Ph.D. from the University of Michigan in 1976. His publications include *Security, Strategy, and the Logic of Chinese Foreign Policy* (1982), *The Sino-Soviet Rivalry and Chinese Security Debate* (1982), and the forthcoming *The Lessons of Coalition Politics: Sino-American Security Relations*.

Bruce Reynolds received a B.A. in Chinese studies from Yale, and a Ph.D. in economics from the University of Michigan in 1974. He lives with his wife and family in Schenectady, New York, where he teaches economics at Union College. His articles include "Two Models of Chinese Agricultural Development" (1978), and other analyses of the Chinese economy and U.S.-Chinese economic relations. He has been a regular visitor to the People's Republic, and spent six months in Peking in 1981 as a visiting scholar at the Institute of Industrial Economics of the Chinese Academy of Social Sciences.

Index

Subject entries in this index refer to People's Republic of China unless subentry indicates otherwise.

Afghanistan, 113, 119, 121, 123, 131, 138, 165, 195, 197, 210; as issue in Sino-Soviet relations, 166, 167; Soviet invasion of, 120, 157, 193, 198, 199, 220

Africa, 22, 73, 117, 187–88, 206

Agriculture, 50, 56, 62, 73, 81, 105–06; growth rate in, 75, 104; price stability, 76; trade in, 71, 82, 87–88, 95, 96, 98; wet-rice, 74. *See also* Grain trade

Air force, 131, 207

Albania, 189

Algeria, 188

Andropov, Yuri, 106, 167, 197

Army, 30, 34, 46, 47, 52, 207

ASEAN. *See* Association of South East Asian Nations (ASEAN)

Asia, xiii, xiv, 112–14, 117; issues in China's policy toward, 125–38; China as competitor and cooperator with, 127–28, 129; China's relations with, xii–xiii, 107–45; cultural center of gravity, 221; polarization of international politics, 157; prospective role of China in, x, 142–45; views of China, 131–32, 138–42, 169–70

Asian and Pacific Council (ASPAC), 118

Asian policy: issues in, 125–38

Association of South East Asia (ASA), 118

Association of South East Asian Nations (ASEAN), 93, 111, 118, 119, 122, 128, 130, 142, 145; China's relations with, 120, 123, 137–38, 140, 143; membership, 113

Australia, 86, 87, 88

Autarky, 83, 113, 129, 191–92, 202–03

Autonomy, 5, 127. *See also* Dependency/autonomy conflict

Backwardness, 35, 67, 111, 169, 207

Balance of power, 130, 143; international, 114, 153–54, 180, 190, 204–05. *See also* Strategic balance of power, international

Bandung, 123, 124, 125, 184, 187

Bandung Conference(s), 116, 188

Bhutan, 138, 141

Border conflict(s), 35, 39, 127, 158, 220; willingness to use force in, 207. *See also* Sino-Soviet entries

Border security, 3, 17, 125, 129, 130, 138, 209; U.S., 2. *See also* Peripheral areas; territorial bounds

Boxers, 26, 27, 31, 36, 188

Brazil, 84, 92, 95

Brezhnev, Leonid, 106, 167, 197

British in China, 9, 10, 28, 29

Buddhism, 7, 15, 20, 34

Bureaucracies, bureaucrats, 26, 46, 49, 58, 69, 78, 80

Burma, 114, 115, 120, 126, 137, 138; revolutionary movement in, 136, 184

Cambodia, 113, 118, 120, 121, 122, 123, 131, 140, 198; China's aid to, 128; government-in-exile, 123; Vietnamese invasion of, 130, 193

Canada, 86, 87, 88
Cancun Conference, 93, 95
Capital, 58, 62, 78, 90–93, 95, 96, 134;
  international flows of, 72, 90–93
Capital-intensive goods, 98–99, 100
Capital stock, 87, 93
Caribbean, 2, 206
Carter, James Earl, 40, 194
CCP. *See* Chinese Communist Party
  (CCP)
Central America, 2, 198
Central planning, 45, 46, 48, 72, 78–79,
  97, 207; relaxation of, 80
Central work conferences, 61–62, 63, 64,
  65
Chiang Kai-shek, 10, 33, 204; *China's
  Destiny,* 17
China: embodiment of strength and virtue
  in people of, 26–27, 28, 29, 34; as
  moral civilization, 44; perceptions of,
  x–xii, 111–13, 131–32, 138–42, 151,
  169–70; as political abstraction, 124;
  political and cultural influence of, 138;
  position of dominance in Asia, 5, 113
  (*see also* Regional power, China as);
  relative weakness of, 29–30; sense of
  cultural superiority, 10, 20, 21, 126. *See
  also* Global power
China Ocean Shipping Company, 128–29
Chinese Civil War, 47, 204
Chinese Communist Party (CCP), 8–10,
  17, 27, 58, 65, 68, 80, 180; centraliza-
  tion of power in, 75; cosmopolitanism
  and populism of, 33–34; defining international position of China, 147–49;
  links with Southeast Asian parties,
  137–38, 139, 140, 143, 144; management of economy, 57; membership, 58–
  59; Northern Expedition, 32; power of,
  45, 58, 59–60, 64, 66, 103; purge of,
  151; and Sino-Soviet alliance, 182–83;
  and Sino-Soviet split, 185–86
Chinese people: embodiment of strength
  and virtue, 26–27, 28, 29, 34
"Chronicle of the Warring States," 7
Closed-door policy, 44, 52–53
Coal, 57, 76, 80, 97, 101, 103
Cold War, 2, 4, 43, 148, 216
Colonialism, 125, 136, 179

Colonization: peripheral areas, 11–14, 18
Communications, 30, 35, 57
Communism, 6, 115. *See also* Chinese
  Communist Party; Marxism-Leninism
Communist countries, 68; of Asia, 120–
  21, 123–25. *See also* Socialist bloc
Compradors, 23, 26
Confucianism, 24, 28
Conservative state, 208; aligned, 192–95
Constitutional monarchy, 25
Consumer goods, 56, 60, 66–67, 75; im-
  port-substitution in, 83, 84
Contact with foreign culture. *See* Foreign
  contacts
Continental economy, 72, 73–74, 75
Continental size, 81, 127, 173, 207; and
  role in international economy, 97, 101
Cosmopolitanism, viii, xii, 6–7, 27–28,
  29, 32, 109, 202–03, 221; of Chinese
  Communists, 33–34; in response to hu-
  miliation, 19–27; tension with popul-
  ism, 36
Cuba, 3, 165, 193, 198, 205
Cultural integrity, ix, 44–45, 64
Cultural relations, xii, 69, 107, 202
Cultural Revolution, 10, 18, 36, 43, 45,
  51–52, 54, 57, 68, 141, 151, 195, 201,
  202, 208, 212; created tensions in political system, 58; effect on foreign relations, 188–89, 190, 191; effect on
  overseas Chinese, 134; emergence
  from, 71; and foreign trade, 90; Soviet
  concern about, 152; xenophobia, 215
Cultural superiority, 10, 20, 21, 126
Culture, 11, 15, 20–21; barbarization of,
  6–7, 36, 203; core of, 11, 17; decline
  of, 23, 26; traditional elite, 26, 206
Czechoslovakia, 52, 152, 190

Dairen, 183
Dalai Lama, 120
Debt, international, 91–92
Decentralization, 75, 80, 104
Deng Xiaoping, 35, 53, 55, 59–63, 65, 86,
  106, 137, 197; economic development
  model, 142; and Sino-American rela-
  tions, 157, 194; theory of the three
  worlds, 117, 192
Deng era, 135

Dependence, xiv, 150, 155, 160–61; cultural, 210
Dependency/autonomy conflict, 4, 27–36, 37, 42
Developing countries, 84–85, 88, 94, 97, 99, 128; China as, 72, 73, 75, 170; foreign debt, 90, 91. *See also* Third World
Diplomacy, 17, 21, 31, 59, 201, 206, 208, 213; Afro-Asian, 116; balance-of-power, 140; bilateral, multilateral, 118; dual-track, 137, 144
Division of labor, 100, 103, 183
Doctrinalism, 213, 219–20. *See also* Ideology
Domestic policy, 27, 43, 156; effect on foreign policy, viii–ix, 43–70, 143, 151, 157–58, 202–03; radicalism in, 215–16, 217; reform of, 59–60, 63, 65, 69
Dual adversary strategy, 152, 153, 217
Dulles, John Foster, 182

East Asia, xii, 222; China's relations with, 97, 100–01, 103; exports, 97–99; horizontal division of labor, 100–01, 103; regional economy, 72, 75; resource endowment, 72–73, 74, 75, 81, 97
East Germany, 103–04
Eastern Europe, 92, 101, 149, 165, 197; economic reforms, 75, 103–04
Economic development (growth), 25, 45, 156, 158, 180, 207, 217, 221; Asian, 113–14; and China as global power, 172–73; debates on, 34; economic reforms and, 104, 105; extensive, intensive, 79–80, 82; factionalism and, 68–69; as goal, 72, 75–78, 81; Maoist era, 49–50, 53–54, 56, 135–36; models of, 36, 115–16, 135–36; post-Mao period, 55, 56–58, 62, 143; and security considerations, 37; and Sino-Soviet alliance, 180–81; strategies for, 46, 51
Economic imperialism, 23–24, 25–26
Economic planning, 65, 75, 183. *See also* Central planning
Economic policy, ix, 72, 82, 96
Economic reform, ix, xii, 59, 64, 67–68, 80, 217; and international economic role, 103–05
Economic relations, xii, 199–200, 202,

203, 206–07, 208; with West, 191–92, 194–95, 196. *See also* Foreign trade
Economic resources, viii. *See also* Resource endowment
Economic stability (goal), 72, 75, 76, 77, 81–82, 103, 104
Economy, ix, 71, 72, 82, 96; administered, 69, 104, 105; constraints on, 67, 72; effect on trade, 72–82, 85, 86, 88, 89, 95, 96; and foreign capital, 90–92; imperialism in, 23–24, 25–26; goals of, 75–78, 81–82; institutions of, 78–81; and new international economic order, 94–95; structural characteristic, 72–75, 81; urban, 56–57. *See also* International economic system
Education, 24, 25, 30, 57, 58, 67, 156
Efficiency, 77, 80, 81, 82
Egypt, 73
Eisenhower, Dwight, 182
Elites, elitism, 15, 18, 28, 49
Energy, 57, 67, 69; export of, 97, 101–03. *See also* Coal; Petroleum
Equity (goal), 72, 75, 76, 77, 80–82, 103
Ethnic Chinese in Asian states, xiii, 16–17, 18–19, 32, 35, 110, 115, 122, 133–35, 139, 140
Ethnic groups, xiii. *See also* National minorities
Europe, viii, 101. *See also* Eastern Europe; Western Europe
European Economic Community (EEC), 79, 99
Expansionism, 5–6, 109, 110, 208; Chinese, 126, 140, 141, 144
Exports, 28, 61, 71, 87, 97–99, 101–03, 128; policy regarding, 84, 105

Factionalism, 54, 55, 58, 68–69
Far Eastern Freight Conference, 129
Feudalism, 1, 3–4
First Five Year Plan (FFYP), 34, 43, 50, 180–81, 183
Foreign aid, 62, 142, 195, 207; China's need for, 24, 30, 34, 36, 156–57, 161, 173, 180, 202; Chinese ambivalence toward, 210–11; supplied by China, 117, 120, 128, 131, 152, 184, 187. *See also* Military aid

Foreign contacts, viii–ix, 28, 29, 35, 37, 45, 64; ambivalence about, 215, 221, 222; changes and continuities in, 177–78, 186, 188, 191–92, 194–95, 199–200, 202, 203, 211, 215–16, 221–22; cyclical pattern of, 215–16; ideological contamination in, 36, 65. See also Cosmopolitanism; Humiliation
Foreign exchange, 67, 102, 103
Foreign investment, ix, 61, 62, 93, 191–92, 210
Foreign policy, vii–x, xiii–xiv, 4, 27, 34, 167, 168, 222–23; ambivalence in, ix–x; anomaly of, 219; changes and continuities in, 177–223; domestic politics and, 43–70; focus on Asia, 107, 110; future prospects, 214–23; globalization of, 206; goals of, 115–25; historical perspective on, 1–42; periodization of, 179–201; power-oriented approach to, 36, 41–42; strategy of, and China's role as global power, 173–76
Foreign trade, ix, 15, 18, 29, 54, 66, 75, 76, 195, 210; with Asian countries, 107, 111, 115–16; during Cultural Revolution, 188; early, 6, 7, 28; effect of domestic economy on, 72–82, 105; level and direction of, 83–87, 95–96; Maoist era, 57–58; partners in, 203, 206–07; ratios, 84; rise in, 206–07; Sino-Soviet alliance and, 181, 185; size of, partners in, 56, 71, 72, 85, 96, 219; state monopoly of, 72, 79
Foreigners in China, 65, 218, 222
Four Modernizations, 34, 43, 62, 63
France, 3, 16, 17, 30–31, 186, 211
Fujian, 11, 17, 21, 134

Gang of Four, 55, 62, 191, 192–93, 202
Generalized System of Preferences, 99
Geneva Conference, 1954, 121
Germany, 16, 31, 211. See also East Germany
Global posture: changes in, 201–09
Global power: China as, 109–14, 125, 154, 169–70, 172, 173, 206, 208, 214
Government, 8, 50, 57, 66, 68, 207; First Ministry of Machine-Building, 79; Materials Supply Bureau, 81; Ministry of

Foreign Affairs, 188; Ministry of Foreign Trade, 100; Russian staff on, 48
Grain trade, 71, 76, 86, 87–88, 92, 96
Great Britain, 15, 16, 17, 24, 31; hegemony, 22–23, 211. See also British in China
Great Leap Forward (GLF), 18, 34, 43, 45, 50, 51, 54, 185
Green Revolution, 74
Gross national product (GNP), 73, 207, 217; per capita, 170, 207
Group of Seventy-seven, 93, 95, 212
Gu Yanwu, 7
Guangdong, 11, 134
Gulf of Campeche, 102
Guomindang, 148

Haig, Alexander, 40
Han, viii, 6, 7, 11, 14, 17, 21, 38
Hanjian (Chinese traitors), 10
Harding, Harry, xiii
Hart, Liddell, xiii, 175
Heavy industry, 45, 60, 67, 79; emphasis on, 49, 56–57, 65
Hegemonism (hegemony), 8, 10; Chinese opposition to, 154, 179, 219; in global politics, 211–12, 223; regional, 109, 110; Soviet, 117, 124, 157, 165, 168, 177, 198, 211, 212; superpower, 114, 118, 125, 146, 192, 193, 200, 214; threat of Chinese, 222; U.S., 168, 198, 211, 212
Heng Samrin government (Phnom Penh), 123, 141
Himalayan states, 18
Historical consciousness, 1–4, 20, 35, 36–42, 173
History: use of, in Asian policy, 125–27
Ho Chi Minh, 121
Hong Kong, 115, 126, 136, 209, 210, 220; export-promotion policy, 84, 98, 99
Hu na, 196
Hu Yaobang, 137, 179, 197–98, 199, 213
Hua Guofeng, 120
Humiliation: by foreigners, 3, 4, 19–27, 38, 46, 210, 214
Hunan, 27
Hungary, 104
Hunt, Michael, xii–xiii, 109

Ideologies, foreign: sinicization of, 33–34
Ideology: and Asian policy, 110, 111–12, 113, 135–38; contamination of, 29, 60, 61, 65; decline of, 139, 144; and economic policy, 82, 85–86, 88, 89, 90, 95–96, 103; flexibility in, 105, 106; and foreign capital, 92–93; and foreign policy, 153, 202–03, 222; and New International Economic Order, 94; radicalization of, 116; revolutionary, xiii, 39–40; as structural characteristic, 72, 74–75, 81, 97, 103. *See also* Marxism-Leninism
Imperial past, 6–7, 37, 38–39, 44
Imperialism, 1, 17, 19, 39, 136, 212, 213; cultural, 32; economic, 23–24, 25–26
Import-substitution, 83–85, 96. *See also* Autarky
Imports, 28, 75, 89, 90, 207
Incentives, 76, 77, 79, 80, 81, 82
Income(s), 80; equality (goal), 74, 75, 80–81, 82, 103; per capita, 73, 81, 97, 99, 100; urban-rural disparity, 73, 75
India, 22, 74, 75, 95, 116, 119, 128, 129, 143–44; anti-Chinese pogroms, 133; China's relations with, 120, 123–24, 126, 133, 143, 220; foreign trade ratio, 84; grain imports, 88; relation with Soviet Union, 210; revolutionary movements in, 136–37; support for Tibetan rebels, 132–33; view of China, 141–42, 222. *See also* Sino-Indian conflict
Indochina, 17, 25, 119, 130, 150, 184, 194
Indonesia, 19, 95, 99, 110, 113, 118, 136, 187; ethnic Chinese in, 133, 134, 135; grain imports, 88; military coup, 188
Industrialization, 24, 73, 83, 89
Industry, 72, 100, 207; growth rate in, 75, 104; state ownership, control of, 75, 78; steel, 57. *See also* Heavy industry
Inflation, 63–64, 77, 102, 104
Inner Asian border, 35
Inner Mongolia (Mongolian People's Republic), 9, 14, 17, 18, 121
Intellectuals, 20, 25, 26, 46, 52, 57, 59, 66
International affairs: China's changing roles in, 177–223; China's objectives in, 180, 201; Chinese analysis of, 211–15; Chinese influence in, 208; effect on

China's foreign policy, 43, 46, 47, 54, 66, 67, 68, 70
International Development Association, 142
International economic system: China's role in, xii, 71–106, 107, 127, 129, 143, 208
International order, 39; China's challenge to legitimacy of, 218–22; China's integration into, xii, 208–09, 214, 215–16
International Monetary Fund (IMF), 92
International strategic system, 146, 147, 149, 153–56, 159; China's role in, 169–76. *See also* Strategic balance of power, international
Interstate system, 5, 7–8
Investment, 69, 77, 78, 79–80, 81, 91. *See also* Foreign investment
Iran, 113, 114, 120
Isolationism, 4, 143–44, 151, 152–53, 180, 188–90, 201, 202, 208; abandonment of, 190–92; attempts at, 36; as future prospect, 215–16; Maoist era, 51
Israel, 198, 199

Japan, 14, 30, 59, 99, 111, 115, 118, 119, 130, 135, 177, 200, 203; alternative to both market and planned economy, 106; and balance of power, 143–44; China's relations with, viii, 33, 47, 123, 125–26, 143, 206, 220; Chinese influence on, 18; conquered Taiwan, 13; cultural synthesis in, 221; development assistance from, 115; economic cooperation with China, 69–70, 119, 129; exports, 99; foreign aid, 128; freedom of the seas, 94; frontier with China, 138, 144; hegemony, 211; horizontal division of labor, 100; intrusions into China, 15, 17, 20; Meiji, 24; military capabilities, 129, 131; occupied by U.S., 112; oil imports, 101, 102, 103; political and economic development, 113; renascent, 149; role in Asia, 109–10; role as global power, 172; savings rate, 77; takeover of Ryukyu islands, 16; territorial disputes with China, 126; trade with China, 57, 86–87, 100, 127,

Japan, trade with China (*continued*)
207; view of China, 139, 142, 222; wars
with China, 31, 209, 210
Jiang Qing, 52
Jin dynasty, 10, 13
Joint equity ventures, 61, 100, 194–95
Jürcheds, 13

Kampuchea, 62, 123, 198, 199
Kang Youwei, 25
Kangxi emperor, 7
Karmal, Babrak, 121
Kazakhs, 14, 18, 132
Khmer Rouge, 123
Khrushchev, Nikita, 48–49, 51, 122, 150,
183, 185
Kim Il-sung, 121, 189
Kirghiz, 132
Kissinger, Henry, 52
Korea, 17, 25, 31, 35, 105, 113, 197;
Chinese invasion of, 207; civil war, 112;
cultural synthesis in, 221; economic de-
velopment, 74, 115; exports, 84, 98–99;
horizontal division of labor, 100; lost to
Japan, 16; strategic crisis in, 39; trade
with China, 127; in tribute system, 15;
truce in, 150. *See also* North Korea;
South Korea
Korean War, 10, 19, 92, 116, 119, 149–
50, 154, 182; China in, 170, 171; em-
bargo against China, 181
Kreps, Juanita, 86

Labor force, 50, 56, 73, 74
Labor-intensive manufactures, 99–100,
128
Lamaism, 15
Lao, 132
Laos, 113, 121, 122, 123, 133, 136, 138,
141
Latin America, 3, 117, 206
Leaders (leadership), ix, xii, 67, 77, 96,
106, 143, 156; analysis of international
affairs, 211–15; defining role for China,
109, 110, 111, 112–13, 145, 147–49,
209; historical consciousness, 2; moderate, 203; need for strong, 68; new
generation, 64, 221–22; post-Mao, 219;
postrevolutionary, 137, 138; and preservation of cultural integrity, 44, 45;

proselytized model of revolution, 115,
116; radical, 212; and resource endowment, 207, 217; and Sino-American relations, 155, 157, 160, 161, 163, 197–
98; and Sino-Soviet relations, 163–64;
in superpower relations, 146, 174;
views of Asia, 112; views of international relations, 116, 129; world view,
4–5, 6
Leninism, 73, 81, 97; as structural characteristic, 74–75. *See also* Ideology;
Marxism-Leninism
Less-developed countries (LDCs), 99,
128; China as, 72, 73, 75, 170; foreign
debt, 90, 91
Li Hongzhang, 29–30, 31, 32
Li Xiannian, 65
Liang Oichao, 23–25, 26, 33
Lieberthal, Kenneth, xii, 37
Lin Biao, 52, 57, 153, 189
Lin Zexu, 22
Liu Shaoqi, 51

Macao, 210, 220
MacArthur, Douglas, 182
Machinery, 97, 100, 105
Malaya, 184
Malaysia, 110, 113, 128, 136, 137, 187;
ethnic Chinese in, 133, 134
Manchu, 13, 17, 20, 26
Manchuria, 13, 15, 17, 31, 32, 210
Mao Zedong, x, xii, 17, 25–27, 34, 45,
46, 59, 60, 63, 72, 117, 156, 202, 205;
arrogated power to himself, 50, 68;
China as political abstraction to, 124;
developmental model, 141–42; foreign
policy, 47, 48, 49, 50–51, 52, 54, 147–
48, 149, 150, 151, 152, 153, 154, 190,
204; purge of followers of, 66; revolutionary ideology, 136; and Sino-Soviet
alliance, 182; theory of the three
worlds, 117, 192; in Vietnam War, 121–
22; vision of international politics, 129
"Mao Zedong Thought," 36
Maoism, xiii–xiv, 39, 60
Maoist period, 47–55, 56, 113, 127; foreign policy in, 219; revolutionary ideology in, 135
Maritime concerns, 18, 110, 126

Market(s), 103, 105, 106; domestic, 74, 100

Marx, Karl, 27

Marxism, 26, 40; India, 141

Marxism-Leninism, 4–5, 6, 39, 148, 212; sinicization of, 33–34, 36

May Fourth, 25, 26, 27

Meo, 132, 133

Merchant marine, 71, 94

Mexican Revolution, 3

Mexico, 92, 102

Middle East, 198, 206

Middle kingdom world view, 5, 36, 38, 39, 41, 109

Military, 60–61, 62, 68, 69; issues, 129–32; needs of, 30–31. *See also* Air force; Army; Navy

Military aid: supplied by Chinese, 117, 136, 184; from USSR, 181–82, 183, 185

Military force: China's willingness to use, 126–27, 131–32, 141, 170, 176, 207

Military power, viii, 107, 117, 144, 156, 217, 218; in China's strategic role in international system, 170–72, 175; as instrument of policy, 18, 34, 85 (*see also* Military force); USSR, 152, 205

Ming, 11, 13, 15, 20

Missionaries, 28, 29, 32, 210

Modernization, viii, ix, xii, xiv, 128, 129, 132, 139, 222; agricultural, 74; considerations in, 158; debate on, 202–03; economic relations with West and, 194–95; foreign policy and, 157; Maoist era, 54, 55; military, 60–61, 117, 130–31, 162, 207, 217, 218, 221; political, 216; and preservation of cultural integrity, 44–45; and relations to superpowers, 176; requires stable international environment, 143; role of overseas Chinese in, 115, 134

Modernizers: all-around, 44–45, 53, 54, 55, 61; differences between eclectic and, 66–67, 69; eclectic, 44, 45, 53, 54, 55, 66–67, 69

Mongolia, 14, 15, 17, 18, 119, 123, 138; China's relations with, 115, 121, 123–24, 126; as issue in Sino-Soviet relations, 166, 167. *See also* Outer Mongolia; Inner Mongolia

Mongols, xiii, 11, 13, 14, 17, 20, 132

Montagnard rebellion, 133

Multi-fiber Agreement, 93

Nanjing, 32

Nasser, Gamal, 187

National minorities, 132–33, 135

Nationalism, 32–33, 35, 85, 144; Asian, 115, 120; of colonized peoples, 18; India, 141; in/of military, 60–61; sinophobic, 35

Nationalist-Communist united front, 33

Nationalist government, 181, 183; in Taiwan, 19, 180; U.S. support for, 148, 150, 204

Nationalists, 8–10, 14, 32–33; Northern Expedition, 32; U.S. support for, 47, 49, 195, 196

Nativism, nativists, xii, 44, 45, 46, 50, 52–54, 55, 66, 67, 221; cycles of, 202–03; xenophobic, 188–89

NATO, 59, 177

Navy, 30–31, 131, 175, 207

Nehru, Jawaharlal, 125, 141, 187

Neo-Confucians, 20, 22

Nepal, 132, 138

Netherlands, 64

"New citizen," 24, 33

New International Economic Order, 72, 93–95, 117, 128, 191, 193, 197, 212–13, 218; Third World's demands for, 93–95, 125, 218

"New life movement," 33

Newly industrialized countries (NICs), 99, 100, 115, 129

Nixon, Richard, viii, 153–54, 155, 190

Nonaligned Movement, xiii, 93, 95

Nong, 132

North China, 32

North Korea (DPRK), 18, 113, 118, 121, 123, 129, 138, 149, 189; Chinese foreign aid to, 128, 131

North Vietnam, 118, 126, 189

Northeast Asia, 119

Northern Expedition, 32

Nuclear capability, 129, 131, 132, 150, 151, 170, 171–72, 175, 181–82, 183, 185, 207; first, 186

Nyerere, Julius, 95

Oil. *See* Petroleum
Oirat Mongols, 14
OPEC, 93, 212
Open-door policy, 45–46, 53, 65, 67, 199
Opium Wars, 10, 19, 209
Outer Mongolia (Mongolian People's Republic), 14, 17, 18, 121, 210, 220

Pakistan, 114; boundary problems, 115, 126, 138; China's relations with, 120, 121, 123, 141, 143; China's foreign aid to, 117, 128
Pan-Asian ideology, 111, 144–45
Panch Shil (Five Principles of Peaceful Coexistence), 116
Paracel islands, 126, 127
Peasants, 22, 26, 32, 33, 49, 50, 56; and agricultural reform, 105–06; as revolutionary force, 27
Peng Dehuai, 50
People's Liberation Army (PLA), 60–61, 123, 132, 141, 144, 177; strengths and weaknesses of, 130, 131. *See also* Army
Peripheral areas, 12–19, 17–19, 30, 39, 132–33, 210
Petroleum, 57, 80–81; export of, 97, 98, 101–03; offshore fields, 46, 94, 102–03
Philippines, 24, 113, 114, 119, 126, 138; exports, 84, 99; revolutionary movement in, 136–37, 184
Phnom Penh, 122, 130, 141
PLA. *See* People's Liberation Army (PLA)
Pol Pot government, 62, 122, 131
Poland, 91, 92, 197
Pollack, Jonathan, xiii–xiv, 205
Population, 11, 56, 67, 69, 74, 81, 138, 169, 170, 173, 207, 217; Manchuria, 13; rural, 221; Taiwan, 11, 13
Populism, xii, 26, 30–31, 32–34, 36, 188; xenophobic, 28–29, 31–32. *See also* Nativism, nativists
Port Arthur, 183
Ports, 209–10; treaty, 9, 28
Portugal, 211
Post-Mao era, 55–66, 107, 111, 134, 143
Postwar world: China in, 147–58
Power: decline of, 16–17; distribution of, 45–46, 54, 55–56, 59–60, 66, 80; emphasis on, as foundation of state, 30; national myth of, 38–39; nativists' view of, 44; in strategic balance, 147; vulnerability to external, 149, 152
Power relations: Asia, 144; world, 148; U.S./USSR, ix, xiv, 5, 197, 200, 205, 214
"Practical statesmanship," 24–25
Prices, 61, 63, 91, 93; set by state, 105–06; stability of, 75, 77, 80–82, 103, 104, 105
Production, 60, 79
Progressivism, 212–13
Protectionism, 79, 97; U.S., 196
Pye, Lucian, 122
Pyongyang, 119, 121, 220

Qian Qichen, 198
Qin, 8, 9, 11, 23
Qing, viii, 5, 7, 8, 9, 10, 13, 17, 18, 19, 32, 196, 202; in Mongolia, 14; territorial agenda, 11; in Tibet, 15
Qinghai, 15
Quemoy crisis, 185

Radicalism, 151, 180, 188, 208, 212; abandonment of, 190–92; as aligned state, 180–84; effect on China's international relations, 215, 217; as independent state, 184–88
Railroads, 14, 29, 30, 57
Reagan administration, 64, 65, 160, 161, 162, 195–96, 197
Red Guards, 188–89
Reformism, 208–09, 218–19; and independence, 195–201; international, 191, 219; as semi-aligned state, 189–92
Reforms: and future, 66–70; institutional, 79–81; opposition to, 68
Regional power(s), 119; ASEAN as, 113; China as, ix, 107–45, 184, 206, 207–08
Renmin Ribao, 189
Republican period, 7, 9, 14, 15, 19, 32
Republican revolution, 27
Resistance, rebellion, 15, 18, 29, 31, 32, 33
Resource endowment, 103, 127, 180, 201, 205–08, 217–18, 222; as structural characteristic, 72, 73–74, 97

Responsiveness to foreign ideas and material culture. *See* Cosmopolitanism
Revisionism, 51, 53, 136
Revolution(s), 3, 14, 25, 27, 47; and Asian policy, 135–38; models of, 115, 116; as tool to reform China, 25, 26–27
Revolutionary movements: Chinese support for, 94, 109, 110, 114, 116, 119, 123, 124, 131, 136, 137–38, 143, 178, 184, 187, 189, 191, 208, 212–13
Reynolds, Bruce, xii, 217
"Romance of the Three Kingdoms," 7
Ruan Yuan, 22
Rulers, 9, 24, 28. *See also* Leaders (leadership)
Rural sector, 60, 73, 75. *See also* Agriculture
Russia, 13, 14, 31, 36; in China, 15, 16, 17. *See also* Union of Soviet Socialist Republics (USSR)
Russian Revolution, 3, 116
Russo-Japanese War, 13
Ryukyu islands, 15, 16, 17, 31

Savings and investment rate, 77, 127
Science, 45, 67, 156
Second World, 192, 193
Security, ix, 34, 37, 53, 107, 110, 115, 136; collective (Asian, proposed), 118; continuity in, 209–11, 212, 214, 220–21, 223; historically derived definition of, 4, 11–12; Japan, 139; Maoist, 147–48; and Sino-American relations, 62, 63, 65, 160–63; and Sino-Soviet alliance, 167, 180, 181–83; from Soviet aggression, 52, 59, 62, 63; threats to, 119, 129–32, 209–10. *See also* Border security
Security alignments, 157, 159–60
Self-reliance (doctrine), 83, 90, 127, 136, 143, 179; economic, 211; effects of, 172–73. *See also* Autarky
"Self-strengthening," 202
Self-sufficiency, 72, 73, 75, 76, 77, 82
Senkaku (Diaoyutai Islands), 126
Shanghai, 32
Shinohara, Miyohei, 100
Shipping, 128–29
Sihanouk, Prince Norodom, 123

Singapore, 84, 99, 113, 115, 133, 221
Sinicization: of colonial territories, 18, 121; of foreign ideologies, 33–34
Sino-American relations, viii, xiv, 34–35, 40–42, 52, 54, 59, 61, 62, 180, 209; changes and continuities in, 177, 178, 183–84, 186, 190–91, 192, 193–94, 216–17; and foreign investment, 62; linchpin of Deng's strategy, 59; normalization of, 63, 64–65; patterns in, 147, 148–49, 150, 151, 152, 153–58, 159–63, 167, 168, 175–76; and security, 62–63; strains in, 195–98, 204, 205
Sino-Indian conflict, 19, 39, 115, 116, 120, 126, 127, 130, 138, 141–42, 144, 185, 207, 220
Sino-Japanese War, 209
Sino-Soviet alliance, 31, 54, 116, 149–50, 155, 180–84, 203, 204; end of, 152; foreign trade and, 85
Sino-Soviet border, 52, 152, 157, 163, 165, 166, 177, 190; Chinese military power and, 171; clashes at, 39, 115, 126, 138, 144, 149, 152, 220; military forces at, 190, 198, 207
Sino-Soviet relations, 48–49, 61, 143; changes and continuities in, 177, 178, 192, 197, 198, 200, 205, 216–17; conflict in, 121, 137, 152–53; in Cultural Revolution, 52; in Great Leap Forward, 50–51; patterns in, 147, 149–53, 154–58, 163–69, 175–76; third party issues in, 167
Sino-Soviet split, 116, 151, 184–88, 204; and trade, 86, 89
Sino-Vietnamese border, 123, 126, 138, 157, 158, 166, 171
Sinocentrism, 6, 11
Sinophobia, 16–17, 35
Snow, Edgar, 17
Socialism: Soviet model of, 47–48, 49, 50
Socialist bloc, 118, 180, 201, 203, 215; rivalry for leadership of, 185–86; trade with China, 85–86, 89
Son Sann, 123
Song, 20
South Africa, 24, 198, 199
South America, 84
South Asia, 112, 113, 120

South China coast, 20
South China Sea, 110, 126, 131
South East Asian Treaty Organization (SEATO), 118
South Korea, 104, 110–11, 113, 119, 128, 129, 135
South Vietnam, 126
Southeast Asia, 15, 16, 22, 99–100, 112, 117, 119–20; China's relations with, 126, 220; Chinese in, 18–19; views of China, 139–42
Southwest Asia, 113, 117, 120
Sovereignty, ix, xiv, 115, 179, 202, 203; concern with, 209–10, 211, 212, 214, 220–21, 223
Soviet Union. *See* Union of Soviet Socialist Republics (USSR)
Soviet-U.S. power balance, ix, xiv, 5, 43, 146, 147, 148, 153–56, 157, 159, 163, 174–75, 176, 184, 197, 200, 205, 214
Spain, 211
Spheres of influence, 20, 31, 210
Sri Lanka, 128
SRV (Socialist Republic of Vietnam), 126, 138. *See also* Vietnam
Stalin, Joseph, 183
Standard of living, 59, 66–67, 69
State Council, 65, 80
State ownership, 72, 75, 78
Straits of Malacca, 110
Strategic balance of power, international, 43, 193, 197, 200; China in, ix, 146–76, 190–91, 206, 216–17
Strategic concerns, 3, 4, 30, 39–40, 120, 136, 158, 159, 175; and Asian policy, 129–32; and economic policy, 83, 85, 86–87, 88, 90, 95–96; and foreign capital, 92–93; and New International Economic Order, 94–95; Sino-American relations and, 153–54, 194; in Sino-Soviet relations, 164, 169
Students: studying abroad, 178, 181, 195, 200; in urban protests, 32, 33
Subjugation, 9, 10, 23, 29
Sukarno, 119, 188
Sun Yat-sen, 25, 134
Superpowers, 115, 117, 210; activity in Asia, 114, 144; China as, viii, 139, 205–06, 217–18; China's alignment with,

179, 182–83, 190–91, 192, 193, 194, 198, 200–01, 203–05, 211, 213, 216–17, 222; China's relation with, xiii–xiv, 117, 118–19, 147–48, 151, 152, 153, 154–69, 171, 173–76, 218; maritime hegemonism of, 110. *See also* Union of Soviet Socialist Republics (USSR); United States

Tai, 132
Taipei, 136, 144
Taiping Rebellion, 15, 26, 27, 28
Taiwan, 17, 18, 25, 30, 104, 105, 126, 135, 210, 221; China's policy toward, 110–11; colonized by China, 11–13; economic development, 74, 113, 115, 128; exports, 84, 98–99; horizontal division of labor, 100; lost to Japan, 16; military capabilities, 129, 131; trade with China, 127; U.S. relations with, 42, 182, 200
Taiwan issue, xiv, 19, 35, 49, 144, 160, 161, 162, 184, 190, 200, 209, 220; compromise in, 61, 63, 64, 65; elimination of, 193; example of superpower intervention, 199; in Sino-American alliance, 195–97; territorial aspects of, 126
Taiwan straits, 39, 49, 207
Tang dynasty, viii, 6, 7, 20, 21, 38
Tang Tsou, 208
Tariffs, 74, 99
Technology, 60, 156, 207; foreign, 36, 44, 58, 66; import of, 34, 61–62, 96, 127, 186, 191, 194, 196, 200; as structural characteristic, 72, 74; trade in, 71, 82, 88–90, 92, 95; transfer of, 48, 62, 131, 160, 161, 181
Territorial bounds, 10–19, 39, 110, 115, 144, 220; and conflict between autonomy and dependence, 35; disputes with Asian neighbors over, 126 (*see also* Border conflict[s]); legacy of past in, 3. *See also* Border security
Textiles, 83, 94, 97, 98, 99, 196
Thailand, 99, 113, 117, 119, 133, 137, 138; revolutionary movement in, 136–37, 184
"Theory of the three worlds," 117, 192, 200

Third World, 110, 156, 186, 189, 193, 197, 206, 208; China as member of, xiii, 112, 114, 146, 199, 204, 214, 222; China's relations with, 107, 184, 219; demands for New International Economic Order, 93–95, 96, 125, 218; international progressive force, 212–13; resistance to superpower hegemonism, 192; reformism in, 191; rise of, 43, 205; revolutionary united front (proposed), 116–17, 118, 187–88; view of China, 170
Three Kingdoms period, 39
Tibet, 14–15, 17, 18, 19
Tito (Broz), Josip, 187
Tongzhi restoration, 21
Trade: domestic, 78; internal barriers to, 79, 82; Sino-Asian, 127; world, 97. *See also* Foreign trade; Grain trade
Trade embargo, 83, 85–86, 89, 151, 215
Tradition(s), viii, 4–10, 35, 36
Transportation, 35, 57, 67, 78. *See also* Railroads
Treaties, 13, 29–30; unequal, 19, 33; with USSR, 47–48, 180
Treaty of Friendship, Alliance, and Mutual Assistance, 180
Treaty of Nerchinsk (1689), 13
Treaty ports, 9, 28
Triangularity, 154–55, 156
Tribute system, 5, 6, 11, 15, 21, 30, 118, 126
Truman administration, 182
Two-China policy, 63, 64, 195. *See also* Taiwan issue

Uighurs, xiii, 14, 132
Union of Soviet Socialist Republics (USSR), 26, 36, 48–49, 101, 118, 165–66, 210; advisers in China, 4, 48; alignments with China, 34–35; Chiang Kai-shek and, 33; China policy, 204–05, 216, 222; China's debt to, 91–92; China's united front with, against U.S., 115, 117, 118; economic assistance to China, 48, 180–81; economic reform, 75, 103–04, 106; expansionism, xiv, 110, 117; hegemony, 117, 124, 157, 165, 168, 177, 198, 211, 212; ideological su-

premacy of, 43, 50–51, 182, 185–86; imports, 75, 88, 89; influence on China, 45, 46; invasion of Afghanistan, 52, 120, 157, 193, 220; invasion of Czechoslovakia, 152; pact with Vietnam, 62–63; participation in Asian affairs, 114, 122, 123, 129, 174; threat to Chinese security, 70, 119, 129–30, 131, 132, 156–57, 161–64, 166, 190, 193, 210; threat to Southeast Asia, 140; trade with China, 86; treaty with China, 47–48; united front against, 59, 124; withdrawal of aid and advisers from China, 51, 185. *See also Sino-Soviet entries*; Soviet-U.S. power balance; Superpowers
United Nations, 107, 187; China in, 191, 206, 208, 209; Security Council, 172
United Nations Conference on Trade and Development (UNCTAD), 93, 95
United Nations Development Program, 128
United States, 22, 33, 75, 86, 94, 99, 116, 130, 136, 141, 143–44, 171; arms sales to Taiwan, 65, 195–97, 200; China policy, 150, 195–97, 200, 204–05, 216, 218, 222; Chinese united front with, 115, 117, 118; conquest of Philippines, 24; containment policy, 43, 210; defeat in Indochina, 137; goals in Pacific, 149; grain exports, 87, 88; hegemony, 168, 198, 211, 212; historical perspective in foreign relations, 2–3; imperialism, 111, 118; as key to China's foreign assistance needs, 62; myth of exceptionalism, 3; normalization of relations with China, 63, 64–65, 209; participation in Asian affairs, 114, 122, 129, 140, 162, 174, 184; presidential elections, 64; relation with Japan, 119; supported Nationalists, 47, 49, 148, 150, 195, 196, 204; as threat to China's security, 182, 186; trade embargo on China, 85–86, 89, 150, 181; two-China policy, 63; view of China, 139, 151. *See also* Sino-American relations; Soviet-U.S. power balance; Superpowers
Urban sector, 33, 49, 73, 75
U.S.-Japan security treaty, 119

U.S.-Taiwan Mutual Defense Treaty, 195
Ussuri River, 190

Versailles, 36
Viet Minh, 184
Vietnam, 16, 18, 19, 31, 35, 39, 119, 129,
    136, 137, 138; allied with Soviet Union,
    19, 62–63, 117, 119–20, 132, 156, 165;
    and balance of power, 143–44; border
    conflicts, 110, 115, 127, 144, 157, 171,
    220 (see also Sino-Vietnamese border);
    China's assistance to, 128, 152, 187;
    China's punitive expedition against, 63,
    131, 133, 207; China's relations with,
    62–63, 121–23, 126, 143; ethnic Chi-
    nese in, 133, 135; invasion of Cam-
    bodia, 193; invasion of Kampuchea,
    62–63, 198; as issue in Sino-Soviet re-
    lations, 166, 167; regional hegemonism,
    198, 199; threat to Chinese security,
    129–30, 210; unified, 113; U.S. involve-
    ment in, 153; view of China, 140–41.
    See also North Vietnam; South Viet-
    nam
Vietnam War, 119, 121–22, 190; China in,
    170, 171; effect on U.S. foreign policy,
    193, 205; U.S. involvement in, 151–52,
    155, 156, 186
Voice of Malayan Revolution, 137
Voice of People's Thailand, 137

Wang Fuzhi, 26
Wang Jingwei, 10–11
War(s), 16, 19, 29, 31, 36, 122, 209, 210
Warlords, 8, 26, 32, 183
Warring States period, 8–9, 23, 24, 36, 39
Weapons systems, 35, 60. See also Mili-
    tary

Wei Yuan, 22
West: China's relations with, viii, xii, 20,
    69–70, 111; effect of Sino-Soviet rela-
    tions on security of, 168; imperialism
    of, 112, 125; influence on China, 177–
    78, 186, 199–200, 202, 221–22; trade
    embargo on China, 83. See also Foreign
    contacts
Western Europe, 59, 86–87, 200, 203, 206
Wich, Richard, 178n1
World Bank, 128
World economy. See International eco-
    nomic system
World Politics, 208
World War II, 13

Xenophobia, 5–6, 31–32, 215; in Cultural
    Revolution, 51, 151, 152, 188–89; to-
    ward ethnic Chinese in Asia, 133, 135;
    Maoist era, 57–58; in military, 60; pop-
    ulist, 28
Xikang, 15
Xinjiang, 14–19, 132
Xu Jivu, 21–23, 24, 25

Yalta, 19, 36
Yangzi River, 11
Ye Mingchen, 28–29
Yellow River, 31
Yuan dynasty, 9
Yugoslavia, 104

Zhao Ziyang, 65, 90, 95, 106, 137
Zhou Enlai, 52, 53, 63, 122, 153, 182,
    187–88; foreign policy of, 190
Zhuang, 132
Zoroastrianism, 7
Zuo Zongtang, 30